Chapter 1

How to Run for Public Office

Making the decision to run

There are lots of how to's and to do's when one finally decides to run for public office at any level. There are official and unofficial documents that can help in making the decision. They also aid in helping the prospective candidate know what to do. All the write-ups by well-meaning government entities are written in a way to sweeten up the candidate's idea of running for office so that they will choose to run.

These are not bad sites. They do not tell prospects for candidacy not to run for office because "your friends will think you are a jerk." But, they might as well say that. Just like my friends, your friends will question your motivation and they will question your ability to beat machine politics in any state.

For Pennsylvanians considering the plunge, there is a wonderful fact-filled write-up that appears to have been written by the state. It is hosted by Wyoming County, PA. You can get to it online through your web browser by typing in *wycopa running for public office*. The actual URL web address is complicated so this search argument in a search engine better help you access the document.

Much of what I present in this chapter is from this document plus I throw in my personal experience as I also do throughout the essays in the book. I went through the whole process as a neophyte in 2010 when I ran for Congress, once again in 2012, as I considered running for the US Senate, and once in 2015 as I ran for Mayor of Wilkes-Barre, PA.

You might say that I have had my fill of such instructions and following them to the letter of the law. But, I am at it again running for Congress in 2016 and the US Senate in 2018 as a write-in candidate. I will talk about write-in options later in the various essays throughout the book.

I got 17% of the vote when I ran for Congress and five years later in my home town, I got just 5% of the vote when I ran for Mayor. I also spent more money in 2015. I have learned many lessons. My net gain from all this activity is that I now get to say that I ran for office. I am glad I did and I am running again but as a write-in, I will no longer have to spend large sums of money (in the thousands) to get on the ballot and conduct any campaign. I run for office hoping to help the City or District in which I live handle the pressures of today more effectively. I know that I can help.

A side desire of mine has always been to get rid of the machine from controlling government at all levels to help bring the government back to the people. So far I have been unsuccessful because the system is rigged. Yet, I continue to have hope that somebody will emerge to take on the bad guys and bring the people a victory. Maybe one day it will be me. Maybe it will be you.

It surely does not have to be me. I would love for everybody who once thought about running for office and hopefully is thinking about doing so again, to promise they will never vote for another incumbent. That is a first step in making the process fair. The people have to get rid of the existing bad guys or as many like to say, "Throw the bums out!" It can become a fair system but not without help from the people at election time. It won't change until we throw out the people that made it like it is.

Government, my friends is bad because we have elected scoundrels to offices that are important for all the people. But, the people we have elected in many if not most cases have become greedy and self-centered. They have distanced themselves from the needs of their constituents.

One of the most important things that a prospective candidate for office must do is a self-evaluation. You must be sure that you are ready both for the possibility of success and the probability of many disappointments along the way.

Table of Contents

Unfortunately a prospective candidate for public office using traditional methods also needs to determine if he or she can afford the commitment of time, money and energy necessary to run for the intended office. Though the official documents make it seem like it is 1, 2, 3, the fact is the incumbents have made the process unnecessarily difficult. Therefore many, once engaged think they cannot really run for office. Let's suppose for a minute that you are certified Mensa (The High IQ Society), but you have minimal resources and even less cash. You are going to have a tough time without donors.

To be successful using the traditional approach of getting on the ballot is very difficult without a pile of money. In my case, running for Congress, I had to buy a lot of yard signs and other material to help myself become known. It cost me about $5000.00 in 2010 and I took no donations to remain free of political encumbrances and entanglements. I wanted nobody to own me. In retrospect, I was too strict as family donating $50 or $100 each would not create an issue.

In addition to money, a prospective candidate must also make sure that he or she is qualified to hold the office being sought. There are no listed qualifications to make sure this is really true, however. My rule of thumb is that if you think you are qualified, you are.

Once you have assured all this, and you want to proceed, your next step is very important. You need to check in with your family and friends, especially your immediate family. You must make sure that they are OK with your running for whatever office. In my case it was Congress. I got reluctant acceptance from my immediate family, which told me that it was OK for me to proceed.

You then need a team of good people to help you. You cannot do it alone. The only thing you can do alone in life is fail. You will need people who can think with you and people who can do work for you. There is lots of work from placing signs, creating fliers, speeches, and essays, building a website, and going door to door to get petition signatures.

You also need one very, very good friend, or if you have some money to burn, a good campaigner who will work for you and be paid to organize your campaign. In my case, Marty Devaney, a very good friend of mine understood the system and he worked very effectively with me. He donated his time and effort to the cause. He was my campaign manager and a great man.

Marty and I put together a team of about forty people from my friend and family group. My brothers and sisters were not happy with the idea and so only a few helped me in the grassroots work. Thankfully, I had a great team of friends and in-laws who were pleased to host a few events and participate as needed as we organized our approach. You'll find that people bring in other people when the benefit to all is better government.

This gave me about three team captains and I could have used more to assure things like signs and nominating petitions were completed. A number for my high school friends asked to help so in the end we had a formidable group. One of the great measurements of our campaign success was that we got over 1500 signatures in three weeks and less than forty were stricken as invalid.

What should first-time candidates know?

I gave you the search argument for the document you should print and read (*wycopa running for public office*). Pay close attention to the instructions provided and check out all the forms necessary to gain ballot access. Make to-do-lists as you read the documents.

In addition, if you plan to spend more than $5000, or if you have more than $250 in expenses, as a first-time candidate you need to become familiar with the Campaign Finance Reporting Law, which is posted on the Department of State's website at www.dos.state.pa.us/campaignfinance.

You might want to ask a friend who is an accountant to help you in this regard, even if they charged you as the details on this huge report are tricky. Remember, all of these things are hoops in a gauntlet that you must traverse in order to be deemed qualified to get on the ballot to run for office in PA.

A prospective candidate should also understand the commitment of time and energy necessary to run a successful campaign for public office and no matter what you thought it would be, it will be even more because incumbents do not ever want to lose and they make the rules.

Try getting on the ballot but make sure you are ready to work harder than it ought to be.

What a Candidate Must File to Access the Ballot

Signature requirements vary depending on the office for which the nomination petition is being circulated. The rule of thumb on signatures is always get twice the number you need. For example, when I ran for Mayor, I needed 100 signatures. My little team brought in over 250. When I ran for Congress, I needed 1000 signatures. My expanded team brought in over 1500 signatures and we checked them thoroughly to make sure there were no gotchas. We lost only 40 in Harrisburg when they were examined by state officials.

You must inform the state what office you are running for and assure they send you a campaign packet with the needed forms before the three-week period for signature gathering for your nominating petitions. You can get your packet early but you cannot solicit signatures before the declared first day.

Obviously one of the forms you need is the nomination petition. If the heading information is not filled in properly, an entire petition can be thrown out during the inspection process when you turn them in. In other words, make sure everything is done right or you can lose as many as 50 signatures in one clip.

Below are some forms you will need. They should all be in your packet. To be sure you have the right contacts in the state to get the packet, visit your county election bureau (voter services) and tell them you are running and they will review what you need. In some cases, depending on the office which you are seeking, such as Mayor or Council, the County group will have all the forms you need.

For governor or senator or congress, you will need to get them from the state. The county people will tell you how to get them. When you visit the county ask about getting the CD of voters so you know who is Democrat and who is Republican. If your office spans counties, ask the county voter services head in each county for their CD. When I ran, there was no state-wide CD.

If you are a Democrat for example, running as a Democrat, you need to get signatures of only Democrats. Republicans get Republican signatures. If you are running for a slot on both tickets, you need to get the minimum number for each party to be on their respective ballot ticket in the primary. The form you use for getting signatures is called a nomination petition. Forms are described below:

The Candidates Affidavit
Each candidate must file with his or her nomination petition or nomination paper an affidavit setting forth information about the candidate, including the candidate's residence, election district and the name of the office the candidate is seeking.

The Statement of Financial Interests
The Statement of Financial Interests is a form that must be filed with the State Ethics Commission, which requires the filer to set forth information regarding the filer's sources of income. A copy of the completed Statement of Financial Interests must also accompany the nomination petition of a candidate for state, county or local public

The Nomination Petition
Each page of a nomination petition contains three basic components: 1) the Preamble; 2) the Signatures of Electors; and 3) the Affidavit of Circulator.

The Preamble:
The preamble is the portion of the nomination petition page where information about the candidate is inserted. The preamble includes the office for which the candidate seeks nomination, the name of the candidate, the candidate's occupation, the candidate's residence and the party affiliation of the signers.

Signatures of Electors:
Each person who signs a nomination petition must insert the following information about himself or
herself: 1.   Signature;2.   Printed name;3.   Address of residence, including street and number, if any; and4.   The date on which he or she signed the nomination petition

The Affidavit of Circulator:
1. Each nomination petition page must include the duly executed affidavit of the person who circulated the nomination petition (the circulator). The circulator of the nomination petition page must swear or affirm the following:
2. That the circulator is a qualified elector of the Commonwealth or of the district, as the case may be.
3. That the circulator is a duly registered and enrolled member of the political party designated in the nomination petition;
4. That the circulator's address of residence is as set forth in items 4 and 5 of the affidavit;
5. That the signers of the nomination petition page signed with the full knowledge of the contents of the nomination petition;
6. That the signers' residences are correctly stated on the nomination petition page;
7. That each signer signed on the date that the signer inserted next to his or her signature, name and address of residence; and
8. That, to the best of the circulator's knowledge and belief the signers are qualified electors, who are duly registered and enrolled in the political party designated in the petitions and are residents in the County set forth in item 1 of the affidavit.

Sorry I had to do that to you in such detail but it is a game rigged for regular citizens to withdraw rather than proceed.

Please note that unless you are superman, you will need multiple circulators for your petitions. These are the people who ask other people for their signatures. Make sure the circulator information is done correctly above. You may have five circulators and each of them may have various nominating petitions. For example, a circulator may get 50 signatures and then need another petition form. A circulator may choose to keep one at his family residence and in the office and in the car, etc. Each has to be filled out properly. Your opponent would be pleased to find a flaw in your work.

Challenges to Nomination Petitions and Nomination Papers

The system is set up that if John W Public writes John Q Public on the petition for any candidate and it is later proven he is John x Public, his line does not count. If your write an abbreviation for Wilkes-Barre as WB or W-B, that signature or form does not count. Pay attention to the rules. I have a copy of the handout sheet I used for circulators at the end of this chapter.

Entrenched establishment politicians like Joe Sestak or Bob Casey, Jr. will challenge regular guys such as Carl Romanelli or like Joe Vodvarka, hoping to scare them into not running. Typically, an individual such as Sestak can challenge the validity of a nomination petition by a good guy like Vodvarka within seven days of the filing deadline for nomination petitions or nomination papers.

Sestak has already challenged the petitions of Vodvarka because he cannot stand the thought of a guy running against him, and he apparently has the resources to squash Vodvarka rather than let him run.

The Candidate List

If you change your mind after you are on the ballot, there is a last day to withdraw or you will be on the ballot regardless. As a valid candidate, you will be asked to come to the state capitol for congress as an example to draw lots for ballot position. If you do not want to go to Harrisburg for example, the Capitol Police will draw your ballot. I chose the latter method and luck of the Irish, I was listed # 1 on the ballot.

After the last day for candidates who have filed nomination petitions to withdraw and after the candidates have cast lots for position on the primary ballot, the Secretary of the Commonwealth must forward a list of statewide candidates of each party to the various county boards of elections. This is how your county knows you are on the ballot.

A candidate of a minor political party or political body will have his or her name placed on the November ballot upon acceptance of his or her nomination paper by the Department of State or the County Board of Elections, as the case may be, unless the nomination paper is judicially set aside as a result of a successful challenge to the candidate's nomination paper. If you fit in this group, please spend some time talking to some experts to make sure this is done properly. Most of what we have discussed so far is how to get on the Primary ballot.

CAMPAIGN FINANCE REPORTING

Who Must File Campaign Finance Reports/Statements?

Campaign finance reports/statements must be filed by candidates for public office setting forth information regarding contributions received and expenditures made for the purpose of influencing the outcome of an election. A candidate may also authorize a committee to accept contributions and make expenditures on the candidate's behalf. The committee must have a chairperson and a treasurer, who may not be the same person. Each candidate and each authorized political committee must file reports of receipts and expenditures, if the amount received or expended or liabilities incurred exceeds $250. Otherwise, the candidate or the treasurer of the authorized political committee may file the statement in lieu of the reports. Candidates are required to file a campaign finance report/statement that is separate from the report/statement

ELECTION DAY

Electioneering
No person, including a candidate, may electioneer or solicit votes when inside a polling place. All persons, except those persons authorized or be inside the polling place (election officers, clerks, machine inspectors, overseers, watchers, persons in the course of voting, persons lawfully giving assistance to voters, and peace and police officers), must remain at least ten (10) feet from the polling place during the progress of voting.

Watchers

Each candidate may appoint two watchers for each election district (polling place) in which the candidate's name appears on the ballot. However, only one watcher for each candidate may be present in the polling place at any one time.

Candidates interested in appointing watchers should contact the appropriate county board of elections for information about submitting the names of watchers and obtaining certificates for those watchers.

Qualifications of watchers:
Each watcher appointed to serve in an election district must be a registered voter of the county in which the election district is located.

In order to serve as a watcher, a person must receive from the appropriate county board of elections a Watcher's Certificate, which the watcher must present when requested to do so.

Rights of Watchers:
When a watcher is not serving in the election district for which the watcher was appointed, the watcher may serve in any other election district in the county in which the watcher is registered to vote.

Watchers may be present in the polling place from the time the election officers meet prior to the opening of the polls until the time that voting is complete and the district register and voting check list is locked and sealed, provided that they remain outside the "enclosed space" (the area in which the voting compartments are located).

A watcher is permitted to keep a list of voters and is entitled to challenge the qualifications of a voter in the manner provided by Law. Watchers should take care to issue challenges in good faith. The Pennsylvania Election Code does not authorize wholesale or frivolous challenges, which are intended to intimidate voters

Chapter Appendix BK's rules for signatures

I developed and used this instruction sheet in my 2010 run for Congress. I have made it more appropriate for 2016. These are not state rules. They were my rules and I gave each circulator and anybody part of the team a copy to help avoid mistakes. When I created this "cheat cheat," I made it one sheet. Look on www.briankellyforcongress.com web site, the mainmenu for a pdf of the form called Signature Rules.

Rules for Signatures -- Brian Kelly for Congress Page 1

1. Get a clipboard, & Black Pen. -- I should have enough here. Put your stuff in the clipboard

2. Get at least one sheet for each county (Luzerne, Lackawanna, Monroe, Columbia, Carbon) in which you may choose to get signatures -- If your streets are in Luzerne County but Mom and Dad's are in Lackawanna County, you need two sheets. Take as many sheets as you think you need (50 signatures max per sheet)

3. Look at the sheet. Note that Item 6 is the County. Luzerne is filled in on some sheets. If you go to counties outside of Luzerne, before getting any signatures fill in the County Name. Do not mix people from different counties on the same form.

4. Look at the sheet. Each sheet holds 50 signatures. You are to observe the person filling out the signature line. Use just one line each to sign and complete their line on the petition.

5. Look at the sheet. The top of the sheet page 1 is already filled out other than county in some cases. [I did this when I copied the forms for Luzerne County where most of my circulators were] The note to the Secretary of the Commonwealth is next. This describes what the signature / line is all about. It is not a vote. It is your agreement that a fellow citizen (me) in the 17th district may run for Congress.

6. Look at the sheet. Lines 1 to 29 and heading. Space for 29 signatures on Page 1.

7. Look at the sheet. In the signature space this is how the signature and information is to be printed / signed. Ditto marks are not permitted anywhere.

A. SIGNATURE OF ELECTOR -- Each signer of the nominating petition is an elector -- i.e. one who has a right to vote D (Democrat) in the primary and is in District 17. (If your case is Republican, make sure the signer is Republican – do not mix Ds and Rs on same sheet)   Observe the signatory <u>sign</u> in that space. The signature itself must be in cursive form - not printed.

B. PRINTED NAME of ELECTOR -- Caution the signatory that the name in the signature and the name printed are the same name - initials or no initials etc. Observe the signatory print their name the same as on their official records -- such as driver's license. Use middle initial if on license.

C. PLACE OF RESIDENCE - HOUSE #- Observe just house # printed in this space.

D. PLACE OF RESIDENCE - Street or Rd. Caution the signatory to place the street or rd with the designator st. rd. or ave. followed by apartment # (apt 1) if there is such a #. Observe the signatory type this information. Street, road, or avenue may be abbreviated but not the street name.

E. PLACE OF RESIDENCE - City, Boro, or Twp. Caution the signatory to use no abbreviations for the municipality. For example WB, W.B., W-B, W-Barre are all invalid and will cause the signature to be thrown out.

F. Date of SIGNING. Observe the signatory print the date while cautioning that it must be correct and within the period of February 16 to March 9, 2010 (check the dates). For example, 02/16/2010 is valid and 02/16/2009 is not. Any date such as 02/15/2010 or before this date is not valid. Any date such as 03/10/2010 or after this date is not valid. Any mistakes on date will cause the signature to be thrown out. Circulators should make sure that the dates on the form are oldest to newest sequence. March 8 should not be before March 1 on the form.

AA. Note on the signature line --- >> If the signatory makes a number of mistakes and it does not look good. It will not be accepted. Draw a straight line through the whole line and ask them to start over on the next line. Do not waste lines.

BB. Lines 30 to 50 are valid spaces for signatures -- thus each sheet can hold a maximum of 50 signatures (29 on front and 21 on back). Get as many forms as you need!

CC. Each Saturday beginning February 20, please call D. Greemez with the # of signatures that you obtained that week. The sooner we get all the forms to Harrisburg the better. 655-5555. Or email <greemez@comcast.net>

DD. On February 27 or March 6, depending on how we are doing, all forms need to be brought to BK's house (candidate) and we will have them notarized. We will have a notary onsite to do this. He or she will do them all at once and charge BK, not the circulator. Circulators must be present to sign in front of Notary

EE. On March 2 or March 9 BK will take the notarized forms to Harrisburg. If you cannot come to get the forms notarized, please have them notarized in your area and BK will reimburse you the expense. BK will come to your house to pick up the notarized form, hopefully before March 2.

FF. Look at the form on the back in the affidavit of circulator. You are the circulator. Do not fill this out the left side at all and do not fill in the right side until all the signatures are on the sheet and the Notary Public is standing in front of you.

GG. Make sure Brian gets as many forms as possible filled with signatures and that they are notarized either at the meeting on Feb 27 or March 6 or by you and your own Notary.

HH. Some have asked for data sheets. Get your data sheets now! Tell Brian what streets / towns you want if your sheets are not ready. Verify that the person signing actually signs their name as it is listed in the data sheet or their Driver's License (should be the same)

II. Can you get anybody's signature? Yes, they know if they have previously signed for Brian so don't worry about it. Get the signature - Democrat -- District 17. Make sure County is correct on the form -- If you get signatures from 5 counties, you need 5 forms.

Rules for Signatures -- Brian Kelly for Congress Page 2

Review ---- Many signatures are thrown out because of small mistakes.
Let's Look at the areas of mistakes that might be made for the meeting

1. Make sure that every detail of everybody's signature is perfect
2. Do not use WB or ditto marks.
3. Make sure you use the Luzerne County form only for Luzerne County Signatories
4. If the signatory makes a mistake, draw a line through it and let them write it again.
5. It helps to check the data sheets vs. the signatures line for errors.

Why would a signature be contested? Here's why:
- ✓ Signature Line Challenges -- the incumbent or other challenger wants to get all signatures thrown out claiming inaccuracies
- ✓ Date on line not between Feb 16 and March 9
- ✓ Signer is not a registered voter
- ✓ Signer resides in wrong district (16 or 18)
- ✓ Signature or data not completely legible -- ask them to do-over.
- ✓ Multiple counties on same form – entire form gets thrown out.
- ✓ Address is wrong / incomplete / missing address
- ✓ Incomplete / missing dates / dates out of order
- ✓ Ditto marks
- ✓ Nickname or initials in place of full name
- ✓ No cursive signature
- ✓ Wrong / fraudulent signature*

*** We will have a meeting at my house on Feb. 27 or March 6, depending on how the signatures are coming

in. I will bring a Notary public to notarize the signature petitions for the carriers. BK will pay for it. Do not get them notarized before then.

Don't forget ask your relatives, close friends and those who you see all the time. We are looking for D, D17
Send Greemez an email so he can communicate with you <greemez@comcast.net>

Essay # 1

Ballot Access: The Game is Rigged!

Try running for office!

Contact: **Brian Kelly for US Congress**
Email   **bkcampaign@yahoo.com**
Date: **April 13, 2016**

****** PRESS RELEASE ******

Like you, Congressional Candidate Brian Kelly is disgusted with the current leaders in our government. He is asking for voters to forget about what big government can do for them. The results are in and the verdict is "0." Kelly is asking voters to write him in twice -- once in 2016 for the House of Representatives, PA District 17, and once in 2018 for the US Senate.

Brian hopes to help release our wonderful country from the grips of the socialists and communists.

In this essay, Brian Kelly demonstrates the difficulty for non-politicians (regular Joe's), such as him, to gain ballot access in a system designed of, for, and by corrupt incumbent politicians.

His essay title is:

BALLOT ACCESS: THE GAME IS RIGGED!

Please enjoy this essay by Mr. Brian Kelly.

Try running for Office in a state such as Pennsylvania, in which the political Incumbents and the establishment have the game rigged. Pennsylvania's corrupt state politicians have slanted the ballot-access table in favor of incumbents and against non-political regular citizens of the Commonwealth.

There are major trials and tribulations facing regular people who attempt to present themselves as candidates on any ballot for any office in the United States of America. The ballot access issue in Pennsylvania is one of the worst in the nation. It should not surprise anybody that the incumbent politicians make the laws that make it difficult for anybody to unseat them. There are many surprisingly restrictive ballot access laws in this country. The average citizen voter has no knowledge or concept of the extent of the problem until one day, he or she decides to put their hat in the ring and they run for office, hoping to give something back.

If you are so inclined, do you feel that you might actually be able to run unimpeded for an important office in Pennsylvania? Would you just go ahead and do it or would you be concerned that the weight of the political machine might be too heavily focused against your candidacy? If you gave it a shot, do you think you would be permitted to run unfettered against a well-established political class whose livelihood and whose continued excessive wealth depends on being elected continually until they die?

I thought I would run for office simply because I am an American and this is America. I have done so but let me tell you the road is unpaved. I ran for Congress and for Mayor. I was on the ballot for Congress in 2010 and on the ballot for Mayor of Wilkes-Barre in 2015. There is a lot of work in running for office and unless you become a politician or the people stop bootlicking politicians by voting for them, a new candidate can expect nothing but misery and failure.

Do you wonder why so few people run for office? Surely you have neighbors who you think would be much better at leading our country, state, county, or city than the same old crew whose names make the ballot every election. I know first-hand why more good people choose to stay away from becoming elected officials. It is because the politicians control the playing field. If you think the game is rigged, you are right! The game is rigged.

There is a big reason why potential candidates for office do not simply emerge into the sunlight when they are so inclined to be the next Mayor, Governor, Senator, or Representative. It is the same reason that even Donald Trump and Bernie Sanders have learned in trying to become president. The game is rigged, at all levels.

The reason is that there are lots of impediments and major roadblocks that need to be carefully navigated. Those currently holding offices of and for the people, think they own the people. Consider that there are no documented cases of an elected official, who in their first term or any term ever calls all citizens of the community together for a meeting to find some other good candidates to run.

It seems logical that we all would have been invited at some time to say, a church hall, so that a great leader could describe to us the process of becoming the next such and such from so and so. If we all wanted the best people to serve, would we not be encouraging our neighbors to come out and be welcomed to consider putting his or her hat in the ring to serve the people?

Why are we deprived of having regular, ordinary citizens such as you and I, rather than machine groomed politicians be the candidates for the offices available in almost all elections? The answer is that over time, the political class through gerrymandering and restrictive ballot access laws, and special rules known only unto them, have made it difficult for anybody other than a crooked politician to get elected.

Politicians play the game and they eventually become experts. It is not by accident that the winners are almost always endorsed by the big Party machines, and let me tell you all, the machines are really big and are really powerful and tough to overcome. Regular Joe's and Josephine's are excluded in the process intentionally but the methods are not entirely obvious. The fact that it costs a lot of money to compete is just one of the first obstacles.

For the money and the major effort, a newcomer has less than a slim chance to gain the nomination or win a general election. Once you put your hat in the ring, there is a lot of unexpected and unnecessary work and expense. It is not an accident that any candidate running for the first time feels that all of the politicians and the minions in government have their hands locked into his or her wallet.

It was not always that way and the founders did not intend it to be that way. Unfortunately, elected politicians have always had the power to make things easy for their next election regardless of its impact on democracy, the will of the people, and the good of the people. The founding fathers expected that the people would throw the bums out but the bums have made it very difficult,

Their path to a reelection and a slot at the establishment perks table is much easier than your path to be newly elected. They use something that I would call a special "incumbent grease." The incumbent grease makes them quite slippery and it helps them to be impervious to the rot they create, through which those not as well connected must traverse.

It was not until the 1880's for example that paper ballots began to be printed by the government. Before then it was private entities who produced the ballots and even before then voice votes were used. In the 1880's official secret ballots came into being by government decree and that is when the ballot access issues for John Q Public began. It is funny how the government broke a system that had worked well for 100 years at that time. Government breaks a lot more than it fixes.

The elitists believed that only elitists should be able to run for public office and they set out to make sure that it was a task that most ordinary citizens would choose not to take up. Today as we see in Congress and the Senate, and even the Presidency, the sense of entitlement to the office held is so strong that the "elite" politicians believe that they know more than the people they serve.

They also know that it is so difficult for a newcomer to replace them that they no longer believe they have a requirement to do the people's will to be re-elected. Of course, that was before the recent populist movement that has Donald Trump and Ted Cruz and Bernie Sanders, ostensibly outsiders to the presidential process, doing so well today. To not be an incumbent in 2016 is now a major advantage for the people. But, will the establishment still have the power and the gall to direct the results? We'll see!

The TEA Party movement of 2009 from its first brew was unfairly defamed by the corrupt progressive media. Yet, it is the TEA Party, a term not mentioned much today that built the foundation for today's populist movement. This movement has brought us candidates who do not owe their allegiance to big donors or the Party machines.

Wikipedia, which sometimes, but infrequently, gets it wrong, got this fact 100% right. It cites that historian Peter Argersinger pointed out that the 1880's reform "that conferred power on officials to regulate who may be on the ballot carried with it the danger that this power would be abused by officialdom and that legislatures controlled by the established political parties (specifically, the Republican and Democratic Parties), would enact restrictive ballot access laws to influence election outcomes, for partisan purposes, in order to ensure re-election of their own party's candidates." Peter Argersinger was 100% correct and my own story as a candidate confirms that.

As a candidate several times who paid a big price to be on the ballot, I can assure all Americans that the ballot access system provided by the states is not designed to let the most competent person through the maze. Thus, the people most often send the same scoundrels back to office rather than helping new blood present its case. First of all, there are no ready forums to present one's a case.

One would presume with no knowledge that the United States would have the most fair ballot access rules in the world of countries that practice a form of democracy. But, this is not true. The United States has been criticized by the Organization for Security and Cooperation in Europe (OSCE) for its harsh ballot access laws in the past. From my own experience, the US has not really lightened up on the rules that prevent ordinary citizens to get on the ballot. The corrupt press never reports on it as it is part of the problem, not the solution.

This is one place in which it appears the Brits have us beat. In their political science model of a healthy two-party system, every candidate for Parliament faces the same ballot-access hurdle-- a simple filing fee. Not only is it free but candidates from all parties are granted two free mailings to all the voters. That's not the end of the fairness. Every candidate also gets some free TV and radio time. It's almost as if the Brits want real people not just politicians to be able to achieve an office in Parliament. We have the same access here if you have the big bucks and lots of spare time. In Britain, they have legal equality between all the parties and it seems to work. Our system seems to be corrupt. As Donald Trump says quite well and quite often: "The system is rigged." Trump is right!

You saw what happened in Colorado, Trump said. It's a fix. We thought we were having an election and a number of months ago, they decide to do it by you know what, right? They said well do it by delegate. Aw, isn't that nice? And the delegates were all there waiting. And, one of them tweeted out today and said today, by mistake, and then they withdrew it, something to the effect of See, never Trump.

Mr. Trump spoke at a rally with over 0,000 supporters who packed the Times Union Center, a sports and concert venue in downtown Albany: I'm hundreds of delegates ahead but the system, folks, is rigged. It's a rigged, disgusting, dirty system.

As a person who has run twice in this dirty system, I more than agree. It is rigged to benefit long term dirty corrupt politicians who in this election, are known simply as "The Establishment."

Even at the local level, when I ran for Mayor last year and was on the ballot, I requested in early 2015 that Mayor Leighton open City Hall for a meet the candidates night twice a month for the few months of the election season. Each mayoral candidate would speak for an hour and each Council candidate would also get time to speak.

The Mayor said the City could not sponsor such events as it was against the law. I have two sons who are lawyers and this simply is not true. Regardless, the Mayor acted like he owned City Hall, not like he was merely renting it with the people's permission until the end of his term. I beg to differ that a Mayor or public official cannot choose to help the electoral process.

But, we all know it is very difficult fighting City Hall. The newspapers are AWOL. Radio stations permit call-ins for brief periods but the local TV stations including Public TV offer nothing for aspiring candidates. The message is to get your wallet out and pay to permit the people to learn to know you. The Fourth estate is dead in Wilkes-Barre PA and for the most part across the country.

In 2010, when I ran for Congress, the incumbent, who seemingly was responsible for funding allocations for Public TV, decided that there would be no public forum or debates on Public TV for the Congressional House Race! Is it not convenient to be the well-known incumbent and have the power to limit your opponent's opportunities to take your job?

The noted scholar John Henry Wigmore, professor of law at Northwestern Univ. from 1901 to 1929, who ultimately was dean of the law faculty had some big-time opinions on fair elections. In his earlier life (1880s) Wigmore had been a leader for election law reform, especially the secret voting method and ballot access laws. His suggestion in my opinion makes sense. He recommended that as few as ten signatures would be an appropriate requirement for nomination to gain access to the official ballot for a legislative office.

For Congress in PA, a candidate needs 1000 signatures plus 1000 more signatures to cover signature challenges. For Mayor, one needs 100 signatures plus 100 more to cover challenges. I dare you to try to get a signature from anybody for anything. See how easy it is. Candidates get three weeks to get all signatures while still going to work every day. Each signature petition sheet of 50 maximum and 1 minimum must be notarized. That is another $5.00 to $10.00 per signature.

So, does that make Pennsylvania law 100 times better than the suggestion of this sage legal scholar who thinks ten signatures are sufficient? Let me repeat myself on the requirement. As noted, in PA, one hoping to become a candidate on the ballot for Congress on the Republican or Democrat side must attain 1000 signatures plus 1000 more for challenges in less than three weeks. I submit that this is regardless of how many snow storms there may have been. All of this hard work, 100 times more than Wigmore's suggestion is necessary to be a candidate for US Representative for either party. Incumbents illegally use their staff to get the signatures or the Party pas as much as $5.00 to $10.00 per signature to have professionals canvas for them. Regular citizens have no such staffs.

At about six to ten signatures per hour, one certainly cannot expect to hold a job and live a normal life if trying to get the signatures by oneself. The clear objective of such as system is to limit the access to the ballot so that normal people say "no way," and politician after politician has his or her way with the people's treasury.

When the signatures are submitted, it is also clear that the objective is to eliminate signatures, not to verify the real citizens who signed the petitions. They may be valid citizens, thereby making their attestation valid but if they make a mistake in their own name or the city or the date or their apartment #, their attestation of a candidate is thrown in the garbage. In the current US Senate primary in Pennsylvania, Joseph Vodvarka's signatures are being challenged by the opportunistic Joe Sestak.

When I first wrote this essay, Mr. Sestak hoped to deny Pennsylvanians a candidate who is of the people and not of the political class. He hoped to chop hundreds of signatures from Vodvarka's submitted petitons. He wanted them marked invalid so that Mr. Vodvarka would lose his right to be on the ballot. That's how bad it is. Since then, I learned that on April 1, the Courts favored Sestak. What a sham. The system is rigged.

Sestak almost immediately took Vodvarka to court so it will cost Vodvarka money to defend his petitions with over 2000 signatures. Sestak, a well-tuned in politician says more than 60 percent of the Vodvarka voter signatures is not known for being a handwriting expert. Yet, he claimed the signatures were flawed and should not be counted. I say if they can find ten good signatures, Vodvarka should be in! Try getting 4000 signatures in three weeks.

Most courts are smarter than the politics often employed by jurists in making decisions. The PA Court ruled against Vodvarka.

U.S. Senate candidates have a tougher time to get signatures than House candidates. Instead of 1000, they need to collect 2,000 signatures to qualify to be on the ballot. Those petition signers must be registered to vote in the county where they reside and be of the same political party as the candidate. Joe Vodvarka had submitted 2,744 signatures, which ought to be enough, except in a rigged system, to have him on the ballot.

Prior to the Commonwealth Court hearing argument on Sestak's challenge, attorneys for Vodvarka and Sestak reached an agreement and stipulated to the court that 558 signatures on Vodvarka's petitions were invalid. As long as he was on the ballot, why would Vodvarka care that he only had 200 or so to spare. That left Vodvarka with 2,186 signatures. But the Commonwealth Court chopped off another 400 signatures so Vodvarka could not run on the ballot with 1800 signatures. What kind of guy does that make Sestak? What kind of lousy system would authorize such a perpetration of justice?

Political pundits have often said that the poll tax is the worst tax possible as it denies people the right to vote. It is my humble opinion that the method of using exorbitant numbers of signatures and arbitrary signature cancellations is worse than a poll tax as it denies the citizens the very candidates that would make an election with just politicians running, into a real election. A politician's objective, such as Joe Sestak, is to eliminate candidates not to verify that they are capable of serving.

Speaking of taxes, to help get 1000 signatures, one can ask for the county database or state database. I called the state and was routed back and forth and then each time, the phone was conveniently disconnected. For my part, I got the pleasure of dialing again but since time is important, I chose not to work with the state. The state database cost $20.00 or so I had been told.

District 11 [Before the recent changes to District 17] in Pennsylvania consisted of all or part of five different counties -- Carbon, Columbia, Monroe, Lackawanna, and Luzerne. To get the databases for these counties, they must be obtained from the counties one by one, for a sum of $50.00 per CD or $250.00. To capture one signature on a petition in each of the five counties--a total of just 5 signatures--would cost approximately $10,00 in Notary Public fees per sheet or $50.00 to have all five signatures notarized.

Why is this a requirement when the State does not accept the notarized affidavit---the word of the Notary, anyway? Vodvarka's were all notarized but the court did not accept the Notary's attestations. The answer is because it is effective harassment for anybody who dares challenge the powers that be. But, you already know that.

Of course each House petition holds 50 signatures so it would take 20 perfect petitions to reach 1000 signatures at a cost of $200.00. Since, at least 1500 signatures is recommended as many will be eliminated rather than verified, this cost is at best $300.00. With signature circulators working on behalf of every candidate, many of the sheets have no more than ten signatures. Of all had just ten signatures, this would be 100 sheets and the cost would be $1000.00 for the notarization of the signatures.

What purpose does this serve?

Additionally, there is a filing fee of $150.00 to be able to submit the petitions and be duly registered as a candidate to be placed on the ballot. They don't take Visa or Master Card. They do not take personal checks. So, I had to go to the bank to get a $150.00 cashier's check made out perfectly to the State of PA or they would not accept it. More harassment. Then, though there were five Voters services offices in District 11, ostensibly because this is a National election, the full petition, a notarized affidavit (another $10.00) and the cashier's check had to be taken to Harrisburg (two hours each way plus mileage cost -- say another $50.00) to a specific room to be processed.

In the directions from Harrisburg, to add insult to injury, I found it comforting that there was a caution after noting that the signature period was from February 16 to March 9. The caution said, "Do not wait until the last minute." In other words, the office is closing at 5:00 P.M. on March 9 so you better be in, processed, and out by 5:00 P.M. When I arrived on a Tuesday, I thought I was OK. Only about forty signatures were discounted. Despite all the obstacles I made it onto the ballot. .

Many citizens do not know how difficult it is for a non-politico to run for any office in Pennsylvania or they would insist that the rules be more reasonable. We have our corrupt state lawmakers to blame for that and they must fix this even before, in our contempt for them, we replace them all. I will do my best, I can assure you to enable ballot access for all so that we the people are not cursed to have only politicians to choose from in our elections.

Speaking of citizens and the requirement for 1000 signatures. It is my understanding that the incumbent merely instructs his staff to get signatures and it is not that big of a deal. If the staff is only minimally involved the incumbent can attend a number of political events during the three week period with hundreds of willing signatures available at each event. The lone wolf, the average Joe, our own John Q. Public, does not have it quite so easy.

In my case, I called a number of establishments to see if I could bring my petition inside and quietly ask people to sign to help grant me ballot access. I learned something in this process. Some establishments are quite gracious and assist in this civic duty of enabling ballot access for citizens of NEPA, who are not part of the machine.

Of course, they would also permit those of the machine and that is fair. Some establishments are not so gracious and they either put me off or took it up the flagpole only to have the owner decree that they did not engage in such politics. For me in these cases, I concluded that they had an alignment with the machine, which I did not have. Knocking on doors is the toughest way to get signatures.

I am running for Congress in 2016 and the US Senate in 2018

Until I die, I will probably be running for some political office. When elected to Congress this year, I will serve one term and then my plan is to serve six years in the US Senate. That ought to be enough, but who knows, maybe one more term... but just one. I spent close to $5000 of my own money to run for Congress in 2010. When I ran for Mayor in 2015, I thought it would be easier. I spent about $6000 but family and friends donated about $3000 so altogether, I am out at least $8,000 and probably more because of PA ballot access laws. I won't do this again this way for sure. I wish I had the cash back for a few family vacations. Yet, here I am

running for office. How am I going to pull that off? Quick-answer --
Write me in!

If voters tuned into write-in ballot laws, and there were a listing
service so that anybody could announce that they were running as a
write-in candidate, we can again have a democratic republic as the
founders intended. It costs nothing to run as a write-in. All you
have to do is make sure that the potential voters know about you.
So, with the listing service, instead of having to get 1500 signatures,
anybody can run for Congress. Because it would be so easy and be
no charge, citizens would have a huge selection of candidates. We
should talk more about this... don't you think?

In the meantime, I bought a web site to handle write-in ballots.
Well, it really does not handle write-in ballots as you still have to
vote at your polling place. However, it is a place in which any write-
in candidate can list his or her name so that any citizen can access
the site to find out who they are. That way, ladies and gentlemen,
we are not stuck with politicians as public officials.
The name of this web site is www.writeinballots.com. I will figure
out how to make it work and it will be available to all. Feel free to
check it out while I am building it.

God bless America!

Vote for the Underdog... Just write in Brian Kelly this time. It's that
easy! Next time, send out a memo like this, and we'll all be voting
for you and it will not cost you a dime I think!

With 64-books, Brian W. Kelly is the most-published and thus the
leading conservative author in America. He is an outspoken and
eloquent expert on solutions to help America and Americans
Though a Democrat, he is a JFK Democrat. One of his pet peeves
is the chicanery and deceit of RINOS and DINOS on all
Americans.

About Brian Kelly:

Brian Kelly is a former IBM Senior Systems Engineer and Retired
Professor of Business and Information Technology (BIT) at

Marywood University in Scranton, PA. He was a candidate for US Congress from PA District 11 in 2010. Kelly was also a candidate running for Mayor in his home town of Wilkes-Barre PA in 2015. Brian still manages his own IT business (www.kellyconsulting.com), and he has recently completed his 64th book, available at www.bookhawkers.com.

Brian is currently running for office as a write-in candidate as a Democrat for Congress to represent the 17th PA District You can check out his two campaign web sites at (www.briankellyforcongress.com and www.kellyforussenate.com). These are both in the process of being rejuvenated for 2016 and 2018. The good news according to Kelly is that when running as a write-in, there are virtually no campaign expenses.

Thank you for being part of the quiet populist revolution to save America.

Essay # 2

Brian Kelly Wants to be Your Congressman

Do you have what you need to assure Brian Kelly is your right guy for Congress PA-17?

Whenever any company or organization evaluates somebody for a position with the company, in addition to a cover letter, and the compulsory employment application, most professionals are asked to provide a resume. In Academia, that resume is called a curriculum vitae, and seemingly, the bigger and thicker it is, the better it is for the candidate.

I know from teaching in colleges and universities for thirty years that academics enjoy puffing themselves up--sometimes literally. Go to a college graduation and look at the plumage as the PhD's are all gussied up in their finest academic garb, checking out each other's pedigree.

A resume is often as simple as a one page biography (bio), the typical form one uses to gain a consulting contract. A business resume is rarely more than several pages. "Curriculum Vitae" is from the Latin and to be short .it means "life's work." When you see my curriculum vitae, you will be able to tell that it includes everything including the kitchen sink. Technically it is to be a brief account of a person's education, qualifications, and previous experience, which is most often sent with a job application. As noted, in academia, however, the document is often more than just a few pages.

About ten years ago, I made the transition from a business resume to a curriculum vitae when I became a member of the faculty of Marywood University as an Instructor. Eventually, I was promoted to Assistant Professor and a few years later, I departed the

University for various reasons. This permitted me to devote more time to writing and to my other professional consulting endeavors.

A curriculum vitae therefore, is often a large document which includes a summary of educational and academic backgrounds as well as teaching and research experience, publications, presentations, awards, honors, affiliations and other details. If you are curious, you may read my most current vita. If I were to choose to apply again, I would update it at

http://www.briankellyforcongress.com/files/bkcvnov172014.pdf Feel free to save the pdf of my resume so you do not have to absorb it all in one sitting. Enjoy!

Since I am running for office as a write-in candidate for Congress, I will explain how to vote for me in subsequent pages. Before I do that let me tell you some more about myself so you know that you are making an informed decision.

About Brian Kelly

Brian Kelly is married to the former Patricia Piotroski and the couple resides in Northeastern Pennsylvania as they have all their married life of forty-one years. They are the proud parents of three wonderful adult children, Brian, Michael, and Katie. Ben, the family canine, and Buddy, the family feline, reside with Pat and Brian, but are loved by all.

Brian Kelly was born and "raised" in Wilkes-Barre PA. He attended St. Boniface Grade School and Meyers High School. Brian was both a pitcher and a catcher on the Meyers High Baseball team and he was active in many school clubs as well as the student council.

Brian competed for an academic scholarship to King's College and was awarded a four year academic scholarship grant, a National Defense Student Loan, and a work-study job. The job in the federal work-study program helped him make up a $50.00 per year shortfall. Tuition was $475.00 per semester. Scholarship was $250 and loan was $200. Brian is most grateful to King's College for the Academic scholarship and to the Federal Government for the loan and work-study assistance. it was the difference between a successful business life and a blue collar job.

Brian graduated cum laude from King's with a degree in Data Processing, the pre-cursor degree to Business Information Technology. While at King's, Kelly was a member of two honor societies, the King's Aquinas Society, and the Delta Epsilon Sigma National Honor Society. Brian played varsity Baseball for the Monarchs as a catcher / pinch hitter, and then as a starting pitcher in his Junior and Senior years.

After King's, he joined the IBM Corporation as a Computer Science Systems Assistant where he spent 23 years before retiring, under a special program, as a Senior Systems Engineer. During his IBM career, Kelly received his M.B.A. summa cum laude in Accounting and Finance from Wilkes University. After his time at IBM, Brian accepted a position with College Misericordia as its Chief Technology Director / Internal IT Consultant. At the same time, he initiated his own IT Consulting Practice, Kelly Consulting.

After building the College Misericordia campus network, its connection to the Internet, its email and its Web servers, Kelly left College Misericordia and moved on to spend full time in his own IT business consulting practice. In 2004, Kelly joined the faculty of Marywood University and, in addition to maintaining his consulting practice, Brian served Marywood as an Assistant Professor of Business Information Technology and as its IBM i system technology assistant to the Business Information Technology Faculty.

Contact campaign@briankellyforcongress.com

An Entreaty to vote for Brian Kelly from Brian Kelly

Fellow Citizens of Northeastern Pennsylvania, I would like to present myself as a Candidate to be your Congressman for the 17h District of Pennsylvania. As you know, this seat is currently held by Representative Matt Cartwright of Scranton, Pennsylvania. I will be running as a write-in candidate, a Democrat against Mr. Cartwright in the Primary Election on April 26, 2016.

I am proud to say that--but for a few years as an independent living in Utica, NY, I would be a lifetime Democrat and a lifetime resident of Northeastern PA. Right after I earned my Bachelor of Science from King's College at the age of 21, I competed in a tough job marketplace, and I had the good fortune of being hired to work as a Systems Engineer at IBM in Utica, New York. For two years, I lived in Utica as a registered Independent.

My dad, a lifetime Democrat, was very conservative and good man. He was a staunch believer in the importance of labor unions to help the working man in America. He worked as heating specialist at R. A. Davis in Wilkes-Barre and then as laborer at Stegmaier Brewery on "Brewery Hill" in Wilkes-Barre for thirty-one years until the Stegmaier label was purchased by the Lion Incorporated. At that time, the Lion proudly brewed Gibbons Beer.

[G-I-B-B-O-N-S, pure refreshing Gibbons. If it's Gibbons, it's good—so the next time you should say gimme gimme gimme gimme Gibbons!]

That is the essence of the 1960's Gibbons commercial.

Stegmaier of course brewed a number of different beers, including Stegmaier Beer, Ale, Porter, and Bach. When I was in my twenties, the "Brewery" brought back Liebotschaner, a finely crafted and aged old-time Stegmaier formulation. The company made its beer from fresh grains and hops and malt and it aged all of its products in huge vats on the left side of Market St. as one headed up Brewery Hill.

[So! If you want a beer that's mellow, a beer that is really grand, say hey make mine Stegmaier, the gold medal beer of the land. And, so at home, or club, or tap room; always order the beer that they cheer. Served just right; mellow, cool, and light, Stegmaier Gold Medal Beer.]

This is the essence of the 1960's Stegmaier commercial.

My dad was pretty good at what he did and he took his work seriously. For a number of years before its demise, Stegmaier had one of the fastest canning machines in Pennsylvania. My dad operated this behemoth single-handedly. For its day, it was an awesome machine. It put out 600 cans per minute. That's even fast according to today's standards. My dad was quite a guy.

My father and I regularly had discussions about beliefs and ideologies and which candidate truly was best for official jobs, at the local, state, and federal levels. More often than not, he and I were on the same page. My dad's philosophy was that you should always vote for the best candidate for the job, not simply the political party. These discussions eventually prompted me to cancel my registration as an independent, and become a Democrat. In Pennsylvania, Independents have no voice in the primary elections.

Lots of discontent is not only brewing; it's boiling-over.

There is a storm of discontent content brewing across the United States. You can feel it wherever you go. Regular Americans are beginning to pay attention to what our Congressional representatives have been doing against our will in Washington, D.C. Politics and government, and their collective effect on what's happening in America have become regular dinner table topics.

I know nobody today who thinks; thinks President Obama is a good president. In fact most see him as the worst president ever. I think they are right! Sometimes particular Democrats do not have it right. It is OK to be upset. It is OK to show some disgust for what these knaves are doing to us. It's OK.

The leaders of the Democratic Party have betrayed the common man, such as you and I, but none of us writing or reading this paragraph are dead and so we can change the Democratic Party to no longer be the party that separates Americans under the guise of diversity. Instead for the sake of American Unity, we can all join together under the huge umbrella of the US Constitution and reject those leaders who have led us down a path to perdition.

What's not OK is to sit around and let these same elitist establishment types come back again in 2017 to inflict more harm on the American people. Vote them out. You have the power! We have the power!

I decided to run for Congress as a write-in candidate because somebody has to represent US. I am a write-in because it means that I do not have to bootlick the rich and powerful for donations.

We need change more now than when we thought we needed change and brought in Obama.

What we do not need is the kind of change that exalts one man and attempts to silence a nation. I ask you to vote "for the people" on April 26 and again in November 8 of this year, 2016. Vote out the proponents of big, intrusive, freedom-taking government and all the politicians will disappear overnight.

It seems the kind of change we have been getting from our anti-American President and the corrupt Congress is good only for the government and the high-paid bureaucrats. It is not the right formula for freedom-loving Americans. While you and I are asking to have government less involved in our daily lives, Congress is throwing one freedom-stealing regulation after another on us on their way to making this a socialist nation. They blame Obama for bringing them up but they do nothing to stop them. This Congress does not represent the people.

We can fix that. All we have to do is vote them out. The people think that they are powerless yet we have all the power. I am running for Congress and I am a Democrat. Please do not vote for Bernie Sanders or Hillary Clinton in the general election. In the primary, because Sanders is at least honest that he plans to destroy America with socialism, he gets my vote over Hillary who will destroy America by selling us all out to anybody that will pay her tribute. In the general election, a vote for either of these America-destroyers is a vote against your won posterity.

You will see this message and hear this message a number of times in this book and on my briankellyforcongress.com website and in my campaign. It is high time that we the people send greedy politicians with self-interests and special interests home for good.

Don't count on other states or other areas of our state to get this job done without our participation. It all starts at home. For US, that is Northeastern Pennsylvania. Our time has come. Good-by to all the incumbents who are contributing to the downfall of America. Good-by to Matt Cartwright and next year good-by to Bob Casey, an embarrassment to Northeastern PA. The 111th Congress was the worst Congress in American History. But, Matt Cartwright, Bob

Casey, and the 114th Congress have nothing good to write home about. Hold your collective noses and then vote them out!

I would hope that by learning about who I am and where I am from and what I stand for, you will conclude that we have unity of purpose. I am one of the regular people in life. I believe that it is my time to serve and if you will permit me, I would be honored to be your Congressman for the people of the 17th Congressional District of Pennsylvania.

Things that are worth repeating are worth repeating

Here is some stuff from a press release by the Brian Kelly for Congress Campaign that is very readable and as mot of Brian Kelly's writings, it calls the people to action. Brian believes that we the people have no choice than to be mere passers-by in a country being drugged into submission by people who hate America.

*** PRESS RELEASE ***
BRIAN KELLY ANNOUNCES HIS CANDIDACY FOR CONGRESS IN PENNSYLVANIA'S 17th DISTRICT

Kelly Says It Is Time To Return The Government To The People!

Brian Kelly, a former IBM Senior Systems Engineer and Assistant Professor of Business and Information Technology (BIT) at Marywood University in Scranton, announced his write-in candidacy for Congress in Pennsylvania's Seventeenth Congressional District on January 26, 2016. Kelly, of Wilkes-Barre, is seeking the Democratic nomination to challenge incumbent Democratic Congressman Matt Cartwright of Scranton. Cartwright, with a huge campaign war-chest is his party's choice and is on the ballot.

Kelly has promised that he will run as an independent write-in candidate in the general election in the event he does not win the Democratic Party nomination. Brian asks all white Democrats to vote for him in the primary as he will serve white voters well. Brian will serve all colors—brown, yellow, black, and red voters equally well. But, as his campaign writer, he told me to mention "white" because nobody else seems to care about white people in America.

Though there may be additional write-in candidates challenging Matt Cartwright and Brian Kelly for the same Seat in the 17th PA District, I would ask your support for Kelly's write-in candidacy. Of the two major candidates for the seat in District 17, Kelly is the only one who is not a lawyer. He is the only one *of the people*. Brian Kelly has worked in the private sector all his life. He hates what is happening to NEPA and the country at large and his solutions can make it all better.

Are lawyers in elected office ever good for the people?

Can't we do better than sending a lawyer to Congress? You may know that only about 5 percent of Americans have ever thought about running for elected office, according to a 2002 survey. Yet another survey shows that 58 percent of lawyers have considered the idea. Why should the rest of us want to be governed by lawyers? Lawyers are in fact nothing more than politicians in waiting. We can do better than sending a politician or a lawyer back to Congress.

They ask the question: What is the difference between a dead skunk in the middle of the road and a dead lawyer in the middle of the road? Who would ever know the answer but a lawyer... A lawyer of right mind would say: "There must be tire skid marks in front of the skunk."

Some others via email ask questions like "How many lawyer jokes are there? And of course the answer is "only two." The follow-on is that the rest of the jokes are true stories."

Even law school students, and I should know because I provided snacks to both of my children, both of whom are great lawyers, while they were attending law school. They paid their own way and had some student loans. My boys know that many lawyers forget their oaths.

From what they learned at home, my children intrinsically know that lawyers are a negative breed of their own. As a group, they are dishonest and mean, deceitful and spiteful, arrogant and oblivious. Even other lawyers think other lawyers are not trustworthy. Not every single lawyer, but most of them. The exceptions don't change the rule. Nobody would consider putting a bouquet of roses on a pile of manure to reduce the stench? It doesn't work. Lawyers are at a minimum not respected in society unless they have provided some specific benefit to some specific person. Most humans expect that lawyers will expel an unpleasant scent.

Brian Kelly expresses his reason for running for public office in these simple terms: "to return our government back to the people." Kelly notes that government spending is out of control and that only a change in leadership can turn government away from more unpopular tax-payer funded bailouts, crippling taxes and government-takeovers. Cartwright, a successful layer of course is for more spending and for more taxing of those who earn a living in Pennsylvania.

Brian sees the solution as "We must create jobs, not destroy them. The policies of Matt Cartwright and Barack Obama are killing US businesses. Like many, I fear the building of a huge, never ending bureaucracy wherever you look."

Kelly finds government as the only "industry" prospering. He deeply fears the seemingly predestined government takeover of healthcare, the disrupting of the doctor patient relationships, and the bankrupt notion of repressive energy tax legislation and the destruction of the industry that produces America's most abundant energy source-coal. He is concerned that all of this excessive government, which the incumbent supports, will make it tough for Americans to live like Americans. "You can be assured that I will work to stop these flawed changes brought about by poor leadership." Kelly said.

Kelly said that in order to restore the economy, "a brand new Congress must be committed to getting government to stop micro-managing the economy." Kelly told his supporters, "Matt

Cartwright, who is on a mission to be the next Paul Kanjorski, has spent his time in Congress pushing for bigger government, higher taxes and what can be argued as tax-payer funded bonanzas and even jobs for the politically well-connected. This is exactly the medicine that we do not need."

Kelly said: "It is no accident that at the heart of the corruption problems in Northeastern PA, a certain few for far too long a time have always been well taken care of—first under the huge 'Kanjo' umbrella, and now the Cartwright umbrella. Umbrellas must be eliminated!

Meanwhile those of us who do not live in gated communities, protected by the Secret Service or others, -- the rest of us taxpayers, waste our ink writing to this Congressman. We are to accept that all "favors" go to special interests near and far. We know that members of Congress such as Matt Cartwright have squandered our economic resources, reduced economic growth, and have operated in a wrong-headed plain unfair fashion.

As good as Paul Kanjorski was for NEPA in his early years, and as good as we all thought Matt Cartwright was going to be, things have not worked out well for NEPA. Can you argue with me? It is time to return this important office back to the people. It is time for NEPA to have a level playing field wherever government touches the public."

Government takeovers, national debt, a huge deficit, and the major job killing regulations of the Obama / Cartwright administration are being rejected summarily by all Americans.

Pennsylvanians will be hurt even more than others by the shutdown of coal and an "energy tax" since many PA communities still have a viable coal industry. Yet, Matt Cartwright has lined up against Pennsylvanians again on this issue. His votes are to kill the energy industry in PA though taxes or restrictive regulations.

Besides being unfriendly to Pennsylvania business and industry, the only creators of lasting jobs, Matt Cartwright is vulnerable in 2016 because his positions mirror those of the unpopular former speaker of the House, Nancy Pelosi, and the worst president ever, Barack Hussein Obama. Why would our Congressman, against constituent write-ins, support Obamacare and other socialist, budget busting legislation?

It's been hard to find Mr. Cartwright lately in 2016 to ask him why he chose not to represent Pennsylvanians in this important legislation. Unlike Paul Kanjorski before him, Cartwright has not scheduled town hall meetings to meet his constituents because it is easier to hide from the people when you are doing a poor job.

Many of us thought ole Matty was done. Check to see how many people thought Cartwright retired before his name showed up as being on the Democratic Ballot for PA in 2016. Big time Matt Cartwright, lawyer first, and friend of the people last, may be good for California and for Nancy Pelosi and Barack Obama but he has lost touch with average Pennsylvanians. That is why I have written about him in the way I did.

Kelly sees the term "culture of corruption" as overworked but it surely fits the 111th through 114th Congress. "It is not enough just to unseat our own Congressman but all the members of the House -- all 435 of them must go, as well as 1/3 of the Senators.

The broom does not necessarily have to sweep them all out at once but that would be good. There are not many of these actors who have been doing the people's business. Too many in Congress have chosen to serve by using their offices to benefit special interests at the expense of taxpayers. A new broom sweeps clean."

Kelly noted. "This is surely a do-nothing Congress," Worse than doing nothing, by their silence they have given President Obama, the authority of an Emperor without being brave enough to even wimper. Whatever Obama gets, this Congress gives him and it is killing our country. Who as a regular guy hoping to keep America OK would ever permit Obama or his designee to control our America again?

Kelly boasts that he has the backing of no political machine and he is taking no political contributions. "It sure should save a lot of time, not having to run fund-raisers." Kelly said. He is proud to say that his total war chest from contributions is $0.00, and he is nowhere close to having to pay the "Obama / Cartwright Rich Tax."

Kelly feels his message will be brought forth now that he has made it known that he is a serious contender for the nomination and for election in November 2016. By writing in the name Brian Kelly, the people will recognize that a regular old "John Doe," not a political operative has made himself available to the people.

Kelly once had a lot of affinity for the "Tea Party People," and those like you and I, who are not part of a named group but who nonetheless have been justifiably enraged at the unresponsiveness of our government. From Kelly's perspectives, the left made the tea party seem like a bunch of life pervert and nobody complained loud enough to know they that it was not the tea, it was the name and it was the people, regular people who the left hoped to discredit but could not because they were simply you and me. .

Kelly said: "At this stage of my life, I see things that can be so much better if Americans had better representation. I feel in many ways like George Bailey from the Building and Loan in "It's a Wonderful Life," seeing the face of the corrupt Mr. Potter in too many hallways of government.

I'd like to take the spirit of WW II Brigadier General Jimmy Stewart (real life) as George Bailey and keep all the Potters out of government for an awful long time--even if it means that I have to put in a few years myself."

Kelly is not interested in a career in politics and when elected will stay for just one or at most a few terms. Kelly says: "A regular person holding an office becomes a politician when trying to be reelected."

Matt Cartwright has an awful lot of money. "I would probably take a few vacations if I had his loot," says Kelly. He will have a dramatic financial advantage over write-in challenger Brian Kelly. Mr. Kelly expects the public to be overwhelmed by the Cartwright media war chest. "The biggest thing Kelly has going for the campaign is that he is very active spreading the word through letters and press releases so that the people know they can write his name in on the ballot and that will be the start of something good.

When the constituents of NEPA get in the "voting booth," no matter how many dollars Matt Cartwright has spent to advance his candidacy, the only thing voters must remember is two words forming one name, Brian Kelly. It is just ten letters and a space. When they write that name in BRIAN KELLY on the ballot, things will begin to change almost immediately.

"The voters will ask themselves, 'is he a politician?' and the answer of course is 'no.' As voters across the US are trying to free themselves from machine politics, with votes to the highest bidders, Brian Kelly is betting that in Northeastern PA, being 'of the people' will matter more than anything on April 26, 2016. " Kelly said.

As previously noted, Kelly, unlike his opponent, is not a lawyer. Like most of us, Kelly sees that as another big advantage. Too many elected officials are lawyers and it is no accident that the laws are unnecessarily complicated for the rest of the people to read. "That may be good for lawyers but it is not good for the people. Look at the poor legislation passed in the last year alone--despite public outcry. Look at the do-nothing Congress pleased to permit Barack Obama to break the Constitution to serve his own agenda. This Congress does not even have enough respect for the people to read the legislation without passing it blindly."

As an independent computer expert and consultant, Kelly is accustomed to solving big business problems. His career in Information technology and his 23 years with IBM and more importantly, his ability to listen and think about the big issues we are all facing, give him the background to figure out the right solutions for US and then fight for them. Kelly thinks Donald Trump offers the same for Americans concerned about Americans.

For most of his life Kelly, like you, has observed the damaging results of entrenched power of all sorts on the lives of those of US living in District 17 in PA and in America. Politics! Politics! Politics! Nepotism! Cronyism! And, then more of the same! We have had it all and we still have it all in Northeastern PA. For Kelly it has gotten too much to take. Along with the mess the Country is in now, the fact that politicians in NEPA are more concerned about their political careers instead of doing well for America is a major motivator for his candidacy for Congress.

As an author, Brian Kelly wishes he was not so old that he has been able to write 63 books, many of which are in the high tech field. He is tickled, however, that he has written twenty-one books since 2010 hoping to convince his fellow Democrats that we must not permit the power brokers in the Democratic Party to ever win again. We can still be good Democrats if we force the power brokers to be more human.

In 2007, Brian Kelly began research for his first book about government. In 2008, he released these first efforts with a book titled, Taxation Without Representation, sold on the Internet at such places as Amazon.com and www.bookahwkers.com. He has updated the Taxation book and wrote twenty-one new patriotic books since then. These are the product of major research as well as his clear opinions as to how the country has gotten off course. Two of his newest books include Wilkes-Barre PA Return to Glory! and The Constitution 4 Dummmies. Those who think the thoughts of the people do not matter, will not read either of these books

On May 4, 2010, when Brian Kelly, considering retiring from his consulting business, first ran for Congress, he released his 42nd book titled, Jobs! Jobs! Jobs! Subtitled, *Where Have They Gone? How Can We Get them Back.* The text of the book is available free on this site in simple articles and the inexpensive paperback is available at www.bookhawkers.com.

Kelly is an ardent defender of the Constitution and in many of his books, he adds appendices with the full text of the US Constitution and other founding documents.

By visiting this website at www.briankellyforcongress.com or by reading his books, available at www.bookhawkers.com, it is easy to know that Brian Kelly stands where you stand on the issues of the day. He sounds like one of US because he is one of US.

Brian Kelly asks all Democrats in NEPA to vote Brian Kelly in the Primary. Two words, both needed for a write-in. He also asks Republicans and Democrats to vote Kelly in the general election. "I promise that you will have change --- this time it will be change that you can live with." And, won't that be a grand day. ---------

Best wishes for a better America from Brian Kelly.

Sometimes it helps to see things again in summary form:

Brian Kelly's Summary Background:

- E. L. Meyers High, W-B, PA, with honors
- B. S. from King's College cum laude
- M. B. A. from Wilkes University magna cum laude
- 23 years with IBM Corporation as Senior Systems Engineer
- 15 Year Ongoing Consultancy
- Business and Information Technology Consultant
- 5 years Technology Manager -- Misericordia University
  - Chief Technology Officer
- 7 years with Marywood University
  - Assistant Professor, Business Information technology
- Author:
  - 63 books,
  - Hundreds of magazine articles

Brian Kelly believes in the effort to restore reverence for God and respect for the unalienable rights to life and liberty in America.

Brian Kelly believes and understands the notion of self-government of, by, and for the people – as well as our moral, physical, and economic sovereignty. Kelly has written four books in this regard:

Taxation Without Representation; *Obama's Seven Deadly Sins* - ; and Healthcare Accountability. Included in each of the first three books is a full copy of the Constitution of the United States, something that we all should keep in our hands in these trying times. Kelly penned another book titled: Jobs! Jobs! Jobs! in 2010. Altogether he has written 64 books. Most were penned between 2010 to 2016. All are available from www.bookhawkers.com.

Brian Kelly is easy to understand. He is an advocate of a complete overhaul of our taxing system and the abolishment of the 16th Amendment, thereby eliminating the tax code and the IRS. The Fair Tax has many advantages over the current income tax system.

The Fair tax seems to have the most advantages of all other options, but even the Flat tax is far better than our current income tax system

- Brian Kelly is an advocate of strong border security
- Brian Kelly is ready to declare our nation's reliance on God as fundamental.
- Brian Kelly will work to protect our unalienable rights to life, liberty, and private property.
- Brian Kelly will help restore and protect our constitutional republican form of government.
- Brian Kelly will work to protect the institution of marriage and the traditional family.
- Brian Kelly will work to protect our national sovereignty, military strength, and border security.

The rest of this book describes Brian Kelly's candidacy so that as had been announced in the past by those against Mr. Kelly, nobody can say that Brian Kelly is not the best candidate for America.

Essay # 3

Since you are not a normal Democrat; why should I vote for you?

Question: I have read a lot of the stuff on your site and, other than that you don't seem to be a normal Democrat, and I am not so sure about that, why should I vote for you?

Answer: Thanks for the question. I wrote many of the things on this site myself so I am not sure if you really read them all. I am not sure that I can convince anybody that I am worthy of their vote. Though the fact that an ordinary guy permits himself or herself to go through this process, I think that unless they have other ideas about a representative democracy that ought to be enough. Let me take a crack at this question though it intrinsically annoys me. Don't hang up early on this... OK?

About being a normal Democrat, perhaps you are right. I don't seem to be one because I am not. The Democrats have changed. I'd like to think that I am how Democrats once were when my dad was a staunch Democrat and he convinced me to change from Independent to Democrat. Perhaps Democrats should be that party again.

The key phrase in all of this is "for the people." Democrats had always been for the people. It was always implied that the people were Americans. Today, Democrats have an extremely hard left agenda like as if Russia was a good place to live. I do not think that way.

Since Progressivism, Socialism, and Communism have proven to be bad for the people, wherever they are brought forth, a Democrat Party that is hard left is for just a few people. It is not for the common, hard-working, regular American person. Your parents and my parents would have disdain for a party that seems as its goal to assure people they can be dependent on government and all will be OK. That is not my Democratic party.

Why should you vote for me? If I were taking big campaign donations from all of the people that could buy a piece of me, I am sure somebody interested in my success would have a better answer to that question. I am answering this question myself and the best I can come up with is because I care about the things you care about.

If you were different and you liked the government running everything and telling you what you can and cannot do, then I would not be the right candidate for you. I am not for an all-powerful government that infringes on the freedom of the people.

If you like having over 50% of the population on the dole, taking from the all the people through the government, I am not the right guy for you. If you want to get lots of real good stuff, other than good spirit, from the government, without ever having to give anything back, I am definitely not the right guy for you.

If you want help in achieving a better life, think of me when you are voting. If you want a government that tries to motivate the people to be self-sufficient and rugged individualists, and lovers of freedom, count me in. if you want an America for Americans first, please include me in your voting plans. I am the right representative for you.

By the way, I am a staunch American. I think that we all should help fellow Americans first and foreigners second. If we choose not to help because our hearts are hard, then that is for the churches to help us. It is not the government's role to force us to be nice to others by taking our wealth without our permission and giving it to somebody else.

Government has nothing to give but that which it confiscates from others. If anybody is going to be charitable, it should not be the government after stealing the fruits of the labor of the people, it should be the people themselves.

Think about all the taxes you pay that do not go for roads and bridges, or to defend our precious country. Should it not be the people and not the bureaucrats in Washington who determine which charity gets your donations, and how much? Do we need the hand of what can easily be a corrupt government to tell us how good we should be to our neighbors? No! We go to churches to get God's message to treat all well, to be charitable with our gifts, and to help all that we can. It is our choice to do so. We go to government for things churches do not give -- such as roads, bridges, security, and defense.

You should vote for me because I will take your vote to mean that all of the freedom robbing bills that are now becoming law, or have become law under the worst Congress ever---the infamous 111th--- these laws that reduce our freedoms and steal our hard earned wages, should all be repealed the day I get in office.

There was no good reason for government, the least efficient and least capable manager of goods and services to be in charge of healthcare. Yet, a Congress more tuned into special interests than the people's interests forced its will on the people. Only those who like the principles of Karl Marx, who want to place government bureaucrats between their doctor and access to care, could go for such lies.

Besides Obamacare, there is no reason for government to levy the destructive energy tax called cap and trade other than to send more jobs overseas and place a major tax on everybody who heats or air-conditions their home or who drives a car or, quite frankly -- anybody who exhales carbon dioxide.

You should vote for me because I will be a voice of common sense against terrorism and I will help the Congress help the President work to combat this threat very seriously, not frivolously, while sparing the lives of American troops. I do not think those thoughts are mutually exclusive.

I will make my voice count in Congress. I will yell loud and clear, I want no enemy combatants tried in US courts. I want Gitmo to be retained as a safe and secure place that helps Americans, even if it may ruin Obama campaign pledges made to other countries. The reasons to close this first-rate facility in a tropical setting are hogwash forms of hard left propaganda.

I think that if you read this and you read the rest of this site, and maybe even some of my books, then you will know that I am your best choice for Congressman in the 17th District. Just give me the word, and I will pick up the challenge and I promise you that I will go, get my job done for the people, proposing as much pro-people legislation as possible, working to repeal those laws, especially the new ones, that hurt the people, the country, our wonderful way of life, and the American Dream. Please ask the same question of Matt Cartwright!

Essay # 4

Why are you running for Congress

Question: Why are you running for Congress?
Answer: That is a very good question?

As a husband and father, my family was very important in this decision. In 2008, I considered running and my family and I discussed it at length and I decided not to run. In 2010, I put a team together, and I saved some money and my family gave me encouragement, though they still had some trepidation about the potential impact on our family unit. We'd like to remain reasonably private and regular people. At the same time, there were other factors.

This year, six years after having the #1 position on the ballot for the Democratic Primary, I am running again for Congress as a write-in candidate, because of a number of reasons. I am running as a write-in because I simply cannot afford to try to outspend the fat campaign war-chest amassed for Matt Cartwright. So, I am running a campaign on the cheap but with your help, I will prove that money does not trump the will of the people.

My family agrees that things are even worse for Americans this time around. I would be happy my candidacy to defer to a like-minded person if one shows up. Short of that there are a lot of things that are wrong, with our country, and I would love the opportunity to get my hands dirty to help fix them. I am at the right time of my life and I see no reason why I should stand by and watch as my family's liberties, both economic and civil, are being wiped out by our own government.

Reagan had a sense of humor

You may remember Ronald Reagan's great sense of humor. Reagan, for example is credited with a number of sayings. Without me offering any commentary, you can learn a lot about why I am running for Congress from the fact that I really do love the following Reagan quotes.

"The nine most terrifying words in the English language are: 'I'm from the government and I'm here to help.'"

"Approximately 80 percent of our air pollution stems from hydrocarbons released by vegetation, so let's not go overboard in setting and enforcing tough emission standards from man-made sources."

"I've noticed that everyone who is for abortion has already been born."

"I am not worried about the deficit. It is big enough to take care of itself."

[Brian Kelly adds that Ronald Reagan never met Barack Obama] "Politics is supposed to be the second-oldest profession. I have come to realize that it bears a very close resemblance to the first."

Does that help you know where I stand on those issues? There is a whole menu on this site. It is called "Platform Points." It discusses just about any point in my platform and offers where I stand on it.

In life, we are often told that we must be for something, not just against things. I am for a lot of things but one of my best ways of describing why I am running for Congress is to speak in the negative. "I do not want the government controlling my life." Yes, there is a corollary to that precept: "I do not want the government controlling your life."

I can recall some great people in my life making comments that now make so much sense. For example Dennis Grimes Senior from Fulton Street in Wilkes-Barre, who, when told that Congress did not get much done this term, would always say: "good!" Then, of course with the twinkle in his Irish eyes, he would add a little priceless gem to make the sentence end well, and I would smile. How profound he was.

Each time Congress meets we lose more freedom. There are too many people who think that you should do this and you should do that. It is bad news when they get into office. They want to make sure you do it and they have the power to make laws to make it mandatory. I want to let you alone to lead your own life, and I hope if you are in similar circumstance, that you will let me alone to lead my life.

I believe that freedom is our most important gift. Our forefathers shed their blood for our freedom and liberty. Freedom has no real limits but being a good person does add restrictions to freedom.

For example, I believe that in many and possibly most cases, a particular individual's freedom ends where another person's freedom begins. So, there will always be disputes between people and so it is OK to have some rules that help arbitrate man's behavior to his fellow man. My favorite rule book was created by the Founders. It is called the Constitution. Barack Obama and the 111th through 114th Congresses think they know better than the rules in this book and that is one major source of the angst in this country.

The fewer impositions of government on the people, the better. Government should get out of lives. We can handle salt, and sugar, and heat and cold. Government should worry about roads, bridges, traffic, and defense and a few other limited items.

I see no reason, for example to have a government law that outlaws beer, or two-ply toilet tissue, or red hair, or tattoos. I see no reason for laws that command that I must do something such as attend church services on Sundays -- or not attend, or turn off my air conditioner in the summer (car or home) because somebody else wants me to save energy. I would not want to be commanded to use Dr. X as my family physician instead of Dr. Y. I surely would not want to have a visit scheduled with Dr. Kevorkian.

I would not want to have to use gasohol when gasoline or an alternative energy source suits my tastes. I would not want to have to buy health insurance, a pair of mittens, blue socks, a notepad, or cough medicine if I am not so inclined. I want liberty. I want freedom to make my own choices in life. On everything but abortion, I am pro-choice. On this issue I am pro Mom and pro Baby!

For me, it really is all about freedom, which is the positive of "no government control." I do not want government monitoring or controlling of my life from womb to tomb or any other area in between. I have written twenty-some additional books between my first run for Congress and now, many of which include a full copy of the Constitution of the United States.

The Constitution was created in order to form a "more perfect union," since it corrected a number of flaws in the Articles of Confederation. It is not perfect but it is lots better than Nancy Pelosi and Harry Reid and Barack Obama making up freedom-destroying rules on the fly, as they go along.

My campaign is a very new campaign and for many it will not seem like much of a campaign. That's OK, the founding fathers would love it. If the truth be known, there is no real "campaign," just a bunch of friends who help me with great advice and my very active keyboard where I pen letters to the editor, press releases and essays for my web site. Thank you for reading this one. I hope to be able to select some "free" events in which to participate, but they are not offered frequently as incumbent politicians know that the more you know about me, the less you will like them.

The vast percentage of the people I know believe that we must fight back against a monstrous, out of control government. Those who know me believe that I would make a difference in Washington, and though they have cautioned that nobody gets elected without putting together at least a little machine, they enjoy the fact that we are doing this without any machine and with no contributions.

In 2010 my little team and I went out over three weeks and brought in 1516 signatures though I needed only 1000. Only! Try and get them. I will never do that again as I had to shut down my life and the lives of too many friends. We were out getting signatures but since all of us have some type of gainful employment, we could not have an exhaustive campaign and did not and will not try to knock on doors. It is tough enough just penning these articles.

I ran once for Congress and once for Mayor of WIlkes-Barre and so I will make some mistakes. My Web site will have some misspellings and I may say things incorrectly. Please point them out to me and I will correct them.

www.briankellyforcongress.com

It is true that most voters (rightly) mistrust their Congressman and Senators. My plan is to be one of a new breed that puts the ordinary person first. My plan is to listen to the people of District 17 and work to help make the founding principles, the very best principles for our country, as the best solutions to make all of our lives better. That's the way it is supposed to be.

Though I am a Democrat, I am very people oriented and very pro-American. Americans first! I have no use for the radical hard left, whose influence is undermining our democracy. As a constitutional conservative democrat, I will work to get us back on track while always listening to the people to know when more track or a few switches are needed.

Thank you for "listening." Don't forget to vote on April 26, 2016

Essay # 5

Do We Really Need Change?

In a word, "yes."

We needed change from a number of the policies of the Bush Administration. All ills are not Obama ills though most of the deadly ones definitely are.

Whether George Bush was really bad or not is debatable but the Country surely was suffering from Bush fatigue and Bush. Eight years or so earlier, the country suffered the same malady with Clinton fatigue.

Nobody, in either the Bush or Clinton Administrations made it seem like it was a good idea for the government to get more active. Nobody asked the government to begin to control everything. We did not need that kind of change.

From unimportant things such as big taxes on juice and soft drinks and small pleasure items to one ply toilet paper instead of two-ply to more serious matters such as no Mammograms for women over 40. The Obama czars are quietly serving but they have been destroying America for their seven year existence.

Socialist bureaucrats have been changing the US to what Russia was before President Reagan ordered the big wall torn down. Most people cannot believe how bad it is but then, others have their eyes wide shut.

So the people don't wake up and find Obama and the 111th through 114th Congresses in their socks, their underwear, their private items, and their bank accounts, this administration and Congress have been hurrying to get the job done before anybody notices that our freedom is disappearing fast. That is not the change anybody was seeking.

It is my party, the Democrats, who have done all this to us and it is time to replace all of the corrupt Democrats in Congress with real people. While we are at it, let's get rid of all the Republicans too. However, in a head to head with Republicans and Democrats, remember Republicans are just ineffective in defending America. Democrats want to destroy us.

It is hard to believe that deep down the Democrats in Congress want to make everybody's life worse. Yet, they are doing the best they can to make the country fall apart. It cannot be by accident.

Democrats under Obama are undermining the country at every turn and they are making America weak? They are not blind. They know what they are doing so we must get rid of them. It is happening before our eyes and it is one of the big things I want to change. If you don't see it, then permit me to admonish you of one thing, "Please pay attention, our freedom is on the line."

As bad as the Bush Administration was reported to have been by the low-ratings media, ole Bush and company never tried to stifle our lives with massive regulations and massive taxes. Bush may have wanted and may have gotten his but he was not trying to take yours. Bush never declared human exhale a noxious and hazardous gas. The hard left--should never be in public office again-- Democrats have been plain silly since they took control and we need to bring sense back into Congress.

Additionally, I do not recall Bush and his cronies changing things so that extreme Muslim Terrorists ever found America an easy target. Democrats will not even use the term terrorist. What is that all about? Should we simply capitulate?

Dr. Thomas Sowell, one of America's deepest and finest thinkers was asked about his greatest fear in a recent interview. You won't believe his response but it is true. He said his biggest fear is that the Iranians will get nuclear weapons and attack not Israel, but the United States. Well, Obama and Kerry have already given them permission for nukes.

Dr. Sowell added that this was his deepest and first fear but his follow-on fear was even worse. He said that what would happen in the US if the Iranians actually attacked us is his worst fear, bar none. He said that let's say Iran fires a nuke and hits a major city like Chicago.

He is convinced that if Obama is president when it happens, that he will surrender. Yes, you heard me right. As commander in chief he has the power to surrender the US to a foreign power. If Iran blew up Chicago, would Obama surrender the US to Iran and dismantle our government and the military so the Mullahs would have no resistance when they came to Washington to rule. Ask Thomas Sowell!

Thomas
Sowell

Yet, this is precisely what the party in charge and the "outgoing" President have done. This group of bad actors have done so bad that I am embarrassed to be a Democrat. Many Democrats and other Americans, including myself are looking at the Bush days as the good old days. That's how inept our 111th through 114th Congresses have been and our President's continual worldwide apology tour has not helped our image at all. "I'm sorry" may have made the day for Connie Francis but it is destroying the notion of American Strength." Even Castro got an apology.

My candidacy to win the Democrat nomination as you might suspect is not endorsed by the established Party Leaders because they would like to give you more of the same corruption and misuse of the people's treasury. My candidacy is the right medicine for the Democratic people of NEPA, not necessarily the "go with the flow Democratic leadership." I do not expect any established politicians to get up any day soon to give a speech that heralds my choosing to run for office. In fact, I am tickled about that. I would be worried otherwise.

It's time for all hard left Democrats to be called home and to be replaced by better Democrats such as yours truly. As hard as it may be to say, even the Republicans in Congress have done a better job over this last year as the Democrats.

Democrats have become socialists, Marxists, fascists, while calling themselves progressives. Most of the people of Northeastern Pennsylvania will have nothing to do with that. That's why they like me as a candidate. I offer a no politics approach to government and I think the people understand that quite well. They are looking for a change they can live with.

The Administration with hard left Democrats in charge has abandoned the American people and along with the 111th through 114th Congress with Democrats in charge most of the time, they continue to siphon the American Treasury to make it more comfortable for trespassers in our country than for citizens.

Why do the foreign nationals who sneak into the US have more rights than citizens and how is it they benefit from our bounty more than we do? I regret to say that Democrats today in Congress have become un-American. That is not the change anybody asked for and it is time to send them home and to clean up the Democratic Party. It starts at Home in NEPA. If we cannot muster the strength to send socialist Matt Cartwright packing from Washington, why should we expect anything to get better?

No incumbent who does not love America better than Lobbyists should be elected. I had been looking for a wholesale 435 representatives exiting but there are some, though very few who still have what's best for America at heart. There are not many Democrats in their lot, unfortunately. That's why we need more Democrats and even more Republicans but very few of the same. The Founders never expected the people to vote scoundrels back into office. We are smarter than to ever do that again. And, while we are creating some good change, maybe we can clean up the Democratic Party so the people no longer fear it!

Essay # 6

Question: Are You a Democrat in Name Only (DINO)?

Answer: First of all—that is a great question.

I may not know the answer to that question but I will tell you how I feel. A long time ago, when I was a kid, I believed the Democrat Party was the party of the people. Though I started out as an Independent, I became a Democrat in my early twenties because of the principles of the Democrat Party. My father believed in these principles also and he taught me them at the time. Democrats represented the ordinary people and the Republicans represented business. The people needed good representation from the Democratic Party because big business already had the Republicans

It was that simple until the notions of conservative, liberal, populist, and socialist entered the picture. I am not liberal. I am not socialist. I am conservative but maybe I am more populist than anything else. I like Donald Trump, Ted Cruz, and John Fitzgerald Kennedy. I guess we would have to ask the party leaders if there is room for good ole conservative or populist thinking Democrats in the party today.

The Republicans have a problem also with RINOS -- Republicans in name only. Good people who are Democrats and Republicans are so fed up with government and dirty corrupt politicians that more and more of us no longer like Democrats or Republicans. Some call us independent thinkers; others call us Populists. We're not ready for Hillary's lies, Sanders giveaways from our pockets, or O'Malley's inability to think on his feet.

We want government changed to benefit the people instead of the entrenched established politicians on both sides of the aisle. Seems to me that is why Donald Trump appeals to Democrats and non-

RINO Republicans. He owes nobody anything and at least we would not have to worry about big money controlling politicians running the US as Trump can afford to love America with his own money. Nobody else can.

More members of my own family have switched from Democrat to Republican than ever before in one election. Why? Because Democrats have become too socialist and are too close to Soviet-type communism for comfort. Why? Because Donald Trump and to an extent, Ted Cruz offer a clarion call to regular people from both parties to let the DINOS and the RINOS behind and become a conservative populist to help America grow again.

The regular folks see Hillary Clinton, Bernie Sanders, Jeb Bush, Lyndsey Graham etc. as club of establishment elites who do not care which Party is elected as long as their perquisites and power remain in tact. And, so, this is a revolt against the elite me-first establishment by the regular John Does out there. At the presidential level, this movement is authored by Donald J. Trump, a real rich guy who needs nothing from nobody. (OK, Anybody!)

Thank you Mr. Donald Trump for setting us free -- Democrat and Republican alike.

I was never a D-Party organizer nor have I had any real affiliation with how the platform of the Democratic Party is created. Yet, over the years as it has evolved, I think I know enough now that this platform stinks. It is a fringe platform and if you are white or you are any color and you work hard for a living, you are not wanted in the D-party today. But, if you do no work, welcome aboard. This is killing America. I see more and more Democrats switching to Republican, not because they are pro-business per se. They are sick of everybody but them having a piece of the pie.

Actually, they are not that selfish. They simply want to keep the piece of the pie that they earned at the workplace and see no value in giving Joe down the street from some other country, the little bit they have. The new American, who is still a citizen, is not a socialist or a communist and they want to put a stop to how our government is killing America. They do not want foreign nationals taking their jobs nor do they want them having a shot at weakening the power of their vote.

Though there is no official word, there apparently is no room for independent or populist thinking in today's Democratic Party and I hope to change that. The fact is that the Democratic Party no longer espouses the values that you and I believe in. The Democratic Party is no longer for the people. The Democratic Party is no longer for the employee as they get their funding from huge crony corporations, even if the worker is unionized.

The Democratic Party chooses the rights of illegal foreign nationals over American citizens. If you are white or of any color and you choose to work, the Democratic Party does not seem to include you in its thinking. It's not only time to change the Country; it's time to change the leadership of the Democratic Party so that it again represents all of the people, not just those with a hard socialist / communist agenda.

Putting a pathogenic liar in the office did not work when her husband was President. Anything based on lies fails. Putting a Communist in the White House means that if you work, you will have to work harder to support the voters needed to keep the Obama-likes in office. I don't like the notion of Obama or anybody like him. He's killing us and Matt Cartwright is helping him stick in the knives.

The Democratic Party wants to take from the employees today and give to the non-employees and even illegal aliens and, they want to give the non-workers far larger amounts of your salary than needed to sustain their lives. Ironically very few of the top Democrats in the party give very much to charity. They are as cheap as it gets. They expect the common man to carry the load rather than the elite. If you work, with the Pelosi / Reid / Obama Democratic party, you better hang on to your wallet.

My father, who was my mentor regarding politics, did not like the slide the Democrat Party began to take against the working man. He did not like that Democrats had completely abandoned the white man. It seems that they began to include everybody who was not a regular worker into the fold -- apparently for the proposition of gaining more votes.

My knowledge of the people of NEPA is that few Democrats are like the San Francisco hard left who now control the party. NEPA people do not think the way Nancy Pelosi or Barack Obama thinks. When I ran for Congress in 2010, Paul Kanjorski was in lock step with San Francisco. But, he was out of step with Northeastern PA -- way out of step. Mr. Kanjorski became rich while in office on the backs of his constituents. When he could no longer utter a sentence that was in tune with the thinking of the voters in Northeastern PA, we sent him packing but we did not do too well when the districts were realigned.

Matt Cartwright, a Kanjo disciple for sure, may not be a thief for his own benefit. But he steals from every worker when he sends their wages to those who choose not to work or are aliens from foreign soil. Matt Cartwright is an enemy of NEPA more than Paul Kanjorski ever was. Kanjorski kept a few bucks for himself. Cartwright wants to take most of what you have and give it to the guy next door who promised to vote Democrat all his life...even if he is not a citizen.

As the one man in NEPA who thought exactly like Nancy Pelosi, Paul Kanjorski voted with Ms. Pelosi 10 out of 11 times. For that, we the people unelected him and put in Lou Barletta. Matt Cartwright snuck into another district and got elected as an unknown.

His ideals are so similar to Barack Obama's nobody would have elected him if they knew him. Cartwright wants to hurt NEPA as much as Obama has hurt us all. If Cartwright were for NEPA, you would be hearing about it. He can't tell you how he thinks because even Democrats for years would kick him out of office. I am a real Democrat. I think you should be able to keep your own money. I think Cartwright is a traitor to the people of NEPA.

Instead of Democrats thinking that I am a DINO, I'd say I am a more traditional Democrat. My philosophies are like those of JFK. The guy who was in office when I first ran for Congress, Paul Kanjorski was a DINO. Matt Cartwright is a DINO. Both became San Francisco hard lefties which makes them both, especially Cartwright lovers of socialism with communism on the doorstep.

Cartwright does not love regular people who work for a living seeking the American Dream in a Capitalist society. We know that with socialism, history tells us there are only nightmares. How have you been sleeping lately in Obama times? Cartwright and Obama share a mindset that you and I reject. Check out their philosophies.

When it is campaign time, like now, we may even get to see our Congressman, Matt Cartwright but few other times. And when he is in public view, we may find our hard leftie appearing to be ambidextrous, which may mean you can pitch lefty and righty but it can also mean deceitful, disingenuous, and deceptive. Because of this, you must remember his record—Kanjo failed us ten out of 11 times. Cartwright is our new Kanjo.

Cartwright consistently voted against NEPA but his record shows that he pleased all the lefties in San Francisco. Let's send him home for a long time this year.

Why should we want to give up our hard earned healthcare and workplace rights so that some politician someplace can have a better life? Have you heard Cartwright screaming at the top of his lungs that he wants Obamacare? He wants you to have it but he won't take it no way no how. He won't trust it to his own family but yours is OK! Congress is exempt and our boy will not put legislation forth to make Congress have the same healthcare they force on the rest of us stiffs.

If you read the campaign site www.briankellyforcongress.com and perhaps one or several of my books, you will see that before Obamacare, everybody had healthcare and this whole thing is just an opportunity for the Socialist / Communist part of the Democratic Party to gain control of Y-O-U and never have to let Y-O-U go.

When they get full control, and I am running so I can stop that, there will be no freedom or personal liberty for any of us. No, I am not a DINO. Look to Nancy Pelosi, Harry Reid, and Matt Cartwright, and you will find living, breathing DINO's. But, don't get too close. They will hurt you.

I know I am not a Republican because I do not own a business with employees and I do not make a real ton of money -- maybe a quarter ton in a whole lifetime. I am not against making a ton of money as I think that is the American Dream for all people. Socialism is the great dream remover of our time, as it takes untamed wild birds and makes Lemmings of them.

Right now, the Republicans have a better crew of America-lovers than do the Democrats... but Republicans are hurting also as protectors of we the people. Rather than become a Republican, I would rather stay a conservative Democrat. Rather than saying I am a DINO and thus worthy of expulsion from the Party, I repeat that Nancy Pelosi and Matt Cartwright are the DINOs. From my set of mostly 20-20 eyes, she and Cartwright belong to the Communist Party. They should both leave the Democratic Party. Hey, they are DINOs!

Harry Reid is another DINO, not far behind Nancy Pelosi. He is leaving the Senate supposedly but we'll see. Nevada clearly thinks Harry Reid is a DINO and he has no chance getting reelected because Nevadans are real people. My bet is that NEPA will expunge Matt Cartwright as Nevada will expunge Harry Reid if he chose to run again. Matt Cartwright needs the same treatment by NEPA Democrats.

Reid, Pelosi and Cartwright are radical socialists who would not be called Democrats in days gone by. They'd be on the first bus out of town and my dad and your dad would be the ones putting them on the bus. They should be sent home and there should be no room in the Democrat Party for them ever again. Regular people, with real people values need to stand up and send Cartwright packing. There is no reason for the Democratic Party to admit certified hard left whackos and their whacko billionaire supporters into a party that wants to be for American citizens. Moreover, what is the Democrat bias against white people? Where did that come from?

No, I am not a DINO, But, if you are looking for DINOs; they are easy to find. Just search on Harry Reid, Nancy Pelosi, Matt Cartwright, and Barack Obama, and you'll get lots of hits. They are DINOs worth removing so we can start this ship up again the right way. They have had their DINO days. DINOS such as these are not good for your idea of America.

FYI -- Check this out
America Rising An Open Letter to Democrat Politicians. It's time.
http://www.youtube.com/watch?v=662R2awSwPQ

Essay # 7

It's Tough Being Unknown!

Everybody knows somebody sometime

It is not such a good thing when "everybody knows somebody sometime" and you are not on the list. When you are the new guy, sometimes the press forgets.

Many of my friends have asked me how I hope to get known in the six counties that make up Congressional District 17. Let me tell you, it is tough without major political financing. But, I will persevere with press releases, letters to the media, and I would be pleased to make a speech whenever asked. To get the attention of the Press, a candidate must first "press" his nose against the glass of the media outlets (Newspaper, Radio, and TV) to get their attention.

Unfortunately for unknown and not-well financed candidates, in my experience in having run unsuccessfully three times, the priority of the management of media outlets is to maintain their viability by bringing in ad revenue and not giving up space or time to citizen candidates. I know that it will not be smooth sailing.

Fortunately, I can set up and manage web sites and I can use Facebook. Therefore, I can reach web surfers without any cost. I will have a Donate Button on many articles and on many sites so that supporters can give what they can. Based on what I get, I will buy whatever media I can afford. Thank you ahead of time for your donations.

In their article, Journalism in the Digital Age, five Stanford (cs.stanford.edu) authors-- Danny Crichton, Ben Christel, Aaditya

Shidham, Alex Valderrama, Jeremy Karmel, take the time to explain the absolute importance of a Fourth Estate (the media) as the most important pillar of our Democratic Republic:
Here is what they say:

"Journalism has long been regarded as an important force in government, so vital to the functioning of a democracy that it has been portrayed as an integral component of democracy itself. In 1841, Thomas Carlyle wrote, "Burke said there were Three Estates in Parliament; but, in the Reporters' Gallery yonder, there sat a Fourth Estate more important far than they all" (On Heroes and Hero Worship).

Four years earlier, Carlyle had used the phrase in his French Revolution: "A Fourth Estate, of Able Editors, springs up, increases and multiplies; irrepressible, incalculable." Carlyle saw the press as instrumental to the birth and growth of democracy, spreading facts and opinions and sparking revolution against tyranny.

"The fact of the matter is that democracy requires informed citizens. No governing body can be expected to operate well without knowledge of the issues on which it is to rule, and rule by the people entails that the people should be informed. In a representative democracy, the role of the press is twofold: it both informs citizens and sets up a feedback loop between the government and voters.

The press makes the actions of the government known to the public, and voters who disapprove of current trends in policy can take corrective action in the next election. Without the press, the feedback loop is broken and the government is no longer accountable to the people. The press is therefore of the utmost importance in a representative democracy.

"Another, related, function of the press is to expose people to opinions contrary to their own. This function is perhaps the most valuable in the Internet age; while people can in theory get information about the actions of their government from online sources, it is all too easy to find opinions online that match one's own. Informed decision-making on the part of voters requires an awareness of multiple points of view, which is not likely to be obtained if voters bear the sole responsibility of seeking out information on relevant issues.

The news media provides a forum for debates to take place, as well as moderating and curating the arguments presented by all sides. It is, of course, idealistic to suppose that media give equal, or even proportional, representation to all opinions, but the fact that many media outlets present themselves as nonpartisan sources of information makes them a better forum for debate than online sources such as blogs, which are typically maintained by one individual or a small group of people with similar opinions..."

It would be nice if the mainstream media took the time to provide forums in their media to inform the public of the candidacies of all citizens running in all elections. Even if it were not every day, and the media used its power to permit short speeches to be carried on their on-line sites. The media's job in our Republic is to inform the public, and let me just say they can do a far better job. When you consider that in the three times that I have run for office,

I have not even been interviewed or permitted to participate in any event on Public Television, even though we the people pay for it. I was interviewed when I ran for Mayor on Election Day but the channel chose not to run the video. Let me repeat, the media do a disservice to the community by not informing the public of its choices.

I have never been endorsed by any media outlet as I have never been well known by their advertising departments.

Reporters and Newspaper Executives are not easy to move to your side. They do not feel obligated to assure that the public knows what each candidate has to offer.

The Press's problem in this primary season for the D17 Congressional seat is that "Nobody expects that a guy 'who nobody knows,' will run for office." And so I know that as a candidate, I will be very close to being summarily ignored.

I do not think that anybody in the Press tries to purposely hurt me. But, my experience in the past has been that even after writing letters to the editor and sending multiple press releases trying to assure the media that I am a viable candidate, I found myself excluded from much of the news coverage. Whether it was intentional or not, no media outlet tried to make up for the loss of publicity my campaigns suffered.

I would hope that regardless of how well known a candidate may be in this upcoming election, the papers and the other news media of NEPA should permit candidates to do things that help the people become informed about where they stand on the major issues of the day. In the past, I have had few vehicles provided for me that would help the people know who I am.

Thus, anybody other than an incumbent or one well-endowed by blessings (cash) can expect to be relegated to the back seat in an election.

The papers. TV, and Radio etc. should permit candidates to submit a short essay, perhaps several times during the campaign. In some media, a short essay per week might be appropriate. In others, a mere mention every now and then would be very informative for the people.

The charter of the press is to provide news to the people, and news about who may be chosen to represent the people is worthy news indeed.

For me, the bottom line is that it is not easy for democracy to continue when the people have a tough time getting on the ballot and then they must fight against mythical forces to convince even their neighbors that they are serious in the endeavor. My political friends say that is the nature of the beast. I say, the beast is the problem.

An attentive press, concerned about the people, is very necessary to help a person not endowed by the machine to get the message out.

I do have this Web site, www.briankellyforcongress.com. I Thank you very much for visiting. I know that people do not just appear on this site. Most have to learn about it from some other media. Then, they can come to this site to learn about me and to learn why many believe that I am the best person right now for the job of Representative of the People.

I think they are right and I am working as hard as I can with the constraints that I have to help you know that I think like you do. Now that you are here, please write down the ten letters BRIAN KELLY on a sheet of paper and take it in the voting booth with you on April 26, 2016. Thank you.

Thank you for visiting:

Essay # 8

Press Release: Brian Kelly Running for Both Congress and Senate

Contact: **Brian Kelly's Congress & Senate Campaign**
Email   **bkcampaign@yahoo.com**
Date: **January 27, 2016**

****** PRESS RELEASE ******

First Ever PA / US Candidate Running for the US House and the US Senate Simultaneously!

WB's Brian Kelly Is Working to Beat the Odds and Win Both Times!

Will PA choose incumbent politicians who hurt the people or a candidate who loves PA & America?

Like you, Congressional Candidate Brian Kelly is disgusted with the current leaders in government. He is asking for voters to forget about what big government can do for them. The results are in and the verdict is "0." Kelly is asking voters to write him in twice -- once in 2016 for Congress and once in 2018 for the US Senate.

Brian hopes to help release our wonderful country from the grips of the socialists and communists.

Kelly ran for Congress in 2010

In 2010, Brian Kelly put a team together so he could run for the US Congress. The full team worked every part of the three cold winter weeks that the state permitted to solicit signatures for the ballot petitions. His team got 1500 plus signatures and he was on the Democratic Primary ballot in Northeastern PA for Congress.

Nobody other than entrenched politicians can get 1500 signatures for anything in three weeks unless they have great friends. One thousand valid signatures were required. When Brian and his Campaign Manager, Marty Devaney, went out together, they averaged about 6 signatures an hour counting the number of cold knocks on doors resulting in no answer or a very cold reception. Kelly offers this as a recount of his next two attempts at success:

"In 2012, needing twice as many signatures (2000) by law. I decided to put a team together to run against US Senator Bob Casey. Very sadly, my good friend and campaign manager, Marty Devaney was quite sick and subsequently passed away. I called off my campaign dogs and asked supporters to write me in.

Two thousand ballot-access nomination signatures were way too much without an organization. Even at full strength, it would have been tough for us to hit 2000. When it was over, even Luzerne County for its own reasons, refused to count my write-in votes, and the state refused to intervene to require any counties to do so."

"In 2015, needing "just" 100 signatures (Just try to get 100 signatures at about 6 per hour in the coldest weeks of the year.), I ran for Mayor of Wilkes-Barre, PA. A small team of family and close friends brought in about 250 signatures and that was more than enough to put me on the ballot. Signatures were tough to get for sure. My opponent and neighbor from South Wilkes-Barre checked my petitions hoping to have me disqualified."

So, as you can see, Brian has had some experience working with ballot access in Pennsylvania. Most Pennsylvania lawmakers are quite happy with ballot access as it is, since it favors incumbents of both parties. "Only those who want to send the incumbents packing should be unhappy at the job our state lawmakers do in making it fair for normal citizens to run for office," Kelly said.

Candidates without ballot access In Pennsylvania as noted above may decide to conduct a write-in campaign. Unfortunately, write-in campaigns rarely meet with success. There are a few exceptions such as when Lisa Murkowski beat Joe Miller for Alaska US Senator in 2010. That means that if we do not want the same Congress and the same Senate that both operate against the people, we too can write in a patriot from Pennsylvania; and like Murkowski, he too can win. His name is "Brian Kelly." If Lisa Murkowski can win; so can Brian Kelly.

"After having spent in the neighborhood of $10,000, mostly my own money in three failed campaigns, it may come as a surprise that I am ready to give it another go. As a write-in candidate for both 2016 and 2018, my plan this time is spend far fewer dimes. Yet, I can't stand the thought of having only politicians who hurt America running for important offices in PA. If you do not want the same losers running the government, please vote out anybody who is holding any office. No incumbents, please -- from either party!"

"I am a citizen who loves America and my plan is to save our country from both the political class and the donor class. Together, they are in the process of systematically destroying America. Barack Obama, Matt Cartwright, and Bob Casey, Jr. are in their ranks. None of them care about Pennsylvania or Pennsylvanians. They say that we cling to our religion and our guns. They have all contributed to the demise of the USA with their love for illegal immigration and their far reaching regulations that have crippled our economy. It is my deep love for this Country as much as I see that our politicians do not, that motivates me to put my hat in two rings at the same time. Therefore, I am making the following announcement:"

"This year, 2016, I am running for the US Congressional Representative seat in the PA 17th District. In 2018, I am also running for the US Senate Seat from Pennsylvania. Matt Cartwright is the current incumbent in the House. His term is over for good (hopefully) at the end of 2016.

When Bob Casey Jr. steps down from office at the end of his second term in 2018, with your grace, I will have served one full term in the House of Representatives.

Then, I will be sworn into office as a US Senator on *January 3, 2019.* *This will be for a six-year term ending on* January 3, 2025. That is my plan."

Brian Kelly wants to tell you some of the reasons why he is so intent on running for both offices. Running for both at the same time is his idea and it is so that he can be better known in both races and when elected, he can make a greater impact for the people Kelly has a few things to say about that:

"Bob Casey and Matt Cartwright might as well be Obama clones. These two "representatives" have no original thoughts as they are plugged into the Obama way 100%. From whichever Party you hail, Democrat or Republican or other, as long as you love America, finally we have all agreed that Obama's policies from the last seven years and into 2016 are destroying our wonderful country.

Only liars and cheats continue to believe in Obama because nobody is dumb enough to believe this President is doing anything to help Americans. We have just one year left to survive the BHO travesty and he will be gone. I sure hope we make it without further damage.

But we may not--unless the people of our great country stay awake. We cannot believe the drivel and the outright lies coming from the corrupt US press. By now, we all know that Obama has no plans to help Americans regardless of how the press props him up. But, this current President does have about a year left to finish destroying the country.

Our country has already been sufficiently weakened. We must clean out all (not just some) of the corrupt anti-American politicians in Washington, DC. Senator Casey and Representative Cartwright must be removed from office through the natural election process. Both have a sickening solidarity on many issues that are not favored by regular people in Northeastern PA. Few in NEPA, for example, appreciate Obama's attacks on the second amendment and his do-nothing response to terrorism. Check out the list below about how these two legislators are expected to vote this year, regardless of how we the people feel about these important issues:

- Both are 100% for Obamacare even though it costs taxpayers more.
- Both are happy giving IRS and the NSA more power over citizens.
- Both want u to pay huge taxes on inherited parents' property.
- Both are against US energy independence.
- Both want EPA to shut down coal plants & increase energy costs.
- Both want to keep spending money we do not have.
- Neither want to limit Obama's executive power.
- Both want same sex marriage -- not just civil unions.
- Both are against a solid US space program-- No NASA!
- Both against Medicare; prefer Obamacare for seniors.
- Both are pro Obamacare as the only US insurance.
- Both endorse Obamacare penalties for young and healthy.
- Both are OK losing America to Mideast terrorists.
- Both believe PLO and Israel are equally dangerous.
- Both support Obama's nuclear weapons gift and $billions to Iran.
- Both are pro Castro even when Castro is against US.
- Both are pro UN even when UN is against US.
- Both are pro terrorist rights & Constitutional protections.
- Both want children of illegals to become citizens by decree.
- Both want illegal aliens to have government-subsidized healthcare.
- Both support no raise in Social Security benefits for seniors.
- Both want amnesty for Illegal aliens and expedited citizenship.
- Both love big government; huge debt ceilings; no budget.
- Both want high taxes to pay for the slothful.
- Both love Common Core Obama educational principals.
- Both want Feds to take over control of schools from the states
- Both have no respect for 2nd Amendment.
- Both want gun control and gun confiscation as in Australia.
  Both are pro-choice and pro-mutilation of womb babies for profit.
- Both OK with live baby dissections and sale of body parts.
- Both want free birth control for the sexually active.
- Neither ask that the sexually active pay for our cigarettes and drinks
- Both see global warming a big threat
- Both ignore science that dictates no global warming problem. .
- Both are Anti-energy.
- Both OK with Americans freezing v offshore drilling.
- Both are happy paying Mideast terrorists for oil and gas.

Feel free to go to their web-sites and ask them your favorite question. From what I have seen when you get the answer from one --- Obama, Cartwright, or Casey, you need not ask the other two.

Keep the faith. Good Americans can defeat this tyranny in our midst.

Essay # 9

Vote for the Underdog!

BRIAN KELLY ASKS PA 17TH CONGRESSIONAL DISTRICT VOTERS TO DO THE AMERICAN THING: "VOTE FOR THE UNDERDOG."

After a lot of thought, Brian Kelly, a lifelong Democrat, not a socialist, or communist such as Matt Cartwright, launched his write-in campaign for Congress in January 2016. Why is Kelly not trying to get on the ballot? In a few words, money and kindness. Kindness because his friends and family need not work so hard for a cause that is highly unlikely to be successful. Though they would be pleased to help, the electorate often does not care how pure a candidate may be. The system must change first before Brian would ask his friends to participate again. Money is obvious. Write-in campaigns permit frugality.

For 1000 verified signatures, at least 1500 would be required. To accomplish this a candidate not willing to pay $5.00 a signature for such a service as most politicians do, would have to devote 250 hours over three weeks (not a minute more) in the coldest weather of the year, to collect the required number of signatures himself. At eight hours per day, this would take about 32 days to accomplish. But, there are only 21 days permitted by the state.

Candidates are not permitted to start early or finish late. They are not permitted to take their three weeks in the summer while on vacation and while most neighbors are easier to find. They are not permitted to do anything that may not force them into spending a lot of money on their campaign. And, so most regular people choose not to run for political office.'

Regular citizens have seen those seeking office with their petitions but most of us do not realize the job they have to do. A candidate must get anywhere from 100 to 2000 signatures depending on which office they seek.

Since only 50 names fit on a sheet and there are many mistakes and often the sheets of good friends may have as few as two or three signatures. it is not obvious that each signature sheet (petition) must be notarized at the candidate's expense.

Then, instead of getting more signatures on the last day, you have to summarize and then drive the petitions to Harrisburg to wait in line for hours to have each signature go through a preliminary evaluation.

If you are one signature short after verification, you're "o-u-t." Sorry Charley! This is a formidable obstacle. The process is designed by state politicians so that only incumbents or entrenched politicians or those who can pay others to do their work can afford the time or expense to run for Congress. Anybody with a real job is immediately excluded.

Brian Kelly told his supporters in 2016 what he was all about and that he believed he had just as good a shot at winning the primary election as a write-in candidate than by having to pay many just to get on the ballot. Kelly's plan of course depends on the media honoring the fact that he is running, and so far the media, other than the Citizen's Voice has completely ignored him. Brian hopes all Times Leader subscribers switch to the Voice. The Voice gives regular Citizens a voice. The Times leader has ignored direct communication to editors and writers.

Kelly believes that what separates himself from Matt Cartwright is that he is not a politician, has never been a politician and does not ever want to be a politician. Moreover, according to Kelly, Cartwright is a socialist on most matters and a communist on many others. He has not represented the people well and he deserves to be thrown out. Kelly is prepared to do his part to assure that this happens.

By all accounts, Kelly is the one underdog in what is now a two-person race in the Democratic Primary. Kelly is not endorsed by the Citizens Voice but at least they help him get out his message, whereas the Times Leader chooses to take in the ad revenue from Cartwright.

Brian Kelly will not be on the ballot simply because he cannot afford to be a politician and so he is the declared underdog. Everybody loves an underdog, especially in this case, in which the underdog is a patriot who pledges to work to undo all of the harm that Matt Cartwright and Barack Obama together have forced on our wonderful country, America.

We can do better. Help Brian Kelly help you by writing to your papers, calling in to the radio, and writing the TV News stations, especially Public TV.

Why is it that just about all elements of the press will have Kelly slotted as a non-entity in the primary? Besides the newspaper coverage, there more than likely will be no TV coverage at all. Even Public TV will choose to stay out of the race in the 17th District. Why is that?   No debates? Which public are they helping?

Kelly thinks he knows the answer to those questions:

"Regular citizens are not newsworthy. A regular citizen may make a fine representative but he or she doesn't sell air time or newspapers. Regular citizens with their paltry subscription fees support the press but the ad revenue keeps the presses rolling."

"Politicians, on the other hand---they are exciting. They are always doing something interesting in their chases for office. They do sell air time and they sell newspapers but that does not help regular Joes'.   Unfortunately, politicians do not make good representatives as we have more than discovered over the past years."

Brian adds:

"I am a regular guy appealing to regular people who do not have to sell air time or newspapers. I trust the people more than the media to make the right decision. For every regular Joe out there who knows they could do a better job for the people, "than the bums that are in office," when you go into the voting booth, look at the ballot position and select write-in [OTHER], and then type in Brian Kelly.

I am a regular person who has had a very successful career with IBM and as a college professor. I am competent like yourself. Like you, I can do a heck of a lot better for the people than the politician that we elected the last two terms. We can do a lot better with you or I in office. This time I am running write-in Brian Kelly." Next time you run, it will cost you hard work and time but if you go the write-in route and more people tune in. you can be elected and it will cost you next to nothing.

This time, Brian Kelly is counting on Americans in PA District 17 doing the American thing on April 26th. Americans root for the underdog. In this case, the voters in Northeastern Pennsylvania can vote for a citizen, not a politician, who has been made into an underdog by the media simply because he is not a politician.

Say no to politicians on April 26. Brian Kelly would be pleased to represent your interests, and not the special interests, in Congress. He owes nobody any favors.

God bless America!

Vote for the Underdog... Just write in Brian Kelly this time. It's that easy! Next time, send out a memo like this, and we'll all be voting for you and it will not cost you a dime... I think!

Essay # 10

The Brian Kelly for Congress Platform

Platform Bullets -- Influenced by Alan Keyes

As Brian was evaluating the items to include in the platform, he used the existing work of Alan Keyes, one of his favorite Americans. This assisted him in quantifying the issues of the American people. The following platform, however, is not that of Alan Keyes. It is Brian Kelly's platform, and as you know, Brian Kelly is hoping to gain your favor as the candidate running in Pennsylvania against incumbent Matt Cartwright for the 17th Congressional Seat for the House of Representatives from Pennsylvania.

Please read the items well as they are categorized in alphabetic order. The items within the categories are arranged in no significant sequence.

If you have questions or concerns about any of these, feel free to start a forum thread or send Brian an email at bk@briankellyforcongress.com. Thank you for your time and patience.

A. Abortion

1. A child has a God-given right to life from fertilization to natural death.
2. All unborn children are persons, not masses of flesh.
3. Abortion is "prohibited" in Declaration of Independence- prohibit abortion.
4. Embryonic stem cell research experiments with human life.
5. Human embryos in such research "gravely immoral" and unnecessary.

5. Need a Constitutional amendment defining life from conception.
6. Abortion is unjust and immoral.
7. Mothers have no right to take a womb baby's life.
8. Only exception is to preserve life of mother.
9. Brian Kelly is pro mom and pro-baby. No mom feels good after killing a womb baby.
etc.

B. Budget & Economy

1. Deficits must be eliminated.
2. Out-of-control spending must stop.
3. Budget must be balanced just like a household.
4. Balanced budget amendment to the Constitution is a great idea.
5. Need amendment to the Constitution to limit borrowing and spending.
6. No company is too big to fail.
7. If your business can't make it, expect no government help.
8. Government can have no stake in private enterprise (GM etc.).
9. No more bailouts period.
10. Eliminate "pork"
11. Cut Spending -- address the Debt

C. Civil Rights

1. Redefine separation of church & state according to Constitution.
2. Protect religion from the state, but not vice versa.
3. Right to acknowledge God is the foundation of all our rights.
4. Public display of the Ten Commandments is a state's right.
5. Official language of US is English.
6. Marriage is between a man and a woman.
7. Civil unions OK without the notion of or the word, "marriage."

C1. Affirmative Action

8. We cannot cure a past injustice with another injustice.
9. Preferential affirmative action patronizes blacks, women, other "minorities.'
10. Affirmative action is discrimination in reverse.

D. Corporations

1. Corporations should not have citizenship.
2. Corporations should not be permitted to become too big to fail.
3. Corporate mergers do not serve the public well-being.
4. Corporations should have plans to use American workers in America
5. Corporations should pay the social cost of "offshoring" jobs.
6. Corporations want cheap immigrant labor to replace Americans.
7. Corporate executives employing illegal employees should go to jail.
8. Incentives should be given corporations to not engage in labor arbitrage.
9. Workers' pensions need to be separate & protected in bankruptcy
10. Create two tier corporate income tax e.g. 10% domestic, 35% foreign
11. Tax penalty e.g. 20% for offshoring jobs
12. $5.00 per hour tax for each hour of illegal alien work.
13. Reduce foreign visas such as H1-B by 90% to dave American jobs.

E. Crime

1. Death penalty is sometimes essential
2. Oppose "hate crimes" legislation -- redundant they are already crimes.
3. Harsh penalties for gang-related crimes in the same vein as RICO.

F. Education

1. Sex education is a private responsibility.
2. This is a Christian Nation.. Prayers to Christ or any god should not be barred.
3. Schools forfeit funds if they expose kids to gay propaganda / pornography.
4. Sex education if it exists at all, should be abstinence-based.
5. Relationship of college tuition rises & taxpayer subsidies is a big problem.

6. Funding for any agency promoting a political entity should be cut--Dept of Education was using taxpayers dollars to promote the President
7. Teachers keep politics out of classroom -- no political indoctrination
8. Federal government may not use dollar incentives to affect state behavior. All states share equally according to population
9. Common Core -- Out! No Fed influence in education

G. School Choice

1. Parents & local citizens know better than educated masters.
2. Empower parents to choose schools that reflect their values.
3. Break up the government monopoly on public education.
4. Eliminate Department of Education -- use parental / local boards.
5. Pro-voucher; keep fed gov't out of K-12 education.
6. Money should follow parents' education choices.
7. Outlaw politically correct brainwashing.
8. Empower parents against the monopoly of public schools.
9. Let communities decide school rules-- such as all-male / female academies.
19. Make & Female restrooms

H. School Prayer

1. Who allowed the judges to drive God out of our schools?
2. Prohibiting school prayer creates a godless, anything goes society.
3. Christian schooling should receive tax credits. Religion taught off hours
4. Advocate prayer wherever you want in schools
5. God in schools may keep Columbine-like shooters out.
6. Constitution does not forbid prayer in schools.
7. Need prayer in schools and by educators.

I. Energy & Oil & Environment

1. Cap and Trade or similar legislation if enacted, needs to be repealed.
2. Need to seriously develop proper alternative fuels but do not force technology while fossil fuels including coal still work quite well. .
3. Drill here, Drill now in the meantime. Assure off-shore safety
4. Build clean and safe nuclear plants in the meantime.
5. Energy impact of hybrid fuels needs to be evaluated.
6. Ethanol burns more energy than it saves and it raises food prices?
7. Explore & exploit ANWR, while respecting ecology.
8. Drill Offshore in all states that permit it.
9. "Global Warming is a hoax" so bad name changed to "Climate Change"
10. A Prophet should never make a profit" Al Gore - an approaching green billionaire
11. Against Copenhagen & Kyoto Treaty
12. CAFE standards kill people in crashes - abolish them.

J. Foreign Policy

1. Speak softly but carry a really big stick
2. Use common sense to make trade agreements that benefit U.S.
3. Evaluate the idea of not so free trade
4. Eliminate Trans Pacific (TPP)
5. Gain International concurrence diplomatically but act for the US
6. Recognize the UN as an anti-US agency.

K. Government Reform

1. Amendment for Initiation, Referendum, Recall at Fed level.
2. Give people a voice to overcome legislators' personal opinions.
3. Strictly limit government to the enumerated powers.
4. Focus on moral sovereignty, tax reform, & sealing the border.
5. No union or corporate or foreign donors to campaigns.
6. Disallow lawsuits that stop public officials invoking God.
7. Churches may identify candidates who favor its principles.

8. Congress should have last word, not supreme court
9. People through Initiation and Referendum get the last word.
10. Obeying the dictate of federal judges means no Constitution.
11. Less Government Control
12. Unlimited campaign contributions, but only by people, & well publicized.
13. Panel to examine constitutionality of executive orders
14. Congress can pick unconstitutional EOs without court appearances and eliminate them w/o Pres. concurrence

L. Gun Control

1. Fiercely defend the Second Amendment
2. Fundamental DUTY of free citizens to keep & bear arms.
3. Gun control mentality means crooks have all the guns.
4. Second Amendment not about hunting, but about national duty.
5. No federal role in gun safety-leave it to states & parents.

M. Health Care

1. Repeal all aspects of Obamacare including the "Porkulus" bureaucracy
2. Euthanasia violates unalienable right to life.
3. Patient in charge; no government-controlled health care.
4. No mandated health insurance and universal coverage.
5. Enhanced EMTALA and Enhanced Medicaid
6. Healthcare Accountability / Healthcare Loans
7. Eliminate pre-existing conditions, policy limits for insurance policies.
8. Protect disabled and vulnerable people like Terri Schiavo.
9. Encourage insurance reward for avoiding tobacco, alcohol, obesity.
10. People should take care of their own health.
11. Sensibly cap malpractice awards --- tort reform.
12. Health insurance purchases across state lines to reduce costs
13. Doctor / patient relationship key factor in any change
14. No Medicare cutbacks in treatment or access
15. Market determines health payments, not bureaucrats
16 Govt. becomes advocate for not v people.

N. Homeland Security

1. Peace through strength.
2. Strong & prepared military.
3. Eliminate political correctness from homeland security and the military
4. Assure Homeland Security Director takes mission seriously.
5. Assure Homeland Security Director believes we are at war.
6. Assure Homeland Security Director is competent.
7. Close up the border.
8. Penalize businesses who hire illegals before Americans - $5 tax per hour.
9. Stand unalterably opposed to all who commit terrorist acts.
10. Killing innocents by terror is same evil as by abortion.
11. Protect military chaplains' right to pray in preferred faith.
12. Allow Christian symbols in national war memorials.
    Country was founded as Chiristian!
13. No student visas to citizens of terrorist states.
14. Coordinate terror watch list with no-fly list
15. Doctrine of terror is killing innocent people.
16. Develop oil independence plan.
17. Drill Here. Drill Now!
18. Don't use Patriot Act to take away freedoms.
19. Send a clear message to the entire terror network.
20. Take preemptive action only if a probable threat exists.
21. Rapidly develop, deploy and/or enhance anti-missile defense systems.
22. Allies share cost of financing terror war efforts.
23. Supports missile strikes against terrorists abroad. (Aug 1998)
24. Establish an effective National Border Guard
25. Seal the borders of the United States

O. Immigration

1. Vigilant maintenance of our sovereign territory and borders.
2. Enforce existing laws against illegal immigration.
3. Sovereignty is betrayed when our borders are not defended.
4. Immigration, yes; colonization, no: oppose guest workers.
5. Control border first, or no other laws matter.
6. Blacks are hurt first by cheap immigrant labor.

7. Excessive multiculturalism weakens American culture.
8. Rescind Bush's order allowing Mexican trucks on US roads.
9. Oppose amnesty
10. Oppose guest workers until unemployment under 5%.
11. Extending privileges to non-citizens invites lawbreaking.
12. Expand orderly legal immigration as appropriate; curtail illegal immigration.
13. No U.S. citizenship for "anchor babies" of non-citizens
14. No immigrants from countries who are controlled of terrorists.
15. Pass the Lifetime Guest Plan for existing illegals.

P. Jobs

1. Provide tax cuts to small businesses to help them provide real jobs
2. Encourage job creation as means to provide health insurance.
3. Work with corporations to undo damage of offshoring
4. Work with corporations to encourage jobs brought back to US
5. Penalize corporations that are bad citizens re: jobs. gov't contracts, etc.
6. No "sexual orientation" in Employment Non-Discrimination Act.
7. Government does not create jobs, only businesses do.
8. Family farms are nursery of moral character.
9. Create two tier corporate income tax -- 10% domestic, 35% foreign
10. Tax penalty to 20% for offshoring jobs
11. $5.00 per hour tax for each hour of illegal alien work.
12. Reduce foreign visas such as H1-B by 90% to dave American jobs.

Q. Social Security & Medicare

1. Keep promises to those who paid so long.
2. Repeal the theft of $700 Billion for Obamacare from Medicare
3. Start Paying Back the SS & Medicare Fund -- generously
4. Tell the truth about COLA and CPI
5. Examine public land and offshore for energy as Social Security and Medicare funding source.
6. Oil companies pay the taxpayers for taking public oil.

R. Tax Reform

1. Repeal the Sixteenth Amendment.
2. Implement Fair Tax
3. Turn off spigot that funds politician's ambitions
4. Income tax has failed. Special people know the loopholes
5. Tax code filled with favors for special interests.
6. Replace income tax with a (1) national sales tax (FAIR Tax)
7. Abolish the income tax and IRS and spend money responsibly
8. National sales tax (Fair Tax) does give control back to people.
9. Augment taxing with tariffs & duties.
10. Income tax gives govt. too much control
11. Excise taxes allow citizens to control tax rate themselves.
12. "Soak the rich" schemes have un-American socialist objectives.

S. Technology

1. No Fairness Doctrine: no equal time if morally objectionable
2. Apply broadcast indecency rules to cable networks
3. Publicly fund NASA
4. Explore space aggressively -- Russia or China in Space is a threat.

T. War & Peace

1. Iraq / Afghanistan -- not best wars -- fight to win or get out
2. Use more technology and less troops.
3. Withdrawing before your enemy stops is called "defeat".
4. Need more countries to share the load
5. Do not go to war frivolously
6. Call Terrorism terrorism and fight it aggressively
7. Do not let Muslim immigrants into US until vetting procedures can be accomplished
8. Defeat ISIS big time by strength and cunning
9. Build areas within Syria & Mideast for returning immigrants to be safe.

U. Welfare & Poverty

1. Constitution does not require separation of church and state.
2. Charity to / from people, not from the government
3. Shift welfare from government to the faith sector.
4. Disintegration of the family causes social ills.
5. Encourage work instead of taking away apartment if one parent goes to work
6. No welfare reward for having a baby.
7. Create a Welfare Accountability System for pay-backs

Matt Cartwright and Bob Casey Jr. and Obama think alike but unlike real Americans.

Our country has already been sufficiently weakened. We must clean out all (not just some) of the corrupt anti-American politicians in Washington, DC. Senator Casey and Representative Cartwright must be removed from office through the natural election process.

Both have a sickening solidarity on many issues that are not favored by regular people in Northeastern PA. Few in NEPA, for example, appreciate Obama's attacks on the second amendment and his do-nothing response to terrorism.

Check out the list in Essay # 8 about how these two legislators are expected to vote this year, regardless of how we the people feel about the important issues.

Keep the faith. Good Americans can defeat this tyranny in our midst.

Essay 11

Brian Kelly is a JFK Democrat

Being A JFK Democrat

You may wonder why I am a JFK Democrat instead of a conservative Republican? The fact is that neither party is perfect for me. I am for business but not for unbridled corporate power. I am for unions but not for thug tactics in the workplace and I am not for forced unionism.

I worked for IBM for 23 years and at the time, IBM never had nor needed a union. Corporations should treat employees right and unions should be for the employees and not on the same team as the managers. At IBM, the founders believed that if you take care of the people, the people will take care of the business. It worked!

I am pro-life and I am against selling baby parts and live brains, though some legislators such as Matt Cartwright, the incumbent, forget this. Deep down most Americans are pro-life. Who wants to kill babies when they are the most vulnerable--when they have not made their first goo or gaw?

I do not believe in protecting smelts and trees if it causes harm to human beings. God made human beings with dominion over all life, and though we must be just caretakers of this awesome responsibility, it should not mean that humans must starve or be cold or freeze in the wintertime to please somebody's twisted agenda.

In many ways some of the great ambitions of the Democratic Party leaders to create an equal world where there is no injustice has placed human beings per se in the back seat and has elevated nonhumans to a status not intended by God. What good is it to freeze in the winter simply because the EPA has chosen to ban coal? I grew up with a coal stove in my living room and kitchen as did my wife, and we are still healthy. Plus, we (the USA) have plenty of coal for the rest of the world. Why shut off the spigot? Why? It makes no sense. China is killing us economically using coal!

Don't you think that protecting unborn babies is more important than protecting turtle eggs? Since it is a crime to destroy turtle eggs, at a minimum, it should also be a crime to kill an unborn child? Who is not pro baby? I think the big shot elite leaders of the Democratic Party have begun to endorse philosophies that give Government, rather than God, supreme power. I believe that God rules supreme above all else. When was the last time you were at a deathbed and heard the grieving family praying to the government?

Though recently I have come to like the philosophies of populists and conservatives like Marco Rubio and Donald Trump and Ben Carson and Ted Cruz. I am not for communists such as Bernie Sanders nor for wannabe communists such as Hillary Clinton. There is no good choice on the Democrat side. Sorry! JFK is sorely needed!

Like the Republican nominees, I do not think that corporations were meant to dominate individuals. I also think that American corporations have an obligation in exchange for the privilege of operating in America to care for their employees and to help do everything in their power to protect and create American Jobs. Hiring illegal aliens must be verboten!

Republicans and many rich Democrats even prominent Democrats such as John Kerry and the Heinz Company have no problem taking jobs overseas. Additionally, they have no problem trying to reduce the American wage to as low as possible by bringing in illegal foreign workers to force the wages down.

Neither party wants to enforce our immigration laws. Republicans want lower wages and Democrats see a huge voter pool in those who are granted amnesty. I am for safe and secure borders and I believe in an America for Americans. If foreigners can live legally within our borders according to our laws, I am for that also. But, American citizens, that's us folks, must come first instead of last.

I would like to share with you information on a site that describes how to be a conservative (JFK) Democrat. My philosophies for the most part fit this description.

http://www.ehow.com/how_2090667_be-conservative-democrat.html
"
How to Be a Conservative Democrat
Contributor: By eHow Contributing Writer
Article Rating: (11 Ratings)

In politics sometimes, it seems easy to categorize a person by their party affiliation. A Republican is conservative and a Democrat is liberal. That is too limiting and shortsighted. Party affiliation does not eliminate individual thought. Defying these stereotypes is not always easy but is what democracy is based on--freedom of thought and choice.

Instructions for being a conservative Democrat

1. Step 1
Believe in small government. Small government means limiting the sprawling bureaucracy that invades people's lives and tries to tell them how to live those lives. Small government also means limiting monetary waste in government that comes with oversized government programs.

2. Step 2
Understand that there are services that the government needs to offer. While the conservative Democrat is against big government, they realize that some social programs are necessary for the country to thrive.

3. Step 3
Realize that a strong military force is a good. While curtailing government spending is prudent, it should not be at the expense of the nation's military. Even in times of peace, a strong military can be a deterrent to other aggressive countries and governments.

4. Step 4

Sympathize with the working class. A conservative democrat understands that the working class is the backbone that built this country. Conservative Democrats keep this in mind whenever taking issue with a policy or ideology.

5. Step 5
Focus on education and family values. Education and family values are an important part of the core values of the conservative Democrat. Education is what made this country a world leader and needs to be the focus of a conservative Democrats political agenda.

6. Step 6
Consider free market capitalism a positive endeavor. A conservative Democrat understands that the free market and capitalism empower the individual to make her own destiny.

For Democrats who feel as I do about life, I am clearly your candidate for the 17th District, and I would appreciate your vote. Matt Cartwright is a socialist / communist, and life will not get better for you or anybody else in the USA, if he and his ilk are permitted back into Congress.

Essay 12

How Brian Kelly plans to win the Congressional Seat in PA D17

Brian Kelly can win the 2016 Congressional Election!

The press will be asking Brian Kelly to comment on how he plans to win the primary election against a well-financed opponent such as Matt Cartwright. Regardless of whether you are a Republican or Democrat, you can write Brian Kelly on your ballot! Just type it in!

Brian Kelly recognizes the road is uphill but he has confidence that the people are looking for honest government and a fresh start. Kelly represents both. This Web Site has much more real information on it than the Cartwright Web Site. Please read what interests you here as Brian Kelly's whole philosophy of what is needed in America today is revealed on the pages of this site.

Nobody is happy with the government today. Along with Barack Obama, Matt Cartwright is just another one of the bad guys, Kelly believes the key to winning this election is to get the message out that he is a very capable yet still a very regular citizen with no political entanglements. Kelly is not an elitist. He does not represent the establishment. He is like all the people in Northeastern Pennsylvania.

Brian Kelly is convinced that it is time to abandon machine politics and bring honest government back to the people. "In fact, for the poor job they did, it would be great if all 435 representatives were replaced. But, it all starts at home in Northeastern PA." We must fire Matt Cartwright, a big friend of big government in order to take back our country from the socialists.

To help answer the media inquiry on how a campaign designed to spend $0.00 can be successful, Kelly wrote a response to answer that probable question. The full text is included below. From the next paragraph forward, these are all press quotable points from candidate Kelly. In this response he explains how he plans to get his message out, and why he expects that his message will be heard, and why he expects to win.

"In a nutshell, the success of my campaign starts with the people of Northeastern Pennsylvania. People are looking for change that we can live with after getting a change we did not expect. Paul Kanjorski's retirement party was announced before he lost but another Kanjo, Matt Cartwright has taken his place and he is serving himself, and I hope to ruin his reelection party.

"I am hoping to get my message out through news articles such as the one you are reading, engaging in talk radio, and making myself available for speaking engagements and debates. My web site www.briankellyforcongress.com is a storehouse of information on all the issues and I have been getting a lot of hits--so much that I rest the site at the beginning of February.

I am asking anybody with an old campaign sign from 2010, to get them into their front yards as it will be too tough for my campaign team to put signs in six counties. Search engines and Facebook will be bringing in more Web traffic soon. Before too long, there will be a buzz in the barber and beauty shops, in the cafe's and the supermarkets, and we all know that word of mouth is the strongest advertising. If you do not see me getting my share of PR, please call the media and tell them to be fair."

"I realize that I am technically at a disadvantage in getting elected by not being able to spend tens of thousands of dollars or more of other people's money trying to become known. But, the people are smart enough to know that I will owe nobody. The machine does not have even a little piece of Brian Kelly. My being in the race may make it a little more difficult for the voters to be aware of all of their choices since I cannot push my message out as the others can. But when elected, it will be a big plus for voters because I will represent to them and not the special interests who paid for the others' big campaigns.

"Matt Cartwright is becoming a powerful guy in Congress, without a doubt. Perhaps he is too powerful for remembering his Northeastern PA roots. The people of Northeastern PA know that Matt Cartwright, just like Barack Obama, is for budget busting big government excessive spending, deficits, and debt. He cannot run away from it. He cares more about illegal foreign nationals becoming citizens than Americans having jobs. He wants terrorists to be able to come in with no vetting. He is not a friend of Israel and he likes the PLO. He is OK with Obama being an emperor instead of a president. Why would anybody send him back to cause more harm to the American people.

"I think voters are real smart and they will be even smarter this time around after the big mistake we all made in 2012. The people will have it easier in the booth this time. Say "NO" to Matt Cartwright. This is the time in America that will prompt the people to vote for somebody they don't know, rather than somebody they know all too well. In many ways the lack of name recognition may very well be a plus for me in this election.

"I am counting on good, solid, Democrat voters in Northeastern Pennsylvania, not socialists and communists, to recognize that there are two candidates but many will know only one of the names as Cartwright is already a well-known politicians. There is a mood of anti-incumbent and anti-politician across the country and this is just as true here in Northeastern Pennsylvania. This will help me in a big way. I have never held public office and so I am completely untainted by political corruption and that is how I like it.

"People are more informed on government now than any other time in my life. Many think we already know more than the politicians. Almost everybody---from engineers to bus drivers to cafeteria workers to police officers to street cleaners to storekeepers are all talking about how bad things have gotten and how bad they are about to get. I am counting on the people to just say no to politicians and machine politics, and anybody who choose to not listen to the people.

Cast your vote for somebody ready to restore the government back to the people. May I again suggest writing Brian Kelly in on your ballot. It is very easy. Bring the spelling of my name with you when you vote, B-R-I-A-N K-E-L-L-Y. Thank you.

"I may miss out on some voters who do no research and who talk to nobody but by April 26, I think most good citizens will make a point of knowing who I am. Quite frankly, the people in NEPA are very smart, and the stakes are too high for them not to vote, and not to choose one of their own. It's time to say no to the entrenched machine politicians. By primary Election Day, the people will know that I am for limited government, fiscal conservancy, limited spending and for cutting taxes. More importantly, I am pro-life in more than name-only. I think none of us are for cutting up baby body parts for sale, yet Matt Cartwright has a do-nothing attitude on this.

"When the folks in NEPA learn my messages and they choose to dig a little deeper they'll find that I also have a real solution for the Jobs! Jobs! Jobs! Problem, not just a bunch of rhetoric. This government fakes right and goes left, way left, so often that the people are sick of the lies and the level of propaganda that would make Joseph Goebbels proud. People want straight talk and straight solutions and they know none of that ever comes from crooked politicians.

"Not only are there no jobs right now, but the government is not even working on the problem. Once the State of the Union Address is finished each year, neither Congress nor the Administration care again that Americans are unemployed and underemployed and that foreign nationals have taken their jobs. While you are wondering when you are going to be able to find a job, Congress will try to convince you that things are getting much better because of their work.

Yet, nobody in Congress or the Administration is doing anything to help you. What has Matt Cartwright done other than kiss-up to Obama? I am not suggesting that government is the answer on jobs. Good capitalism is the answer. But, good capitalism cannot occur when the Congress favors corporations and foreign workers and rich cronies over American Citizens. People are smart. They see the lies. Who does the 114th Congress represent?"

"While checking what my message is all about, the folks may also find that I have a unique solution for illegal immigration that can help the jobs picture. Once the word starts to spread that as a candidate, I am for real, and that my message is for real, the people will know, and the people will have their say. The Press surely has a responsibility in assuring that Brian Kelly, a regular guy running for Congress does not go into History unelected because the Press chose to ignore a regular guy's candidacy."

"It is the people, not the machine, who are the ones who run the government, and we do that by voting. As I said in my opening, the voters of Northeastern Pennsylvania want change they can live with, and they will get that for sure when they cast their write-in ballots for Brian Kelly in the primary.

"When something needs to be replaced, whether it be a leaky faucet or a bad representative, one who has stopped representing the people, shall we agree that the sooner it be replaced, the better. Citizens of Northeastern PA, why wait until the Fall when we can remove the incumbent on April 26th. Democrats have the power of the vote. Send Matt Cartwright back home. Elect Brian Kelly by writing him in.

"My message will get out and when it does, the people will make history. On May 18th, 2010, a candidate, whose campaign contributions and expenses are so trivial the last time he ran for Congress, that he was not required to fill out a financial disclosure form, will have prevailed."

Essay 13

Replace Congress Today!

Start Fixing Congress Forever By Replacing It Today!

My Name is Brian Kelly. I am not the coach of Notre Dame. I am from District 17 in Northeastern Pennsylvania and I am running for Congress as a write-in candidate to help return government to the people.

Representing the people is not and never was intended by our founders to be a career. The current system creates politicians such as Scranton's Matt Cartwright from ordinary people when they choose to be in Congress for life representing their careers instead of the people.

Fixing Congress starts at home! Matt Cartwright and Bob Casey in Pennsylvania are not immune. In fact, they are examples of the problem. Members of congress from both parties after three 2-year terms or two six-year terms should immediately be sent home. It starts right here in Northeastern PA, District 17.

Today's Democratic Party led by Barack Obama and backed by almost 100% of the Democrats in Congress have enacted policies to kill America and especially regular Americans, especially white Americans. Good people who love America must take over the Party and bring some sense to America. A good number of Republicans should be voted out also but they are not as bad as our Party. Democrats are single-handedly destroying everything that's made this nation great.

It is OK for Democrats to be values-oriented and have conservative principles. When anything goes, you get anything and the anything is typically not good. A group called young conservatives has put together a simple and understandable list of nine different ways the Democrat Party has managed to ruin America.

I regret to say that Matt Cartwright, who currently holds the House seat in the 17th PA District is a disciple of this nine point philosophy and must be replaced. Cartwright has proven he is not one of us. Now that it is election season again, if you watch closely, you might even catch a glimpse of him in NEPA. He shows up this time of year to get reelected. They say every now and then he sneaks out of his secure gated community to get a latte.'

Here are the nine points killing America. These are backed by Democrats in Congress and at all levels of the bureaucracy. Ask Matt Cartwright if he subscribes to this list. I suspect he will honestly say yes, because it is the way he has voted. What does Matt Cartwright and other Democratic leaders really want?

1. Let criminals out
2. Let illegals in
3. Let boys in girl's locker rooms
4. Let women kill their offspring
5. Prosecute innocent police officers
6. Persecute Christians
7. Accept barbarity in the form of Islam
8. Over tax the hard working
9. Coddle the lazy

That just about does it. Matt Cartwright and Bob Casey Jr. liberal progressive socialists from Pennsylvania share many philosophies. They are well documented in essay #12. . You won't believe how radical Matt Cartwright actually is because he does not often engage the people with his radical philosophies. But, it is how he votes and how he says he will continue to vote. We must stop him. Feel free to add Bob Casey's name to this greatest hits list above. We cannot afford either. We must defeat him.

Essay # 14
Mr. Smith Goes to Washington

Mr. Smith Goes to Washington

Ladies and Gentlemen, I would like to present myself. My name is Jefferson Smith and I am going to Washington—if you select me of course.

Jimmy Stewart is one of my favorite actors of all time. He is as Americana as it gets with the perfect touch of honesty that makes even men admire the actor and the character the actor is playing. My favorite movie of all time is "It's A Wonderful Life." It gets me every time. Remember the big pot of cash the neighbors brought in to George Bailey so he could keep the Building and Loan going. Well, that's how I think America should be. Every hard working American deserves a break.

What George Bailey did not need was the government stealing from his neighbors so that he could go to college and to heck with Pottersville. Well, it would have been Pottersville if George had not stayed to help all the people in Bedford Falls with his dad's Building and Loan Company. Government intervention creates Pottersvilles and good neighbors create the likes of Bedford Falls. Let's let good people be good people again rather than taking so much from them that Mr. Potter is the only one left with any money.

Mr. Smith Goes to Washington exudes the same emotion from the viewer. It was another of Frank Capra's big hits and Jimmy Stewart as Jefferson Smith is as down to earth as George Bailey. I don't propose that I can do as good a job for Northeastern PA as Jefferson Smith did for his constituency. However, I am as much a babe in the woods as far as politics go as Mr. Smith.

I am running for office to help fight the same type of corruption that Smith faced when he went to Washington. I am up to the task and

I am ready to fight to make America, America again. There is nothing separating me from my chance other than two elections and your two votes. I thank you very much in advance for the votes.

You may know that *Kelly* is the second most common family name in Ireland (after Murphy). It is the 69th most popular surname in the United States. Kelly in many ways is like Jones and Smith.

And so will you indulge me please as I say again. My name is Mr. Smith, and I am going to Washington. I can't get there without your help.

Think of the corrupt conditions that existed in this famous movie as Mr. Smith, played by Jimmy Stewart was a bumpkin when he first went into this Washington den of iniquity -- for him it was the Senate. He was the naive and idealistic Jefferson Smith, the leader of the Boy Rangers. In Washington, Smith soon discovers many of the shortcomings of the political process as his earnest goal of a national boys' camp leads to a conflict with the state's corrupt political boss, Jim Taylor.

Taylor first tries to corrupt Smith and then later attempts to destroy Smith through a made-up scandal. Smith conducts a filibuster and finally sways everybody to not pass the ~~healthcare bill~~. Wouldn't that be nice! (It was the Boy Rangers Bill). Smith would be working to get the bill repealed if it were passed, and the movie would have taken a bit longer. Kelly will make the repeal of the 2700 bill a priority and will replace it with an EMTALA-like bill in the neighborhood of 4 to 8 pages.

Stranger things have happened. I hope to be like your Mr. Smith if you select me. And, so, I ask you to send me to Washington to serve in the House of Representatives. I hope there are approximately 434 additional new Representatives sworn in when I have the honor to take office in January, 2017. I want to thank you all. Thank you very much.

Essay 15

George Says It Ain't Fair

It just ain't fair!

Right after I wrote an essay on the American tax system, my e-mailbox was graced with this note from George.

Who is George?

I think George is John and Jane Doe's long lost brother who has come to life after taking the cattle prod from the Congress one time too many.

Let's let George say it from his email today!

Subject: My Feelings on Our Income Tax System

Broken, complicated, corrupted, expensive, destructive and unfair are the words that best describe the federal income tax system after almost a hundred years of being treated like the personal piggy bank of tax lobbyists and members of Congress.

This is not simply a plain old pig sty. It is one that is so complex that it costs taxpayers and American businesses more than $300 billion a year in just paperwork costs. I am saying this costs is a given-- even before a penny of tax is paid. What people owe but don't pay amounted to more than $400 billion last year—a shortfall that, to make up, increased the average taxpayer's bill by more than a third.

In Washington, D.C., however, a new American aristocracy made up of political insiders, profits immensely by buying and selling pieces of the federal tax code. It is routinely used to buy votes and pit Americans against each other. This explains why almost half of the nation does not pay income taxes while the other half carries the entire load. Does such pandering represent the 'Achilles Heel' of our Republic and spell inevitable economic ruin?

Our tax system makes members of Congress powerful and it makes tax lobbyists among the richest and most influential people in Washington's elitist ranks. In a nation that threw off the power of pampered aristocrats in our founding, we need to recognize that these bastards are back and they are dining out on our money.

Meanwhile, the nation continues to stagger under unthinkable, suffocating levels of national debt. Between promises to spend more and more to buy votes, coupled with insider deals to sell off more and more of the tax code, we the people are always left holding the bag.

Obviously corrupted, our nation's tax system caters to powerful schemers with access to Congressional tax writing committees at the top and ignores the just plain dishonest down below. More than a trillion dollars a year in America's "underground economy" escapes taxation. Drug dealers, prostitutes and gamblers revel in a taxation dead zone along with at least 10 million illegal immigrants. Millions enjoy the fruits of honest Americans' labors as their tax dollars go to pay for highways, our nation's defense, schools and every other federal program, while they pay no federal income taxes.

Well said, George

By the way, the FAIR Tax solves this problem 100%

Thank you!

Essay 16

Congress Needs to Be Sent Packing Today!

If we ship them home immediately, our pain is over!

My Name is Brian Kelly. I am not the coach of Notre Dame. I am from District 17 in Northeastern Pennsylvania and I am running for Congress as a write-in candidate to help return government to the people.

I support the idea of an eight point fix for Congress. It is enumerated at the end of this essay.

There are a lot more problems than the solutions that it would take to solve them. For the most part, the solutions involve sending our self-centered greedy representatives packing out of Washington as fast as we can get them the transportation. That alone would solve mostly everything that is wrong.

Representing the people is not and never was intended by our founders to be a career. The current system creates politicians from ordinary people when they choose to be in Congress for life representing their careers instead of the people.

If I gain the favor of the people in the 2016 primary election and in the general election, one of my first acts will be to introduce a bill that has some good language or very similar language into the House of Representatives to get us back on track.

Remember this key point: Fixing Congress starts at home! Matt Cartwright and Bob Casey in Pennsylvania are not immune. In fact, they are examples of the problem. Members of congress from both parties after three 2-year terms or two six-year terms should immediately be sent home. It starts right here in Northeastern PA, District 17.

I am a Democrat. My father was a Democrat. The Democratic Party that we see today is not our father's Democratic Party. It is not even for regular Americans. As A democrat myself, I know that we must clean out our Party of the elements that are blatantly trying to destroy our great country.

In 2016, I see lifelong Democrats switching to the Republican Party today just so they can vote for Donald Trump and get away from the fringe-loving Democratic Party of today. If you are a regular hard-working American, the Democrats of today have no room for you at their table.

Today's Democratic Party led by Barack Obama and backed by almost 100% of the Democrats in Congress have enacted policies to kill America and especially regular Americans, especially white Americans. Good people who love America must take over the Party and bring some sense to America. A good number of Republicans should be voted out also but they are not as bad as our Party. Democrats are single-handedly destroying everything that's made this nation great.

It is OK for Democrats to be values-oriented and have conservative principles. When anything goes, you get anything and the anything is typically not good. A group called young conservatives has put together a simple and understandable list of nine different ways the Democrat Party has managed to ruin America.

I regret to say that Matt Cartwright, who currently holds the House seat in the 17th PA District is a disciple of this nine point philosophy and must be replaced. Cartwright has proven he is not one of us. Now that it is the election season again, if you watch closely, you might even catch a glimpse of his eminence in NEPA. They say every now and then that he sneaks out of his secure gated community to get a latte'.

Here are the nine points killing America. These are backed by Democrats in Congress and at all levels of the bureaucracy. Ask

Matt Cartwright if he is the author of this list. What do Matt Cartwright and other Democrats really want?

1. Let criminals out
2. Let illegals in
3. Let boys in girl's locker rooms
4. Let women kill their offspring
5. Prosecute innocent police officers
6. Persecute Christians
7. Accept barbarity in the form of Islam
8. Over tax the hard working
9. Coddle the lazy

That just about does it. Matt Cartwright and Bob Casey Jr. share many philosophies. They are well documented. You won't believe how radical Cartwright and many Democrats are since they have stopped being around the public.

Some things are eternal. I received this email on March 6, 2010. It still applies

From: "Friend" <friend@msnx.com>
To: "Brian Kelly" <campaign@briankellyforcongress.com>
Subject: Fw: Fw: Fwd: THIS IS HOW YOU FIX CONGRESS -
Date: Sat, 6 Mar 2010 11:17:41 -0500
X-Mailer: MSN 9
Seal-Send-Time: Sat, 6 Mar 2010 11:17:41 -0500
X-OriginalArrivalTime: 06 Mar 2010 16:17:48.0748 (UTC)
FILETIME=[902A80C0:01CABD48]

THIS IS HOW YOU FIX CONGRESS!!!!!

In the meantime of course, we must send them home. This notion needs to be an amendment, not just an Act of Congress, just so they can't change it again.

I have copied, pasted and sent this email to virtually everybody on my e-mail list and that includes conservatives, liberals, and everybody in between. Even though we disagree on a number of issues, I count all of you who received this email as friends. The proposal is to promote a "Congressional Reform Act of 2009." It would contain eight provisions, all of which would probably be strongly endorsed by those who drafted the Constitution and the Bill of Rights.

I know many of you will say, "This is impossible." Let me remind you that Congress has the lowest approval of any entity in Government. Now (At the time it was 2010 but still applies) is the time when Americans must join together to reform Congress - the entity that represents us or the representatives we elect will overrun us with their assumed power.

We need to get a Senator to introduce this bill in the US Senate and a Representative to introduce a similar bill in the US House. These people will become American heroes. Please add any ideas on how to get this done. Would any member of Congress give up their worldly life to help their constituents? Ask Mark Cartwright and Bob Casey Jr. their thoughts to get a feel for whether the people can ever count on these two greedy bastards to help their neighbors? You can count on my when you elect me to Congress in 2016.

Thanks,
A Fellow American (with editing)
****
Congressional Reform Act of 2017

The Eight Point Fix for Congress

1. Term Limits: 12 years only, one of the possible options below.
A. Two Six-year Senate terms
B. Six Two-year House terms
C. One Six-year Senate term and three Two-Year House terms

Serving in Congress is an honor, not a career. The Founding Fathers envisioned citizen legislators. Serve your term(s), then go home and back to work.

2. No Tenure / No Pension:
A congressman collects a salary while in office and receives no pay (no retirement) when they are out of office. Serving in Congress is

an honor, not a career. The Founding Fathers envisioned citizen legislators, serve your term(s), then go home and back to work.

3. Congress (past, present & future) participates in Social Security:
All funds in the Congressional retirement fund moves to the Social Security system immediately. All future funds flow into the Social Security system, Congress participates with the American people. Serving in Congress is an honor, not a career. The Founding Fathers envisioned citizen legislators, server their short term(s), then going home and back to work.

4. Congress can purchase their own retirement plan just as all Americans.
Serving in Congress is an honor, not a career. The Founding Fathers envisioned citizen legislators, serve your term(s), then go home and back to work.

5. Congress will no longer be allowed to vote themselves an "automatic" pay raise. Congressional pay will rise ONLY by the approval (vote) of the people they represent. Serving in Congress is an honor, not a career. The Founding Fathers envisioned citizen legislators, serve your term(s), then go home and back to work.

6. Congress loses its current health care system and participates in the same health care system as the American people. If it must be Obamacare, a system Congress enacted, so be it! Serving in Congress is an honor, not a career. The Founding Fathers envisioned citizen legislators, serve your term(s), then go home and back to work.

7. Congress must equally abide in all laws they impose on the American people.
Serving in Congress is an honor, not a career. The Founding Fathers envisioned citizen legislators, serve your term(s), then go home and back to work.

8. All contracts with past and present congressmen are void effective 1/1/17. The American people did not make this contract with congressmen, congressmen made all these contracts for themselves.

Serving in Congress is an honor, not a career. The Founding
Fathers envisioned citizen legislators, serve your term(s), then go
home and back to work.

Essay 17

The Founders Expected US to Throw The Bums Out!

Hello America!

The global recommendation is to throw all the bums out.

In every district and every state in America, we cannot permit our own legislator to go back to Washington. Do not think that your representative is the exception because he or she brings the pork back to town. The pork you get back may not be worth the price of the pig you send back to Congress. Their actions again have been nothing short of treacherous for this country and no matter how much pork anybody gets, if there is no America left in which to enjoy the pork, what good is it!

The global recommendation is to throw all the bums out.

Intrinsically, that may sound unfair. So, I vote that we keep Jeff Sessions. You may contend that some legislators, though very few, really have represented America and Americans in the two years of the 114th Congress or the last two years of their time in the US Senate. However, most Americans would be pleased for them to voluntarily exit--stage left. All Democrats should go and any Republican who voted for Paul Ryan as Speaker and Mitch McConnell as Senate Majority Leader.

The default is that it is time for them all to go! America would not be hurting and Barack Obama would not be mocking us all if Congress were doing its job.

The Congress (House and Senate) on both sides, Democrat and Republican enjoy a very, very low approval rating. Your

Congressman from wherever you live, contributes to that low approval rating. So, the sentiment in the country is to not send them back. Get rid of them all! It would make America a better country for sure if we got together and decided to not send any of these treasonous rascals back to Washington. Few people who love America would argue with that.

In NEPA, I hope my fellow Democrats have had enough of incumbency and the pain it lays on Americans. We in NEPA definitely do not want to send back to Congress our socialist representative Matt Cartwright. In just two terms, he has become a hard core socialist / communist. Check out how much he loves Hillary Clinton by examining his web site.

The problem with most people, who claim that they want all of Congress dumped, is that they cannot get up the moxie to dump their own representative. Matt Cartwright knows this. Sometimes constituents who are favored by their Congress person are greedy and want to make sure that their nephews and nieces can get jobs even though their neighbor's kids cannot get the jobs because the system is rigged. The privileged keep incumbents in power because it pays off for them. This is wrong. Ask not what your country can do for you!

So, we do have people across the land who want to dump all incumbents but their own. They would like to dump yours and keep theirs but that cannot be done. The risk of keeping yours is that none of these scoundrels get dumped when the objective is for all to be dumped.

The message is that it starts at home folks. For District 17 in the State of Pennsylvania for example, it is our duty in 2016 to dump Matt Cartwright. He does not represent the people of PA even if he sends you some personal pork every now and then!

The global recommendation is to throw all the bums out.

Essay 18

I am not a Politician?

Please do not call me a politician just because I choose to speak up!

I regularly engage in arguments with people who call me a politician. I am not a politician. When most people think of a politician they mean a person with few values other than greed, narcissism, and me-first attitude. A formal definition of the word politician in this light is as follows:

"A person who acts in a manipulative and devious way, typically to gain advancement within an organization"

I have another definition of my own: "A politician is a person who once elected, decides to go for a second term."

There is a respectable definition and I cannot deny that under this definition, I do qualify since I have been a candidate for public office several times. Here goes:

"A person who is professionally involved in politics, especially as a holder of or a candidate for an elected office." Synonyms for this definition are as follows: "legislator, elected official, statesman, stateswoman, public servant."

My sincere hope is that by my taking a shot at an elected office, I can better help my city, state, and country. Last time I checked, things are not going too well for we the people, and it would be nice if all of us paid a little more attention to candidates to help assure that we get the best people to steer our government. In other words, elected officials should work to help the people rather than serve their political greed.

In that light, here are some very funny but too true humorous definitions of the word politician by some people you probably know or at least once heard about. This list surely is too true and it can be a lot longer:

If God wanted us to vote, he would have given us candidates.
~Jay Leno~

The problem with political jokes is they get elected.
~Henry Cate, VII~

We hang the petty thieves and appoint the great ones to public office
~Aesop~

If we got one-tenth of what was promised to us in these State of the Union speeches, there wouldn't be any inducement to go to heaven.
~Will Rogers~

Politicians are the same all over. They promise to build a bridge even where there is no river.
~Nikita Khrushchev~

When I was a boy I was told that anybody could become President; I'm beginning to believe it.
~Clarence Darrow~

Politicians are people who, when they see light at the end of the tunnel, go out and buy some more tunnel.
~John Quinton~

Why pay money to have your family tree traced; go into politics and your opponents will do it for you.
~Author unknown~

Politics is the gentle art of getting votes from the poor and campaign funds from the rich, by promising to protect each from the other.
~Oscar Ameringer~

I offer my opponents a bargain: if they will stop telling lies about us, I will stop telling the truth about them.
~Adlai Stevenson, 1952

A politician is a fellow who will lay down your life for his country.
~ Tex Guinan~

I have come to the conclusion that politics is too serious a matter to be left to the politicians.
~Charles de Gaulle~

Instead of giving a politician the keys to the city, it might be better to change the locks.
~Doug Larson~

Essay 19

Brian Kelly Is Pro-Mom and Pro-Baby!

Contact: **Brian Kelly for US Congress**
Email   **bkcampaign@yahoo.com**
Date: **April 9, 2016**

****** PRESS RELEASE ******

Like you, Congressional Candidate Brian Kelly is disgusted with the current leaders in our government. He is asking for voters to forget about what big government can do for them. The results are in and the verdict is "0." Kelly is asking voters to write him in twice -- once in 2016 for the House of Representatives, PA District 17, and once in 2018 for the US Senate.

Brian hopes to help release our wonderful country from the grips of the socialists and communists.

In this essay, Brian Kelly examines a "tough" issue many believe is settled law. Kelly believes legalized murder cannot be a valid law in any country. When we kill someone, have we committed murder? Regardless of the "settled law," we are continually asked by our own consciences if killing a baby in or out of the womb, or killing an adult who is powerless or not is ethically and morally proper. Should we kill grandma off when we really need the inheritance and it would be inconvenient to live without it? If we choose yes to that, should it be legal?

Moms and their Babies are Loving and Both Need Love!

Please enjoy this essay by Mr. Brian Kelly.
His essay title is:
Yes, I Am Pro-Mom and I Am Pro-Baby!

BRIAN KELLY ASKS PA 17TH CONGRESSIONAL DISTRICT VOTERS TO VOTE FOR A CANDIDATE WHO SUPPORTS BOTH MOMS and BABIES!

I am happy to tell the world that I support protection for the unborn. I am father to three wonderful grown-up babies and I would not trade any one of them for the whole world. A baby is a heart melter for sure. Yet, in America, the same baby, if it could be reinserted into its mother's womb any time after birth, would again be eligible for the executioner's knife.

When I ran for public office, first to become a Congressman and then again to become a Mayor; I took notice to the legal rights of the unborn, and the lack thereof. I learned that a baby in the womb has fewer rights than most all other living beings. A baby can be killed at will and tortured in the process as long as it is in a proper setting; and there is not one law to assure that it will not happen again and again and again. Millions and millions and millions of times!

Ironically, there are laws about killing other forms of life. Yet, none of these life forms will ever grow up to be anybody's son or anybody's daughter, and none of these life forms will ever grow up to be President of the United States. For example, it is a fact that a turtle egg has more legal rights than an unborn baby, even though the baby is inside a mother's womb, and a turtle egg is buried in the sand on a beach someplace.

Under the Endangered Species Act, It is criminal to disturb in any way a turtle egg since it may become a living turtle. However, In Roe v Wade, the Supremes said that aborting a perfectly formed unborn human baby is perfectly legal. But, it is not a moral right! We all live under God, the top Dog in the Universe. Tell God that killing one of his created and recently inserted souls in a womb-baby is OK if you dare.

Would you consider it torture if a prankster intentionally stomped on a turtle egg or worse yet, poured acid on the egg? It would certainly be against the law.

We may not hear it but a baby's first cry may happen in the womb long before its abortion in what some might call a delivery room.

Why would the baby be crying? New research shows that babies in the womb may learn to express their displeasure by crying silently while still in the womb as early as in the 28th week of pregnancy. What if they knew their eventual fate? Would we then hear their cries? Can we hear turtle eggs crying?

What if our laws changed and we were now forgiven if we chose to kill adults who were inconveniencing us in any way? How about a nasty neighbor law? If it were legal, and adults could be killed on a whim, as long as the venue were a hospital or a nice delivery-type room in an adult abortion clinic, we would surely want the death to be as painless as possible? "Sorry grandma, but I can't really wait ten more years for the inheritance. Thank you for the power of attorney that lets me have my inheritance now."

Suppose for example that it were OK for you or another adult to be dropped into an acrid solution that was so strong it would burn your skin initially; then eat your flesh; and then consume your organs until you stopped breathing. Would that be OK? Would it be torture? Would you prefer to be water-boarded? Ask a baby who survived an abortion how that saline solution felt before they exploded out of the womb to possible freedom.

Would any of this be even worse than water-boarding since, when it is over, unlike the "victim" of water boarding, who surely would have had a deep scare, you or the victim in this case, would not be alive.

Well, guess what one of the most common methods of abortion is? You may already know that it is to use a saline solution, which is harsh brine, so to speak. When used in the process of a saline abortion for example, the acrid brine scalds the child from the outside-in. With constant contact, the intention is to have the solution cause the layers of the baby's skin to peel off; then, the flesh, until the solution reaches the organs and causes death.

It is not an immediate process. It takes time. It's almost as horrific as you or I being dropped in a vat of that bad stuff. The difference of course is that it is just a baby, whereas you are an adult. But ask yourself: is that a valid difference? If there were a microphone in the womb, would cries be heard by those outside the womb until the baby's throat were so damaged that the little woman could make no more noise before the rest of her organs were destroyed?

By the way, some of the little tykes that are supposed to be aborted swim like hell and they actually make sure that they are born alive, though they obviously have some body-damage from their painful journey. Barack Obama in Chicago chose not to vote to keep them alive if against the rules, they lived. After all, where did the term wrongful birth come from if not from the poor souls crying and running from the dangerous womb as fast as they could?

Perhaps it is more sanitary to discuss babies that are just about ready to come out of the womb to be born than scalding babies in the womb. When we make such a discussion as sanitary as we can, perhaps we can put aside the fact that a baby dies in almost every abortion. For those that almost make it, we may still use the term abortion, though the child is for the most part, already out of the womb at the time. But, to be more accurate, it is better that we use the term infanticide to describe the killing of a baby when it no longer is in the womb or it is only partially in the womb, and despite all odds, it is looking for a caring human being to help make it alive.

These horrific acts upon our smallest and most defenseless human beings can be performed legally, as they can euphemistically and conveniently be called late term abortions. You may know that at the most recent DNC convention the delegates voted to keep all forms of abortion legal by removing restrictions and protections for the unborn. Did you hear Republicans stand up in opposition?

Before Congress decided not to inject itself into the baby organ harvesting debate, the infanticide methods such as partial birth abortion, in which the baby's head is pierced or perhaps crushed by forceps, though the latter may occur in the womb also were not described well by the press. Yet, some of those, who decide to kill a baby in this fashion sometimes are able to convince themselves that there is no torture involved in the process.

But, they still cannot convince me or the baby who feels the pain of that! Well, at least it is not as torturous as the saline solution abortion? Who really knows maybe it is especially when at the end, the abortionists tools suck the brain out of the baby's head. I wonder what that feels like. It sickens me so I do not wonder long.

If the baby is not killed before it gets out of the womb in an in-womb abortion, the person that chooses to abort their child may even have a second chance to rid themselves of this potentially lifelong problem, i. e. an unwanted child. Once the baby is fully out of the womb following a botched abortion, and it is deemed to have been born wrongfully, some hospital caretakers, in some hospitals may even help out by not feeding the infant.

In this way, your baby girl starves to death instead of being killed in the womb. It is the same result but starving takes a few days or a week or so. Because it is not instantaneous, it may keep you tied up longer than a quick saline abortion that actually works. So, do we think it is torture to deprive a newborn of lifesaving nutrition? I vote yes and the baby if given a voice would vote yes. Do you think water boarding is worse? Maybe it is? Perhaps that is why the US has laws against water boarding.

For those who need a refresher on human development, since human children are not born in eggs and are not listed in any law as being in danger of imminent death, and thus are not protected by the Endangered Species Act, it might help to know when it is (exactly) that a baby becomes a person. I mean exactly. If it was never, even your humble scribe would not be able to write about anything.

Why wouldn't God just tell us unless, like me, the Almighty thinks that it doesn't really matter? Why would God think that anybody would ever use such knowledge to hurt one of His innocents? There you have it--finally we have the proof that God was not born in the twentieth or twenty-first century or he would know that answer for sure. Choice! We have choice! Is this a choice that any of us think God has given us?

Perhaps it would be easier to kill little unborn babies if the slayer knew exactly when person-hood arrived. But then maybe it would not matter at all to the abortionist. If we studied the issue, we might just learn that those who kill unborn babies in the womb really do not want to know the answer to that question.

Maybe God will never tell us, but I have a feeling that if pressed, and we could squeeze it out of Him somehow, our Lord would say that life begins at conception, if not sometime even before that.

After all, who knows when God builds those nifty little immortal souls that he eventually and so quietly installs in all the newborns while they are in the womb.

Most God-fearing people would agree that person-hood occurs when a baby is conceived. Some would add that is when God gifts the new life with her unique and immortal soul. Others, such as adults looking to expand their choices in life might use technical terms to cover up the murder of an innocent. But, I have a feeling God would call it, "Murder," no matter how assured the Supremes may have been.

If we can check back into the refresher course on human development for a minute here, you may learn that by 20 weeks, halfway through the fifth month, a live-born baby's lungs may be developed enough that the baby may breathe for an hour or so on its own before dying outside the womb if unattended.

By 23 weeks, which is just into the sixth month, 1/3 of the babies survive the birth process and become normal people. Unfortunately, we never really get a full sampling on who would live and who would not, in other words, we cannot tell which given baby would have been part of the one-third that make it. You see; before the live-born baby even has a chance to cry, during the partial birth abortion, her skull is punctured and her brain is removed, unless of course there is value to cutting off her head with the moral equivalent of an ISIS machete.

More often than many of us would believe, a live-born baby from a botched abortion is starved in a hospital. It could be counted in the third that make it, even though this already handicapped baby will get to live only a few days to a week before, with no care from the well-instructed, caring staff, the little lady starves to death.

After all, this baby already survived an experts attempt to kill it painfully in the womb. If it were not for lack of nutrition after such an unwanted baby is placed on a hospital shelf to starve to death, it would not be too many years for her to be just like any other toddler when she learns about the miracle of Santa Claus. But, she will have not have any Christmases and there will be no presents and nobody will pay for her death. This is the real war on future women.

There is a group called the Center for Medical Progress. It has chronicled a Planned Parenthood abortionist in Texas, who freely admitted that she systematically alters the position of the baby during an abortion to not risk hurting the baby's brain. In this way, they are able to surgically remove the baby's brain in its full head while it is alive. They do what they call "harvesting an intact baby head."

Since nobody claimed foul when the abortionist would pierce the head to cause death, there would be no reason for these profiteers to believe there would be a problem in severing the head at the neck as long as they knew the "art of the harvest." This is a necessary act in the abortionist's quest to sell the baby's head to the highest bidder for human organ procurement purposes. They get paid for the abortion and for the extracted parts. Such a deal!

Nobody wants to believe it but this is the latest morbid reality that seems to get no attention from the mainstream corrupt press that would abort their very own mothers if their ideology demanded it.

If somehow, this same group, Planned Parenthood, found that they could sell the yolk of a fertilized turtle egg for more money than a human head, just so they could watch the little turtle embryo starve to death, the media would be outraged. However, showing that human life does not matter, since it is only a baby, nobody in the corrupt press, driven by the perverted ideology of the new Democratic Party, seems to care.

The abortionist in this death play, just one of many dramas that will never be on TV, happens to work for Planned Parenthood in Austin, Texas. Dr. Amna Dermish has been recorded telling a guiltless, emotionless tale about how she was trained by the abortion business senior director of medical services, in the art of harvesting the body parts of babies during abortions to assure the most money for the harvest.

The "art" was not to minimize the pain of the baby being killed, but to assure the company would reap a hefty fee for the baby parts that were bagged and chilled in a for-sale scheme much like Tysons trying to preserve only the best chicken wings. This gruesome "art" of course is more real than fictional. Boris Karloff, if he were alive and the film were made, could have played all the parts, but he probably would have been too outraged to accept the "parts." Hollywood, however would have found another actor.

The objective of the profit-seeking abortionists is to use a "legal" partial-birth abortion procedure to terminate living, late-term future babies. This "clever art" can provide intact fetal heads for brain harvesting and ultimate research. Perhaps with all this research, a nice head transplant will be possible in the future as the human race outdoes itself by creating the first FrankenBaby? Can any of this be true? Don't we wish it were not?

To help these little people that are killed indiscriminately so that other more worthy adult humans can have more choices, I am an advocate for both the baby and the mom. I am pro-baby and pro-mom. Unfortunately, the laws of the United States currently do not support my stance that a baby is a human being.

The pro-death crowd, or the pro-choice crowd as they euphemistically like to be called, insist that abortion is a valid and positive reproductive choice, but none would agree to giving the baby a choice in the matter, while in the womb or even afterwards. Afterwards, for example, in just a few days after a live-birth, a disease eliminated long ago in the US gets to afflict the child. It is known as starvation to many. It sets in and takes the baby's life. It comes about from a process known as neglect.

Logic dictates, and we all know it intrinsically, that a baby in the womb or out of the womb would chose life if it were able to be asked. And, so to give more meaning to the reckless killing of millions of tiny people each year, I decided to change the words describing my stance from pro-life to pro-baby. I want the little guy, who is forming his or her life in the mom's womb to be the focus of the argument of whether she lives or dies.

Unfortunately, the notion of killing live babies in the United States has become very political. From the last Democratic National Convention, I got the sense that all Democrats wanted the right to kill unborn babies at any time right up to the time prudent people would call it infanticide, and perhaps even after that. Yet, I am a Democrat and I do not feel as the DNC Democrats. I do not want abortion or infanticide.

I think that just a small group of choice at any cost advocates, want their choice to kill babies legalized by the rest of us, who do not feel as they do about the matter. I know there are many Democrats just like me who think that a baby, in or out of the womb, is a person and therefore should be protected by law, not killed so some adult someplace has the opportunity to exercise a choice.

Unfortunately, the # 1 Democrat in the country, Barack Obama is not on my side. Back in his days in Illinois, todays President Obama was the only Illinois Senator to not only vote against babies, but he actually rose up and gave a speech against a bill that would have protected babies who survived late term labor-induced abortions. He also voted against a bill designed to prevent partial-birth abortions. I know I would not have spoken up against that bill and I would not have voted the way then State Senator Obama voted. What would you have done? Would you have voted for the right to kill or the right to save babies from a torturous death? Ask yourself that question if you dare.

Yes, I am pro-mom.

Pro-baby and pro-mom are synonyms. Aborting female babies is clearly a war on the future of women. Aborting black babies does nothing to enhance the "Black Lives Matter" movement. Obviously, the greatest friends to live babies in America are their moms, and I commend all moms for all they do. Besides the moms, one of the greatest friends of babies in America has always been one-time Congressman Ron Paul. I have a little story about the Congressman coming up shortly.

Thumbs up or thumbs down? As hard as it is to believe, there are many who think that fully grown adults ought to decide the fate of newly born babies who "wrongfully" survived abortion attempts.

You remember the gladiators in the Colosseum. Thumbs up or thumbs down? Life, or death?

While running for office in 2010, I wrote an article that I titled, "The Butcher of Lyon" as my perspective on those who would prefer to butcher the newly born survivors of abortions, rather than save them. You can access this on Google or another search engine by typing in: The Butcher of Lyon and Brian Kelly. Perhaps you would be surprised to find who thinks that babies are not people, and who thinks babies born-alive and living outside the womb should be starved in hospitals.

When we think of a baby, don't we all project the virtues of kindness and innocence? Of course we do! Would you not bet that if the babies were given the choice, they would make better and more pure decisions about whether adults should live or adults should die? Would babies vote to kill their parents if they were permitted to do so?

Can you not see babies always giving thumbs up as to whether elders should live or die? Don't you think? Ask yourself who is it that has given man such power over God's precious creations? If your answer is nobody, then you and I are on the same page.

My mother was as nice to me as any mom to any child, and I love her for it. My wife was as wonderful to our children in the womb, out of the womb, and on through life as any woman could possibly have ever been. I love her intensely, and her care for our little ones was an eye-opener for me.

As much as I loved my wife as I asked her to marry me, her selfless caring for our children was just awesome. She was a professional person with a college degree, but the three little ones were more important to her than anything else. That's probably how most moms feel when they make the big decision to have a baby, and they are fortunate enough to have a husband who can pick up the slack.

Sure, some people get caught in the middle of their lives with unwanted pregnancies. Some would suggest that because I love babies that I do not support the individual liberty of a potential mom to decide. I would never want to decide who lives or dies under any circumstances. Thumbs up or thumbs down? But, if somebody wanted to kill the mom, I would fight against it with the same intensity that I fight the notion that sinless babies in the womb can be killed. Babies and moms should both live. That is the natural plan.

Is the abortion pill RU486 safe for women?

Treatment with Mifeprex (mifepristone) and misoprostol, both part of the RU486 phenomenon for the termination of pregnancy is seen by women with unwanted pregnancies as a miracle drug.

Sometimes real miracles are hard to come by. Those looking for babies to adopt might think that a new baby with a soul from God is a miracle. Unfortunately for women who are unaware, RU486 has major some issues and if it were not politically incorrect to say so, the abortion industry might even call it dangerous. For example, to help assure that the mom does not die in the procedure, it *requires* three office visits. It is a documented, dangerous drug and nobody would take it if they were not about to abort a child that would have no home if born.

Mifeprex (RU486) is a synthetic steroid indicated for the medical termination of intrauterine pregnancy through 49 days of pregnancy. It stops growth and causes the death of the womb baby. Mifeprex Tablets are also available in generic form. Side effects of this drug are not trivial and must be checked out to assure the mother remains healthy. The effects include pelvic pain or cramps, nausea, diarrhea, stomach pain, dizziness, tired feeling, or back pain. Other side effects of Mifeprex include allergic reactions such as closing of the throat, swelling of the lips, and tongue, or face. Seek emergency medical attention if any of these allergic reactions occur.

The FDA, not trying to alarm a community that would prefer to throw warnings and precautions was careful to release a recent report without any fanfare. It showed conclusively that 14 women in the United States alone have died from using the mifepristone abortion drug and 2,207 women have been injured by it. Being pro-mom, I would advise against putting a woman in harm's way.

Having a baby is a tough road for a family but especially a mom. Then again, we must remember that nothing in life worth having is easy. Moms go through the arduous process of a nine month pregnancy, the trauma of birth, and then the first two years. Wow! It is tough! But let me say again nothing in life worth having is easy.

Giving birth and raising a child is an intrinsic part of a mom's life, and the dad's role is also a huge part of the dad's life. If nobody chose to do what was right, the world would be extinct of people.

If there were not another living being involved in whether a baby should live or should die, I would agree with those who value choice first that there would be a denial of liberty and in this case, the mom should decide the baby's fate. But, again this would be only if the baby were not a baby! But, the baby is a living baby in or out of the womb and this living being is unbelievably dependent and helpless. Just because it is helpless does not mean that a powerful adult has a right to determine if such a living child is to be terminated. So, I am very comfortable in being pro-baby and pro-mom. I want both to live and to live well.

I am convinced that the individual human beings, the smallest Americans, our mom-womb babies, whose liberties are most vulnerable, are the unborn. We must agree to protect them and their right to be born and to live. No human has the right to take another human's life, regardless of how fragile or in need of care the other human may be. I am pro-baby and I am pro-mom.

I certainly support a woman's right and freedom to choose whatever she wants in life. I would submit that the decision to abort a human, causing its death is not something any man or any woman has a right to choose under God. Death is murder when an innocent child is killed. Women, men, and babies, in and out of the womb, are equal in Gods eyes. How can they not be?

Is not the womb of a dog or a cat sacred until it produces its offspring? Even then, what American does not feel that the living puppies are sacred? Who thinks killing puppies or kittens is a good thing? How much more sacred is a child in the womb, especially when the conclusion is that it is a human, with the same DNA as other members of the family?

The choices humans make, both women and men, with regard to humans cannot include the termination of the life of another human. God has not given any of us that right. An aborted / killed unborn baby, whose soul had just been placed in the womb by God, would not have chosen death. Who are we to take away the purpose for that soul?

I have a picture of Ron Paul that really melts me and it shows his inner goodness. It is of Dr. Paul in his hospital scrubs delivering a baby. While a Congressman from Texas, Ron Paul, an Obstetric M.D. both before and after he was elected to Congress, would go home on weekends from Washington to Texas, and deliver his patient's babies. He is a clear champion of liberty, and if I may be so bold, I am talking about your liberty as well as the liberty of a ton of little babies.

In a campaign picture from December 18, 2007, Dr. Ron Paul is shown with Baby Liberty, wrapped in an American flag, shortly after Dr. Paul delivered the baby. The picture was submitted by Michael Nystrom and it can be seen on the Web by doing a simple search. It is impressive. Who would be so bold? I agree with Dr. Paul about how precious is a baby.

I am 68 years old and not many things affect me in the same way that they did when I was younger. Ron Paul is a bit older than me but he offers the best thoughts that I have heard in ages on the humanity of a womb-baby. When I saw the picture of the flag-draped baby it just hit me how important this issue really is for all human beings.

The Democratic Party platform, which unsuccessfully tried to remove all references to God in the last presidential election has become the abortion always is right Party to the point of infanticide with partial birth abortion. I do not agree.

When babies are partially born alive, right when they should be making their first big cry, they are killed in a very cruel and painful way. A game of whack-a-mole is more civil than what happens to the little baby's head, before harvesting was made profitable, once it pops out of the womb and harvesting is not the objective. On the way out, the baby, whose faculties are developed probably thinks it is her birth process. President Obama is a Democrat and he approves the killing plank in the Democratic Platform. What does that say about him?

The overriding message that you have been reading in this essay is for moms to love themselves and to give birth to their babies. Then, mom needs to know that God will help you love your baby intensely.

One day your baby will make you so glad that you chose the light of God by choosing life. Your baby will love you, and you will be blessed. Life is real. Babies are real. Moms are real. Dads are real. Moms who give babies their opportunity for a real life are the most wonderful people on earth and this act pleases God for God surely loves his little children.

In your heart, you know that all babies are given their souls by God so they can live and serve the world and the Lord. Let us permit the babies to live. I am pro-baby and I am pro-mom. How about you?

Essay 20

Brian Kelly's 64 Books Available at BookHawkers

This book and others help Brian Kelly Survive!

If you would like to see other articles on a number of patriotic topics, feel free to visit www.brianwkelly.com. Brian's 2016 plan is to serve one term in Congress in the House and follow it up with one term in the US Senate. Recent work by Brian was once hosted by conservative action alerts, but they did not make it as an entity. This patriotic site unfortunately did not survive. To keep his editorial content alive, Kelly moved it to his personal web site at www.brianwkelly.com. Enjoy!

Brian made his first run for Congress in 2010, and with no fund-raisers, he was very pleased to receive 17% of the district vote in a three person race for the Democratic nomination. Since then, Kelly has written many more patriotic books that I would bet you would enjoy. He has written 64 books in all with this book and a great book about Notre Dame in process. When you read any books by Brian Kelly, you will quickly agree that many of your friends actually need to read his books to help light the fire of patriotism in their bellies-- just as it exists in yours.

All sixty-four of Brian Kelly's books are listed at www.letsgopublish.com

Hey, even those books of Brian's that were published by other companies are out there in the list. You can see these sixty-four book titles much more easily by clicking right here. The link takes you to a comprehensive list of Brian Kelly's many books.

By the way, you probably would like to know that this particular Brian Kelly is not the coach of Notre Dame; but he privately second guesses many of the coach's plays and decisions. Our Brian Kelly coached a number of Little League championship teams and non-championship teams.

Moreover, his ladies soccer team, who when under 8 years old, won zero games and whose imperfect record was destroyed only by a 0-0 tie, went on to win County Cup titles three years, always called Mr. Kelly, "Coach."

Our Brian Kelly, who is running for Congress in 2016 and plans to run for the US Senate in 2018 ran for Mayor of Wilkes-Barre in 2015. Kelly mistakenly thought that Wilkes-Barre citizens no longer wanted the City to be run by politicians. Brian was wrong.

Kelly's mayoral candidacy site at www.briankellyformayor.com is still accessed by many who wonder how he did not do better than 5% of the voters. It still shows great ideas for the City. Nonetheless, Kelly got shellacked in his run for Mayor. His principles for the people actually stood better in 2010 for the Congressional District as he received 17% of the vote and shattered the plans for one politician to succeed another in Congress.

Thank you for visiting this site and for supporting Kelly for Congress.

If you would like to help out Brian Kelly by supporting his publishing activities, it all helps. Buy a book! Buy 100 of this book and give them to your friends. It all helps. Give a run out to Brian's book sale site at www.bookhawkers.com, and you may find something else to stimulate the conservative in you.

It all helps! If you would like to make a direct contribution to the campaign, you may send a check to Brian Kelly (Kelly for Congress), PO Box 621, Wilkes-Barre, PA 18703. Of course, if you are online, you may simply click the button below to donate on-line by credit-card. If you go to www.bookhawkers.com, you can also donate there. I am still paying off debt from my last Congress venture and that is what I use the contributions for. Thank you for your interest in Pennsylvania, America, and in the Brian Kelly campaign for Congress. We cannot achieve a govt. for the people without the people helping in whatever way we can.

DONATE

Essay 21

Some Great New Ideas for Term Limits

A New Idea for Term Limits!

Many Americans feel they are facing poor government in 2016 because of the political leftovers who are making the decisions for all of US. Normal people can fully sympathize with the notion that all of the members of Congress, no matter whether corrupted in their first term or their third term are corrupt nonetheless. So, what are we doing giving them multiple shots at the nations treasury? If you really look at it logically, we are the fools.

Let me tell you why we do what we do. No matter what bad actors they are when we do not see them, they come back each election cycle and again they are magnificent. They wear their robes of importance. They are addressed as "the honorable," and they are clearly the best we ever could get from our meager population. Some of us are actually ready to thank them for deceiving us and taking our money and spending it unwisely. Are we fools? Maybe! I will regret to say. I say, we are fools because we have the power to vote them out and we do not.

We assign to these nasty creatures of self-indulgence the same attributes as a far-off brother or sister who comes in for the gala graduation as an example. In our hearts, we know that this particular brother or sister is not what mom and dad would have wanted, but, hey, they are ours! We are so glad they came! For Congressmen, the graduation occurs every two years; for Senators, six.

Though they mostly ignore our letters, when they do respond, they often demean our arguments to come see mom and dad, when they show up for the next graduation / election many of us somehow can't wait to share the best wine and the fatted calf with our kin (whoops, our prodigal representative). But, then again they have returned, and is that not all that matters. So we can't cast them away, though we should.

Sorry, Charley, that only occurs in real weddings, real graduations, and real relatives. The fact is these guys are creeps, sponges, and exactly the kind of people we would not want at our fests. Yet, we feel honored that these rats have chosen our den, rather than where they belong. I think you got my point by now.

How many graduations, first communions, or weddings can a rat attend without ever being seen as a rat? I regret that it can go on for at least thirteen terms as it did with Kanjorski and it is going on with Cartwright who is at two going on thirteen terms. I am here in this essay to tell you that I see it as my job so that the number two does not easily roll into three or thirteen. .

You don't really think I want to have to behave like a rat?

Term limits addresses the problem of lecherous career politicians. Yes, there are such things! Some might suggest that this is just a symptom of voter apathy and disinterest. I disagree. I see the notion of limiting terms in office to reasonable numbers of terms as desirable. It would be nice if the office holder recognized they were no longer welcome, but there is a fat chance of anything ever overcoming their greed.

Why do they keep getting in when smart people like you and I do not want to bring them back? You and I have other jobs. Their job is to snooker us into thinking they are the best... and that any change would be like suicide on our parts.

For the macho among us, the other deal is that they assure the reelection of the undesirable by bringing back the victory of say, '05', and '07,' and the wonderful victory party. As they always do, they make a contest out of the upcoming election and if they have not really messed up (not whether they did a bit of good) , or they just messed up a little, the same guys who were for them last time are for them again this time. We will win! Rah! Rah! And then they disappear again until the next election.

And so it seems in this scenario, that it will always be corrupt. The only solution against this scenario is to think and then vote them out. Voting out the long-term politicians is the best term limit methodology. It works. Rather than complaining two days after the election that the guy you voted for is a creep, check it out ahead of time and send the creeps packing before the election. Don't go winning the big game for the creeps just because it feels good and you had a drink with them at their reelection party. !

Give US an Idea!

I would suggest that each time a candidate for Representative wins a particular office for the second time, in order to be reelected for the third time, they should be required to have 6% more votes (one for each year) than their opponent. Each subsequent attempt at reelection should require a cumulative 2% additional vote separation. If their popularity increases, they stay in office, if it goes down, a lesser person with no giveaways, no people in her pocket, or in their bag, gets to represent the people. The bad guys, the incumbents become easy to throw out.

So, let's say that there is a 13-term Congressman running in your district. That would mean that this Congressman would need to get 6 + 22 = 28 more points than the challenger in order to continue in office. A three term Congressman running for # 4 would need 6 + 2 = 8 more points than their opponent in order to win. For Senators, it would be based on years. So, to run for term #2 after having served 6 years, a senatorial candidate would need 6 plus 6 = 12 more points than their opponent. For term #3, after having served 12 years, a senatorial candidate would need 18 more points than their opponent.

Many who cast deciding votes believe that this is not their problem. They are America-astute enough to vote in each election and vote for the best person. Politicians often argue that they would support term limits if the people of their district really wanted them. Unfortunately, politicians do not address the underlying issues that lead to a lack of participation by voters in the election process.

Some argue that term limits remove the voter from his/her responsibility to hold elected officials accountable. Some others argue that when term limits is applied strictly, good politicians (perhaps an oxymoron) are tossed out with the bad, strictly based on their years of service. The truth recently is that if the few good politicians were to be thrown out with this lot of mostly bad actors in Congress today, it would be for the good of the country. Our country is falling apart and we have all 435 members of the house, and all 00 Senators, claiming to represent we the people. But, they do not represent us or America would no be so messed up right now. We need to even the score by helping non-politicians get elected. If the politicians are that great then it should not be a big issue for them to get six or even 18 more points than an unknown challenger.

The Founders thought the people would be smarter than we seem to be. They could not imagine that we would put the same corrupt representatives in office time and time again. Term limits were supposed to be determined by the people by not reelecting scoundrels back into office. We the people are at fault for that. We are to blame for sure.

If we limit salaries of representatives, that would make it hard for the middle class to represent us. That is therefore a bad idea. Then, only very rich people could hold office because they'd be the only ones who could afford it. So, we have to be careful. I do think, however, that setting the salary lower for each year in office might be a natural way of creating term limits. I think that would be OK even on a regressive scale. For example, years 2 through 20, $5,000 per year less cumulative. Years 21 through 40, $3,000 per year. I think that would be OK. If after 40 years Congress must work for no salary, fine. Maybe that would be OK. Perhaps a combination of points and dollars would work best.

I would look for other natural mechanisms but again the best control is the people who, hopefully, would be paying attention and keeping the bums, once discovered as bums, from ever getting reelected. Yes, it is our jobs to pay attention to our officials and not to pretend that just because they are on our team, they must be reelected. Bad people are bad people. Corrupt politicians are corrupt politicians, and the longer they get away with corruption, the more corrupt they become. Many of us wish to believe that everybody is honest. Yet, unfortunately, the longer our public servants serve, the longer they want to rule and not serve.

Another issue such as term limits in the House and Senate may have regarding voter perception is that the committee system in place now is seniority based. Therefore, if everybody is getting pork, none would come to Northeastern Pa. -- if, say that Kelly guy became a "first termer."

Good point for sure. But, how about this. Even Kelly would not have run for Office if the only concern was local pork. Why send money to Washington to get a few pork chops back? We could set up a citizen's pork advisory that must study each bill or perhaps something like that.

Things have gotten so bad that most of us will be second guessing our election decisions. Few, even Democrats like me, think Obama has served us well. Few think Senator Bob Casey has done his job. How much is all the pork in the world worth if you are not free to enjoy it at the exact moment of time that you want it. Is it possible that the liberty and freedom to choose such things are part of this coming election? Go ahead, I dare you to go out and place your tongue on that salt-lick when nobody from the government is looking and when the shakers are no longer lawful.

Term limits, in theory, may result in committee chairmen, such as me if you will vote for me. SO what if we are relative rookies. That could create an issue but would it not be better than the corruption we have now. The committee system should be based on merit anyway, and not necessarily based on seniority alone, Like most well managed businesses in the information technology age, we can figure something better than the system we have. . Anyway, if Americans are all alert, there will be 435 new Congress persons. Would it not be a shame if District 17 made it 434?
T
he key thing for all of you and I is to assure that the voters are involved. Yes, that is up to all of US. Though in normal elections this would not matter; this time we must make sure all are tuned in enough to be part of the overall process. The objectives of this process are simple: keep 'BAD' politicians from getting voted in again on election day.

In my book, Taxation Without Representation, (www.bookhawkers.com), I spend a whole chapter discussing the notion that "We get the government we deserve." The objective from now on should be that we need to be part of the process so that we deserve better than the poor stock or the recently corrupted stock of politicians we have in office. Then we will get better representation.

So, the solution is probably not limited only to term limits, which puts the election process on an 'autopilot' to no place and in many ways disengages the voter.

Yes, you and I will say, But in many ways the voter may have been bought off by jobs, promises and future opportunities. Since most voters admit to not tuning in, my notion, as discussed above, that would extract an incumbent penalty for each year in office, would clearly accommodate voter apathy.

Thus, the notion of incumbents requiring more votes is a very good idea to reduce the advantage of the incumbent entrenched career politician over a challenger from the people. Unless the people really fell for the politician year in and year out, the margin of victory would replace them.

Regardless of whether the government wants to fix this problem or not. The message to us all is that we must pay attention. It is our fault that it got like this and more importantly, it is our fault if it keeps getting worse with our choosing to keep the same bums in office.

Essay 22

What happened to the Democratic Party?

An Essay by Brian Kelly

Something happened to the Democratic Party since I first joined. Before my dad passed away, we both noticed the big change. The change was not good. It moved the party into being more and more socialist. In many ways, it was so far left that it left the liberals far behind in the rear view mirror.

My father, though never a rich man, loved the American dream. He loved what was his and envied nobody. As part of those who believe in the dream, my dad believed deeply that we should all work hard, get the best wage that we can, and we should be able to keep what we earn. As a Brewery worker, my dad thought much like other hard laborers in Northeastern Pennsylvania, and that included the miners.

A number of my uncles earned their living from 5 AM to 5 PM in the mines, often never seeing the light of day in the short daylight of winter. The miners, the brewery workers, the coal men, and other factory workers in Northeastern PA were rugged individualists. They all loved freedom and they worked hard to enjoy the small breaks in the action. Their love of freedom and family helped them get up every day to put in that long day's work. And I can attest there are family members that even under such seemingly circumstances managed to be overweight. But, it just wasn't so bad!

Work Is Good for the Heart

My career was not as tough as what these men had to put up with in their highly physical jobs. Unions were what helped them all even the score with management so that their wages were higher than mere subsistence. I did benefit from my dad's notion of work. As a very young boy, he picked coal along the railroad tracks to assure there was something to heat the family home. I had a similar youth experience.

When I was five years old, I am not joking when I say that my first job was as an entrepreneur. I used an old Radio Flyer Wagon or an old wheel barrow or a well-used baby carriage to collect papers and rags from my "customers" every Saturday. I worked within a five block radius and I would knock on doors or ring the doorbells of my "customers." to pick up their old newspapers. I would take them to the junkyard that was less than two blocks from my house. I made about a quarter to thirty-five cents a week. It gave me an understanding of what it takes to work and it put something in my pocket. It was a great life lesson.

I later moved on to shoveling sidewalks, cutting grass, working in a 5 & 10 (Huntzinger's 5 & 10), and then I spent time spotting pins in a bowling alley (WB Republics Club). I finished my high school career working on a soda truck (Eagle Bottling Works -- Zep-Up) and I inherited my older brother's paper route, which I turned over to my younger brother Joe when I graduated from Meyers High School in 1965.

At King's I was fortunate enough to get a work-study job in the maintenance department, and as I was scraping gum from the bottom of the tables in the library one day, I was invited to join the student aide's in the Computing Center. That was my first white collar job. One summer before I graduated, I had the pleasure of doing the payroll for the sellers and the cashiers at Pocono Downs, another white collar job. After King's I began my career with IBM, which was most challenging and exciting.

I tell you all this because I hope to give you the right picture. I was doing manual labor from the time I was five years-pls, though nothing like the miners of yesteryear, and I always had a blue collar job or a clerical job or I had no money. It was that simple. My father taught me of the value of unions for the working man but when I joined IBM, there were no unions. All I had to do was my job and when I did it extremely well at IBM, I was rewarded with more than I had ever dreamed of in high school or in College.

Working for IBM was an experience of a lifetime. I have not stopped working but times have changed for me. I am ready to take on the challenge of representation for the people of Northeastern PA. I am a Democrat, but I am a traditional Democrat like my father, not one who longs for the day when an America of the future is ruled by communists.

One of the big differentiation factors between me and the Democratic Party Leaders and our own Congressman Matt Cartwright is that I believe that if you work hard, you should keep what you earn. You should not be obligated to pay the freight for someone whose only problem in life is that they do not want to work.

In our democracy, in our freedom, in our American dream, those who are able to amass a huge bounty and those who are able to earn even a meager living do have obligations to the poor and the sick and those struggling with life. Even though we are morally obligated to try to help the helpless, income re-distribution by government is not the way. Another objective of a country is to create a set of rugged individuals like our parents and grandparents that are prepared to help keep America strong. Yes, I am for helpless people but I am not for making people helpless.

Having watched the Democratic Party evolve from the party of Harry Truman and Henry Scoop Jackson when I joined the party in the early 1970's, to the party of Harry Reid and Barack Obama, I would say one can only come to the conclusion that it has become an immoral, corrupt party. The party has lost its moral underpinnings and basic understanding of its roots.

In the past, my party, the Democrats, were not afraid to defend and promote the freedom and rights of every American. Now in what I would have to call a contaminated state, they support the abandonment of the Constitution; the power of the government to force an unwanted and unpopular health care system on the American populace; the diminution of black Americans through abortion; money laundering of taxpayer funds through unions, and using documented Saul Alinsky strategies to demonize their opposition with the help of a one-sided corrupt press.

Is it Democrats or their leadership or both? I wonder. I know who I am but I do not claim to know all Democrats. I am a Democrat but I do not think like the new fringe-loving Democrat Party. I ask myself for example, why would Democrats seem to love Al Sharpton? I am white and Irish. Sharpton does not make comments about the Irish but he is always chipping at the dignity of white people in America.

Mr. Sharpton is anti-white, anti-Semite, a liar, a con man, and a hustler who extorts millions from corporations. On top of that he is a habitual tax cheat with continual White House visitation privileges. Al owes millions to the IRS but they have given the Reverend a pass. I bet if I tried to find real examples, I could prove that Sharpton is anti-Black among his other scourges. To me he has few redeeming qualities. Yet he keeps appearing as the face of the Democratic Party. Is it so? Is Al Sharpton, white or black, all we Democrats have in our foot locker? What is the Democratic Party? Maybe it is not worth talking about? Maybe it is just in need of resuscitation?

Why does the Democrat Party embrace Al Sharpton? Willie Nelson lost his farm for owing the IRS millions just as Rev. Al. Nelson did not have all the money so the IRS took everything except his guitar, which his daughter had shipped out of the country before agents arrived. Is this the new Democratic Party?

What's different between the favored Rev. Al and the singer who produced FARM AID and many other benefits that helped Americans? Is it no longer OK in the Democratic Party to be a good guy to be permitted to live OK? By the way, Nelson is a major supporter of the Democratic Party. Too bad it does not know it. Too bad for Willie, nobody told the IRS. Or was that a Republican?

This is not my father's Democratic Party designed for the working stiffs in the US. Instead, it has morphed into an institution that is beholden to its public-sector union clients, elite academics, the Eastern aristocracy, and of course the crony capitalists who take from the government and give the Party its major funding. Hey, the next contract must come from someplace!

Obama ran so far left that it took even the hard left factions of the Democratic Party time to catch up. He simply repudiated the Bill

Clinton New Democrat idea which embraced business because business was good for the country. Obama never cared what was good for the country--just his ideology. He never really liked America, even as a community organizer and he has shown disdain for John Doe Americans every day of his presidency. Few are really sure if seven years of a lavish lifestyle on the backs of the American taxpayers have yet to help him like America!

Mr. Obama knows he is the boss. That is for sure. He helps his cronies and that is how he makes it financially / politically. Yet, he has attacked private equity, a cornerstone of capitalism, from which his personal wealth springs. Obama is his own man and to hell with America. For example, a Bill Clinton Democrat would have chosen a non-Obama path and would have championed the Keystone XL Pipeline.

Obama did not care that it would help the country and our feeble economy. It did not matter. He teamed with faux environmentalists to resist it. His duplicity was so obvious that even his clone appeared to be speaking the same exact Obama language. For example, before he was known as a repetitive liar, he campaigned in coal country as a friend of the industry, knowing inside his very being that he hated coal country and all the jobs the people who supported him counted on. Then his EPA intentionally created such tough regulations that there were administration officials who admitted, "if you want to build a coal plant you got a big problem." The folks who loved Obama always felt he was rooting for them. Not so!

Workers affected by such policies were swing-state voters, who are still keenly sensitive to values issues. Yet, they were sucked in by his energy and charm and they voted against themselves for a person whose unspoken intention was to kill their jobs.
Once having conquered through chicanery, the energy workers, Obama then went on a social spree with mandates on contraception that were to help him with single women and urban voters. It did not matter that it might hurt him among Catholics in places like Pennsylvania and Ohio. Even Catholics loved him so much they would not believe that he was actually who he was.

Clinton had already signed the Defense of Marriage Act; but Obama stopped enforcing it, and then declared himself a nouveau supporter of gay marriage the day after North Carolinians voted a traditional definition of marriage into the state's constitution.

Obama could flip flop on any issue and then blame Bush or someone or something else for the reason it took him so long to come around. And, the people, wanting to believe in him, believed him as they today are believing Hillary. No blame ever sticks to Obama because he is always working for the good of Americans even if he is the one who created the problem. He is the perfect "American" to sell anybody the Brooklyn Bridge.

Mr. Obama held his own on his flip-flops because he is the energizer bunny. Despite being killed off numerous times but people, including Sarah Palin, he simply does not accept it, picks himself up undaunted, and he keeps going and going and going. Eventually some who had begun to change their minds that he may not be the great guy they had once thought. After seeing him on TV for the 1000th time again started thinking he was the real deal. He is a Pied Piper for sure and he is very good at it. And that is why so many smart people appear dumb at his feet.

This President goes out every day with a major propaganda message and he helps convince the masses even as his poll numbers drop that he is still the Messiah. He simply looks sincere and repeats his drumbeat of lies more often than fact-checkers can refute them. When the people once loved him seemingly at even higher percentage, all the Democratic leaders backed him and loved him and looked for his coattails.

Even with a funk of an economy and morass as everybody's new wake-up code word of the day, Obama still manages to pretend that he is the reigning emperor and king of America. He does not acknowledge that he has screwed up America. He is Obama!

There are still suck-up Democrats who will follow him to the ends of the earth despite the carnage he has left in his wake. One of them of course is Hillary Clinton. Ironically, Hillary had to abandon Clintonism for Obama's brand of Nihilism for her own survival... or so she thinks.

Democratic analyst and pollster Doug Schoen often gets it 100% right as he does not wear his liberal ideology on his chest, and he does not appear to live on the far left. He says that Obama has substituted class warfare for Clintonism." Americans can feel it. Black v White. Minorities v traditional Americans. Christians v Muslims. Establishment v Outsiders... etc. etc. etc.

Many Clinton New Democrats wish they had gotten a New Democrat President for a few more years before hard left Obama took over. But, they also seem afraid of Obama, who has been known to be vindictive. So, they do not make waves with this ideologue who has captured everybody's Democratic Party to the point that it is no longer recognizable. Hopefully, most Democrats are beginning to see the folly in the ideology and hopefully, they will not vote for more of the same in 2016. But, Obama will definitely be there coaxing his once loyal constituency and there will be those who fall for it.

Help People Help Themselves

Too bad Obama was not what he once seemed to be. He cares little about any of us. Yet, we have a natural duty to help those who need help, but we should do so without institutionalizing their neediness and putting Obama in charge of the institution. Creating a permanent needy class by government taking and redistributing the small holdings of struggling citizens is not the way to truly help the poor.

It is a way, however, for politicians to gain get credit for giving unearned gifts to the "needy class." As such it is no wonder politicians, mostly Democrats, through Obama have opted for a major redistribution of wealth. Oh, and of course it does help the newly dependent to prefer to cast their vote for the person who gave them their grab bag full of goodies.

The greed of politicians is a huge problem today and we all know that at their worst, politicians are the lowliest of the lowly in spirit and goodness. The welfare state, the needy state, the dependent sate, gives the political class the opportunity to buy votes using the public treasury. This is a sin unto itself and instead of saying that is how it is, our representatives should end this practice.

The politician's disdain for being thrifty with public funds is manifest and disgusting. "Gifts" of other people's wealth from politicians is stealing and it is unconstitutional. Even if you have received such a gift, please know that it did not come from a politician. It did not come from the government. It came from your neighbor.

Gaining without working is a way government breaks the spirit of rugged individualists and freedom lovers. Once on the take, it is tough to become rugged again and get a job. The largesse does not help American citizens. Instead, it makes us all weaker. Being lumped into this human receiving pot takes Americans further from ever becoming self-sufficient, rugged individuals and contributing members of society with a real stake in the American Dream. It is a way of forever darkening spirits as the receiver quickly calculates that it is better to take from the government than to work.

Regardless of how good it makes Joe feel, the government's role is not to take from Harry to give to Joe. It is Harry's obligation to help Joe as a human being, but not by degrading Joe into a dependent of the state. Likewise, it is Joe's obligation as he sees the hard work of those who help him, to stop taking from them as quickly as can be, and to become a part of the American Dream.

Unfortunately, many in my party believe that government is the panacea. Government is the big pill bottle and the only medicine for whatever ails you. I submit that it is too much government that has created and encouraged much of what is wrong with America today. The Democratic Party unfortunately is today's drug pusher if you know what I mean.

Common Man & Democratic Party

In today's Democratic Party, the most liberal and greedy politicians appear ready at the drop of a hat to take your hard earned dollars and squander them in full daylight. They will argue "that is the way politics works." They take your meager wealth and liberally distribute it for projects that are so full of bad, spoiled, pork, that they stink. Any given day, you can expect your favorite politician to appear unknowingly with the face of the trichina worm, rather than his own, showing his true liberal, greedy self. Too bad we cannot see politicians in the mirror for what they really are.

It is no longer the common man for whom the Democratic Party Leaders work. As much as I regret to say it, at the national level, my party's leaders seem to work instead to enrich a whole host of "others" than "we the people." These include first and foremost, themselves, the extreme left, special interests, Harvard faculty and graduates, and more recently, Chicago faculty and graduates. The common man is not even on the list. Their major goal of today's progressives is to grow the impact of the government in our daily lives, stealing as much of our small holdings and our freedom with each casting of the ballots.

There is virtually no Republican opposition that has numerical significance. The seven years of Obama have demoralized establishment Republicans to having become the me-too party. As long as the "me" is satisfied, they too are OK with the plight of America. The leaders of the party of Lincoln have nestled in with Democrats to enjoy the life that Obama has given them. They do not have to fight to make it better. And, so, they seem quite content with Obama's leftovers.

Moreover, there really are few Conservative Democrats willing to stand up and be counted. I am a Conservative Democrat and proud of it. Though in my own community, even the press thinks I am unworthy because I am not endorsed by anybody.

I believe government is to help the people to do what we cannot do ourselves. Even the faux Blue Dogs are no longer willing to think for themselves anymore. In recent legislative battles almost all Democrats, even those who would have once labeled themselves as "blue dogs," gave up their individual vote to Nancy Pelosi's wishes or to Harry Reid's. This is not why you sent them to Congress and so it is time to call them back.

Worse than that perhaps, there is nobody on the opposition side brave enough to speak up. Even the Speakers won't speak for Americans. John Boehner, Paul Ryan, and Mitch McConnell have apparently decided that they need only follow the leadership of the minority party. They have yet to do anything to help Americans though they have the power. The power was given to them by the conservatives, who they now bad-mouth regularly. And, so that is why there is so much disgust in the Republican / Conservative ranks and why Donald Trump is making his mark, and why nobody cares that Ted Cruz is not loved by his fellow Senators. They favor treason and Cruz favors a bright and shiny City on the Hill.

Only Republicans, I am sorry to say stood up to challenge the freedom-stealing steamrollers from my party in both the House and the Senate. Though some, there were not many. There were few on either side with the guts to stand up to the Party Leaders steering a bad course for America. Some even took bribes for their districts in exchange for their votes. If that is politics as usual then it is time to never invite a politician back to be your representative of the Democratic Party.

Conservatives

There are many conservatives in the Democratic Party but their voices have been shut off by Party Leadership. Don't let the big shots do this to you. When you have the time, look closely, and you will see that today's Democratic Party Representatives, once a super majority in both the Senate and the House, and now serving in a minority role, may not give a damn about you! Make sure you check that out!

You will notice that our own cast of actors from Pennsylvania are stealing more of America from the people with each of their votes. The people and only the people can hold these representatives accountable by denying them their most precious reason for being -- your vote and their reelection. Though they no longer pay homage to the electorate, remember, until they actually shred the Constitution publicly, you can vote these bums out of office whenever you have the chance. And you should.

These corrupt representatives and their leadership are not stupid people. In fact, they are very smart. They hear Americans from both parties as well as Independents screaming to slow down. Take it easy! What's the hurry? Are they afraid that so many Americans will wake up that their sinister plots to change America into a Banana Republic will be foiled?

They cannot help but hear every-day Americans pleading for them to take the time to read the anti-American and the unconstitutional legislation that their minions and their computers have conjured up for them. They do hear but they are compelled to ignore because the people no longer matter to them. The hard left agenda trumps everything, even human life. Those on the right choose to be powerless.

Look at our Northeastern Pennsylvania representatives and tell me the truth. Of the lot of them, who is worth keeping? We are now suffering through over seven years of the worst recession since the Great Depression and the Congressional Leaders have created Lemmings out of our PA Legislators. Our brood from PA are for whatever Harry and Nancy command, even though Republicans theoretically have the power.

They think the solution is to tax the people and to spend, spend, spend. Throughout the history of America, recessions have always gotten worse when taxes were raised and government spending of the people's tax money was the order of the day. No wonder there is no recovery for the people. No wonder seven years later there are no jobs and 85% of recent college graduates go back home to live with mom and dad.

We're Broke

Though we may joke about it, our representatives, especially the bulk of the Democrats in the House, and all of the Democrats in the Senate (shame) are actually spending dollars loaned by Chinese peasants living behind the Great Wall. America is broke. We have no money. Our politicians spent it on their friends. They already sent too much of it to China!

We cannot tax and spend our way out of this mess. China is for China. Try telling your representatives you don't believe in how they are voting. Go ahead! You will be surprised at their arrogance. If you have tried reaching one of these emboldened elite paragons of intellectuality and maturity to offer your opinions as I have, you will be favored by a returned note that confirms your worst suspicions. The raw fact is, "What you think does not matter."

The response always explains your legislator's opinion in a bully-type response. It is always well written but the verdict is always the same. Their opinion trumps that of the people. Coincidentally, their opinion always seems to match that of Harry Reid and Nancy Pelosi, Chuck Schumer, and others who are the only real masters they serve. It is no longer a euphemism to say that our representatives no longer represent us. It is reality. And it is one of the worst reality shows that any of us can ever get to see.

Coins for Congress?

I am convinced that if there were a "Coins for Congress" program to unseat the whole lot of them, many of us would quickly get our nickels and dimes out to pitch in to make the program a success. Wouldn't it be nice if they were all gone and the new guys were already in place and the new guys chose to work for the people and not for themselves?

Our "representatives" do not serve us and so, simply, they have got to go, starting right here with our own long-time actors in Pennsylvania. Not getting elected is a sure cure for too many terms. It is the ultimate term limiter.

Hold on to your nickels and dimes. I have a better way. "Just throw the bums out!" And, hopefully, sooner than later. You do not have to pay a nickel or a dime to have these folks extricated from their seemingly entitled comfortable seats in Washington DC.

Today's Congress, especially the Democrats have made a big mistake. They have forgotten to take away your freedom to vote. Was it a mistake? Is it possible they have plans so that they will not need your vote? Maybe they are hoping to bring in millions of new voters from other countries to enshrine their ability to keep their spots in Washington.

Is Congress for Americans?

Maybe there are thirty millions of these folks; maybe there are sixty millions. They are already living in America and can be called in to vote merely by being declared citizens? If the Democratic politicians have these new voters, maybe they do not need you or me. We are simply regular Democrats. But, it is possible the Party may think they won't need our votes. Will we ever be able to get rid of this Congress if they create replacement voters this year, next year, or in subsequent years? Are we looking at an Invasion of the Body Snatchers that never seemed so real?

You know deep down that they hope that by having all these new voters, who do not contribute, even to our churches, they will always be elected. They do not mention that the love of giveaways from the people's treasury, which give the politicians their re-elections, are the rationale for their favor.

The Democrats especially know that these new citizens will pay them back with votes. So, your regular citizen votes will be discounted and not count much in future elections. This may be the last time that the people actually can take action with their votes. If not this year, it is coming soon. In 2016, do not miss the opportunity to take control of the government back from the politicians. Do it before the replacement voters take control.

The fact is that in 2016, your vote still does count. In 2016, voting is a much more valuable right than ever before in the US, and we all must use it in the Primaries and in the General Election to return America to a Representative Democracy (a Democratic Republic).

It all starts at home. Every unresponsive legislator, at least 60 and probably more in the Senate (though only 1/3 are up for office) and the majority of the members of the House, need to be given their pink slips. In Northeastern PA, that means that Matt Cartwright needs to go, regardless of who we elect to represent us. It all starts with cleaning the House at Home.

Republicans had their chance for years and they blew it, big time. But, and this is a big but, Republicans, have not tried to turn the US into a post-Romanov Russia. The Reid/Pelosi combo, out of power now but still exerting more power than McConnell and Ryan, want to create a new Communist Russia.

This is perplexing but it is clearly their intent. Republicans to their credit have yet to appoint even one Communist Czar. The Democratic controlled Administration seems to be able to find only

Communists to serve in their US Government unofficial councils. As witnessed by Van Jones, the deposed Green Czar, these folks are not quiet Communists, but a crew of Czars happy to have their ideology displayed along with their full names.

Finally, the Republicans have not and are not stopping the movement of the country further and further to the left to fight the Democrat's stifling regulations. Unfortunately, Republicans are moving the country in no direction at all as they have cowarded out of the foray. All of these Democrat regulations are being infused into de-facto law with impunity from a complicit Republican-controlled, Democrat principles dominated Congress.

I regret to say that it is the Democrats who are doing all this to the people. If I am elected, I will do my best to stop this move post haste. Without changing philosophies or enabling millions and millions of new voters, Democrats will not be able to win another major election for twenty-years. Enough is enough.

My candidacy offers the Democratic Party an opportunity to get in line with the thinking of the vast majority of Americans and to stop flirting with another Bolshevik Revolution.

Tea Parties?

There is nothing wrong with being a Conservative Democrat. The Tea Party once got a lot of tracking as a real political party. It was never a political party. It was simply a means for the white members of the middle class to express frustration at the biased government and the press who somehow and for some reason did not like white males.

Today the ideals of conservatism are embraced by the populist movement that favors Ted Cruz and Donald Trump. I cannot believe all of the one-time staunch Clintonites, who I see switching parties so they can vote for Donald Trump. This is encouraging as it shows that even Democrats have come around to understanding that we must be nice to America for America to be able to be nice to any of us.

Congressional Leaders in both parties, and right now mostly the Democrats have an effective but freedom-stealing agenda. Congress has chosen not to listen to the voices of the people. Instead, they are stealing away our basic freedoms, rights, choices, and also a good part of our incomes.

Obama's executive actions to undermine the Constitution have been heralded by Democrats and permitted to stand by gutless Republicans. Our representatives in the Democratic Party have hijacked the Party and because they have almost absolute power (dangerous as that may be), they have also hijacked our government.

Anybody paying attention sees the government leaders changing the idea of "change we can believe in" to the "Nightmare of Change." Please pay attention. Watch as there is less and less democracy in this constitutional republic. It is a shame that there is more of each of the following: Progressivism, Marxism, Socialism, Communism, Fascism, etc. We must stop it, whether we are Democrats or Republicans, Conservatives, or Liberals.

In order to get the right recipe for this new style of government--a government that would like to take over our very lives, the Congress and the President are currently trying to mix all of these "isms" into a big brew and throw them down our throats. Rest assured, the mixture will not taste good.

As the old joke ends, we will all be inclined to want to bring it back up for another vote. In the words of President Barack Obama, the best virtual crisis creator since the Eggplant that ate Chicago, "it may be too late." Be warned that "if he's still hungry, the whole country is through." Where is Norman Greenbaum, the songwriter who penned the 1950's spoof tune, "The Eggplant that Ate Chicago!" when we need him most? Obama, from Chicago seems not to be content until he completely destroys America.

Naming Names

It's time to name some names. Besides our own Matt Cartwright and Bob Casey, against whom, I am pleased to run for Congress, and then in the Senate for the 2018 election, there are others at the national level that must be defeated.

Senator Harry Reid may not be on the ballot but his minions will be looking to replace him in 2016. He was not for America. Instead, Harry, or as Rush Limbaugh called him, Dingy Harry used his power for outlandish hard left special interests. The word is that many of these have benefited good ole Harry himself.

Yet, in 2016, as active as they are for their own agendas, Senate Majority Leader Reid, and Speaker of the House, Nancy Pelosi have been a veritable tag team of neglect for the needs of the American people since having gained control of Congress and subsequently losing it. They have chosen a radical, socialist agenda that favors non-citizens over citizens. If you are not a citizen, you should be quite pleased with Democratic Leadership. If, as a bona fide citizen, you need a job in the United States, you should be disgusted.

Harry Reid cannot read the news or he would not say the illogical things that he utters. For example, Reid says that those opposed to his government take-over of health care are on the "wrong side of history." Out-of-touch Harry doesn't realize that a majority of Americans and a majority of his constituents and the vast majority of we the people in Northeastern PA opposed and continue to oppose his health care scheme and now we want it repealed and replaced.

Neither Harry's deals nor Nancy's deals and schemes are built to help the America we know. They think that a cut of $500 Billion from Medicare has added to the benefits to which Senior Citizens are accustomed. Yet subtraction is not addition. When Congress steals from the people, there are no benefit increases.

Al Gore thinks he invented the Internet but he did invent the term fuzzy math. Taking lots of a lot from anything cannot make it more than it once was. Sorry Harry. Taking from Medicare has not helped the program to provide more benefits.

The Reid and Pelosi team, with help from the most radical socialist President since Woodrow Wilson, have taken from the people to hand out huge bailouts, and multiple humungous pork stimulus packages. Even China is worried that they will not get paid back. And, of course, you know the bill will come due in time to assure that our grandchildren have to struggle to get by.

Harry Reid and most of Congress do have their own "Nightmare of Change." They do not want their roosts in Washington changed. Their worst dream is for the public to understand that they do not care a darn about America. They want to keep their digs and their perks and their cushy salaries and they want to do so without having to care what you think about what they choose to do. Then, when they retire they can write the gospels about how they planned all along to have that 5 $million dollar job as a Washington Lobbyist. Hey; they can keep their apartments.

Harry Reid was not doing well in his home state until he promised the unions the world. By the way, you and I are paying for that world and Harry has received a large chunk of it from the US Govt. He is about ready to write some gospels that will not be good news for Americans.

Northeastern PA

So, now that we have discussed a number of things that are wrong with the Democratic Party, let me tell you how I would change government and the Democratic Party if the citizens of NEPA favor me with their votes.

If I am fortunate enough to be elected as your Representative for the 17th District of Pennsylvania, I will proudly work to defend life and prevent taxpayer dollars from being used to fund abortion. I will actively work to protect our 2nd Amendment rights. I will consistently vote against pork spending and will work to roll back the unprecedented growth of government and its impositions on all of our cherished, hard fought freedoms. Obamacare will be repealed and Healthcare 2017 will be remade into something better with less government control and bureaucracy -- and no stealing from Medicare.

I will work to repeal all of the lousy, anti-American legislation that was passed this year by our sold-out Congress. I assure you that among other things, I am opposed to any tax increases and I would be happy to sign any pledge that I will not vote for any new taxes and I will vote to reduce the taxes that are already smothering our economy and those that are about to try to remove our air supply.

We are near the end of this important essay. Please indulge me for a page or more while I hit on a number of other issues that will help the Democratic Party and will help the people of NEPA if I am elected.

Obamacare

Way back in 2010, a completely Democratic-controlled Senate and the House passed a health care bill. The purpose was not to make health-care better as there are no paragraphs in the legislation that discuss medical advances that are needed and that will be funded. Instead it was a bureaucratic bungle of do's and don'ts to remove the doctor as the caretaker and replace him or her with the government. My party, the Democrats were thrilled and heralded this major theft of individual freedom from the people.

The legislation simply took control of healthcare from individuals (Doctors and patients) and gave it to the government. Anticipating being the big winner, the government had already hired enough bureaucrats to institute health care rationing and that is a big part of the new Democratic health care agenda now known as Obamacare.

Moreover, the bills in Congress provided taxpayer funds for abortions. Just in the last week of March 2016, the Little Sisters of the Poor were before the Supreme Court as Obama tried to slap a $27 million fine on their charitable work which would have ended their existence as a charity provider.

Bart Stupak who was the stupidest Congressman in 2010 agreed to an amendment that theoretically would tentatively hold the abortion line in the House, but he was aware it would more than likely not hold when the Senate / House Conference Committee finished its work. It did not or the Sisters would not be pleading for the ability to continue to exist.

Congress does what it wishes regardless of the wishes of the American people. Because Paul Kanjorski and now Matt Cartwright follows the corrupt Nancy Pelosi's wishes, Cartwright is part of the problem. He is not part of the solution for NEPA nor the Democratic Party. I will work very hard to change this. It is a top priority and it will be done.

It is time to send Democratic Leadership -- whatever is left running in 2016-- all the phony Representatives from NEPA and elsewhere in the country, back home for good. It's time for Democrats to put up some good candidates who come from the people and are for the people.

Campaign Spending

Originally, I thought I could get by not spending a dime on my 2010 Congressional Campaign v Paul Kanjorski. I was wrong. I am a regular citizen who happened to be a computer consultant by trade. Until after my first campaign, when I chose to support Lou Barletta for Congress, I served Marywood University as an Assistant Professor of Business and Information Technology.

I won't spend a bundle v Matt Cartwright but I can handle this modest Web Site that cost me about $10.00 for the domain name per year. This year I will spend no more money unless I receive some unsolicited donations. I am counting on gaining name recognition for free. Hopefully, the press to whom I send this release will help for the sake of democracy!

I am taking donations for past campaigns but not this one. I still need about $8000 to break even from my mayor campaign and the prior Congress campaign. Feel free to go to www.bookhawkers.com and make a small donation.

I did not plan to make the Wedding, Bar Mitzvah, Baptism, or Funeral circuit in NEPA in 2010 and I will not do so in 2016. I did spend almost $5000 on signs and cards and a few ads. It mounts up fast. I plan no media buys in 2016 so that will not tickle the press in NEPA. I don't think a candidate of the people should have to do that. I have sent out a number of press releases for the past few months about my candidacy but there has not been one story about it written in any local paper or media outlet. Ask them why?

With today's modern technologies, I don't think that a person willing to break out of the mold of regular person in order to represent his or her community should have to go broke to get elected. I also do not believe that a regular person should have to become a politician to run for office. I don't believe that a candidate should have to solicit money from others or spend other people's money on an election campaign. That is not my idea of a representative democracy.

So, I will spend little of my own money and none of anybody else's. I will take no donations to my campaign. In my 2010 campaign I spent under $5000 of my own money. I do wish I had it back for my next vacation. I will take some free radio spots and TV spots that are offered to all candidates and I will make myself available for newspaper interviews that are available to all candidates. But, I will not be in your face every time you turn around, asking for your vote.

Yet, I do want to be elected as your representative so that I can help begin a turnaround of a government gone sour. I'd like to spend the next few years sweetening the smell around Washington by removing as muck of the dirty politics as I can.

Team for Action

I hope to build a team and a mechanism to create as much high impact, yet simple to read legislation as possible and I hope to shepherd it to get it passed for the good of the people. That's why most of Congress has to be thrown out this year or nobody's legislation intended for the people, will have a prayer. Though I am a Democrat, my recommendation is to select the best candidate, hopefully a conservative Democrat such as myself. Please do not vote for a hard left Democrat such as Matt Cartwright to replace a hard left Democrat or you will have little return for your vote. The entrenched politicians have a history of protecting their sponsors. It is time for them and their sponsors to get out of Washington.

More Information

There is lots of stuff on my web site, briankellyforcongress.com. It will tell you about me and my ideas for a better America for Americans. If you want to read even more, I have written 63 books, many of them about the issues of today. The books are published by Lets Go Publish! (www.letsgopublish.com) and are available for purchase at www.bookhawkers.com.

Help!

I do need your support to get elected but you don't have to invite me to breakfast or dinner. Just vote for me by writing my name on the ballot after selecting OTHER. Tell all of your friends, family, and co-workers to vote for me for Congress. I promise honest conservative, Democrat representation. Tell them to visit the site at www.briankellyforcongress.com.

I know that I am the biggest contrast to anybody in Congress that you'll find in this race or any race -- ever. I, like you, am an ordinary citizen. I will serve one term if elected, though I do reserve the right to try for one more. After my one House term, I plan to be a Senator for six years before i retire from public life. I will vote for term limitations so the people do not have to purge Congress regularly of people who have lost track of their real mission -- for the people.

Paul Kanjorski & Matt Cartwright

I think Paul Kanjorski may have been an OK guy. I never met him but we in NEPA all knew him. I had no personal beef with him. He was for a lot of good things, including being pro-life (though only when convenient). I credit him mostly for that. But, he was also for a lot of bad things, the things conjured up by the Leader of the House, Nancy Pelosi-- such as Obamacare and Cap and Trade.

Paul Kanjorski was defeated. His successor is more socialist than Kanjo could have ever dreamed. I am talking about Matt Cartwright, an otherwise nice guy. He just is not good for you or I or regular Americans as our representative. He is aligned with Obama. Need I say more? Cartwright is not the right person to represent the 17th District. We can do better! Why settle?

The Plan

My plan is to proudly represent the people of Northeastern PA when you choose to elect me.

If you would like to learn more about how I think on critical issues, and I encourage you to do so, feel free to purchase any of my major patriotic books. As you can see by the titles, they are quite germane to the issues of today. Even if you are philosophically opposed to my candidacy for your own reasons, you can learn a lot about the environment in which we live by reading any of the following books. This should help you be better prepared to pick your own candidate for the 17th District if you believe I am not the proper candidate for you.

Books by Brian Kelly

(available at www.bookhawkers.com)

- Lifetime Guest Plan: A long-term immigration fix puts Americans first Let's Go Publish! (LGP!), an American Publisher, 2015
- Geoffrey Parsons' Land of Fair Play, LGP! 2014
- Sol Bloom's Epoch Story of the Constitution, LGP! 2014
- The Bill of Rights 4 Dummmies! LGP! 2014
- The Constitution 4 Dummmies! , LGP! 2014
- America 4 Dummmies!, LGP! 2014
- The Federalist Papers by Hamilton, Jay, and Madison, LGP! 2014
- Bring on The American Party, LGP! 013
- No Amnesty! No Way!, LGP! 2013
- RRR: A Unique Plan for Economic Recovery and Job Creation LGP! 2012
- Americans Need Not Apply, LGP! 2011
- Kill the EPA! LGP! 2015
- Jobs Jobs! Jobs!, LGP 2010
- Healthcare Accountability, LGP!2009
- Obama's Seven Deadly Sins. LGP! 2009
- Taxation without Representation LGP! 2011

* all books published by Lets Go Publish! www.letsgopublish.com
* all books are available at www.bookhawkers.com

Don't you think it is time that NEPA and the rest of the Country got some real representation? Thank you in advance for your support.

Sincerely,
Brian W. Kelly ---

Essay 23

Media in NEPA do not serve as Fourth Estate

Press-Media does not serve the people

In this essay, Brian Kelly asks why there was no coverage of his congressional campaign, launched on January 26, 2016 for a Primary Election to be held April 26. He is inclined to forgive the press for their slight as long as they post this disclaimer on all their future work:

"Disclaimer. Though we may appear like a normal media outlet to serve the people, we are not! Our primary goal is ad revenue and so we do not follow the precepts typically attributed to the "fourth estate."

Please enjoy this essay by Mr. Brian Kelly.

Media in NEPA have totally ignored Brian Kelly's congressional candidacy

A *write-in candidate* is a *candidate* in an election whose name does not appear on the ballot, but for whom voters may vote nonetheless by *writing* in the person's name. That's pretty simple isn't it. For its own reasons, the newspapers, radio stations, and TV stations, including Public TV feel that they can exclude bona fide candidates from their lists of candidates simply because a particular candidate has chosen not to go through all of the hoopla and expense of getting his or her name on the ballot.

In order to get one's name on the formal ballot in Pennsylvania, a candidate for state or federal office must meet a variety of complex, state-specific filing requirements and deadlines. These are intended to keep regular citizens from running for office. The founders did not decide that a candidate should need a huge war chest to run for office. Incumbent politicians trying to keep all the John Doe's off the ballot that they can, thus thwarting the fairness underpinnings of our democratic republic, have devised a number of ways to assure their continual reelections. One such way, and the easiest, I might add, is to legally discourage any and all people who may decide one day to challenge the "God-given-right" of a politician to be elected and reelected until that politician retires.

These regulations in Pennsylvania are known as ballot access laws. They simply determine whether a candidate or party will appear on an election ballot. They do not inhibit the ability of an individual to declare her or his candidacy and have the general public write their name in on the ballot on Election Day. This is a hallmark of our democracy and it is the law in Pennsylvania. A write-in candidate is not a *write-in schlepper*. He or she is a *write-in candidate* and all candidates may become either nominated or elected depending on the nature of the election -- Primary or General.

Ballot access laws are set at the state of PA level; not at the federal level. A candidate must prepare to meet ballot access requirements well in advance of primaries, caucuses and the general election. It is so much work put in front of regular citizens by incumbent politicians that most people opt not to run for office ever in their lifetimes--even if they might have become fine representatives of the people. It answers the question as to why the choice of candidates is often poor.

The reason is simple: Politicians do not want the general public to become competitors against their quest for gaining and keeping political office. It isn't fair but it is so.

The formal notion or excuse given by lawmakers is that the state lawmakers have developed ballot access procedures in an effort to prevent non-serious candidates from appearing on the ballot; meanwhile, critics contend that stringent ballot access requirements discourage candidate and voter participation in the electoral process.

Please count me in as a critic as there is no other option given other than the write-in. Feel free to be an active critic yourself. The Press

/ Media have chosen to no longer help the people understand that they have options other than the candidates thrown at them by the political money machines, the major donors, and the entrenched establishment parties. The people are sick of their lousy choices.

The Press is deemed as the fourth estate and highly regarded when they execute this major responsibility. In the United States, the media is often called the fourth branch of government (or fourth estate).

That is because from the founding of America, its job has been to closely monitor the political process in order to ensure that political players don't abuse the democratic process. The job of the fourth estate is not to ignore candidates who have chosen not to play by the rules of the politicians. In fact, it is the press's job to fight for the people by making us all aware that our state legislators have snookered us on ballot access laws.

In my case, there is no reason why since January 26, when I announced that I was running for Congress, there was not one piece in the media of NEPA about my candidacy. Does our fourth estate in NEPA think their only mission is to collect ad revenue from candidates? Why, when the PA Constitution gives write-in candidates an opportunity for election, should a declared write-in candidate not receive the same press coverage as those who worked the moneyed class to get on the ballot? Here is a brief excerpt from a Stanford Article about a free press that you should enjoy:

Consider the following excerpt from Journalism in the Digital Age http://cs.stanford.edu/people/eroberts/cs201/projects/2010-11/Journalism/index7f0d.html?page_id=16

"Journalism has long been regarded as an important force in government, so vital to the functioning of a democracy that it has been portrayed as an integral component of democracy itself. In 1841, Thomas Carlyle wrote, Burke said there were Three Estates in Parliament; but, in the Reporters Gallery yonder, there sat a Fourth Estate more important far than they all (On Heroes and Hero Worship). Four years earlier, Carlyle had used the phrase in his French Revolution: A Fourth Estate, of Able Editors, springs up, increases and multiplies; irrepressible, incalculable. Carlyle saw the press as instrumental to the birth and growth of democracy, spreading facts and opinions and sparking revolution against tyranny."

"The fact of the matter is that democracy requires informed citizens. No governing body can be expected to operate well without knowledge of the issues on which it is to rule, and rule by the people entails that the people should be informed. In a representative democracy, the role of the press is twofold: it both informs citizens and sets up a feedback loop between the government and voters. The press makes the actions of the government known to the public, and voters who disapprove of current trends in policy can take corrective action in the next election. Without the press, the feedback loop is broken and the government is no longer accountable to the people. The press is therefore of the utmost importance in a representative democracy."

When you see this essay by Brian Kelly, a write-in candidate in 2016 for the 17th Congressional District, in print any time in the future, write to your state legislators and tell them to make the ballot access laws in PA favor the people-- not the politicians. While you are at it, write or call your friendly media outlets (Newspapers, Radio, TV) and let them know that you will no longer buy their product or listen/watch their spew if they do not treat all candidates for office fairly. Ask them to put a disclaimer on their work in the future if they deny your request. My recommended text for the disclaimer is:

"Disclaimer. Though we may appear like a normal media outlet to serve the people, we are not! Our primary goal is ad revenue and so we do not follow the precepts typically attributed to the "fourth estate."

My bet is that no media outlet in NEPA or elsewhere dares to print this essay in this the age of a waning free press.

Thank you in advance for your support.

Sincerely,

Brian Kelly

Essay 24

Should Government Be Left to the Politicians?

Question: Who the heck do you think you are coming out of retirement, never having been in government or politics, and after challenging one of the longest serving representatives in NEPA, Paul Kanjorski, and losing in the 2010 primary to the incumbent, you now have the nerve to take on Matt Cartwright, one of Scranton's finest lawyers—once from the firm of Munley, Munley & Cartwright? Shouldn't an opportunist like you just stay retired?

Answer:
Thank you for the question. I ask myself that all the time but not exactly as you have asked it. Why should I run for the US Congress as a write-in candidate? The short answer is that I care and I am deeply concerned that the current government is selling us all out for their own benefit. I am suspicious of anybody who is part of the current administration, Democrat or Republican! How's that for a start?

By the way, I am running as a write-in because it allows me to bypass the political machine and conduct a quiet campaign that costs me nothing to run. I am not following the method prescribed by incumbents to dissuade potential opponents from the citizenry at large from challenging them. This campaign should cost me about zero dollars v several hundred thousand, unless you count my time, which I am pleased to donate. I count on the media to get the word out about me and what I stand for. After all, I am running for Congress. Let's see how well the media does on this one! They have all received this press release. Moreover, my platform is clear and it is listed on www.briankellyforcongress.com.

Though I have chosen to put my hat in the ring, I am really not excited about the prospects of picking up, uprooting my family, and heading to Washington. I worked for several years in New York when I was with IBM, and I was very happy to come back home to Northeastern PA, where I have lived ever since. Yet, I feel I have something to offer and I think it is my time to serve. I do not want to be a politician and I will not become one. But, I think that a government of the people is too important to leave it just to politicians. Maybe that gives you an idea of who I am.

If I were not so upset with our National Government, and its elite demeanor, and its unresponsiveness to the people, I would not feel the need to run for this important office. If I did not think that I could help in a big way, because of how differently I feel than the people who now claim to represent me, I would not even think of taking on this challenge. I would not bug you with my thoughts and opinions.

If you do not like me because you do not know me, I ask you to kindly think about your prospects of ever getting somebody to serve you in Congress who is not a politician. Unless you really know why you may choose to reject me, you, unfortunately for you, are doomed to vote for entrenched politicians and complain forever that they care more about themselves than they care about you. If it is because I am not already in government, think about those who are already in government and those in official offices and how well they serve you and the general public.

I know there is a perception that those who have never held political offices should start at low offices and work their way up the ladder. My thoughts on this notion are that this is the perfect way to create a politician and keep government in the hands of a political class of elite know-it-alls. Meanwhile, the people more or less are told to eat cake. I agree that any politician looking for name recognition should start small at an early age and then go after more important offices until their political career is over.

However, I am not a politician and I do not want to become one. I was once a professor on Marywood's faculty, and now I teach an occasional IT course when asked. I am a computer specialist, a writer, and a businessman. At my age, 68, and with my experience, I know a lot about a lot. In recent years, I have learned more and more about government, our Constitution, and how our democratic republic should be working.

From what I have learned, it is not working the way it should. So, I think it is time to retire most of the politicians and put some hard working, competent, ordinary Americans to work for the people. I think I fit the bill on that one. I just completed my 63rd book. Three of my very recent patriotic books are

- America 4 Dummmies
- The Constitution 4 Dummmies
- The Bill of Rights 4 Dummmies

This gives you an idea of what I care most about.
I know that there is a perception that it helps to have legislative experience. I have heard the rhetoric over and over, from the grocery store to the barber shop to the town tavern: "A new guy in Congress will not serve the people well. We need to bring back the ones who are on the big committees so that our area can be well represented in the Congress of the US." How has that been working out for you?

I do not buy that argument. If it were true we would have the finest Congress there ever was. Instead, we have the worst, and our own one-time Congressman from the recent past got very good at gaming the system and profiting from it. Paul Kanjorski spent 13 precious terms not representing NEPA. He was not a leader but a dedicated follower. He was once a good Democrat for several terms but then for survival, he got in lock step with the hard left socialist faction and Nancy Pelosi became his master so that he could hold important committee chairs.

Matt Cartwright has followed diligently in Kanjo's footsteps. We see Matt only at election time. Look at Cartwright's platform and you will be shocked at what he is advocating for the people of Northeastern PA. As a good citizen, you must check out his far left ideological ideas for NEPA. It is more than likely not how you think. I ask you to learn who he is before you vote him in again.

This is the kind of representation Northeastern PA does not need.

The approval rating of Congress is in the toilet because of the quality of its work - for special interests vs. the people's interests. I am a candidate for Congress to help end poor quality representation and be part of a Congress that realizes that its roots are the people and the people are who all of the representatives are to serve.

The perception that big time experience counts in Congress may be correct. It may be correct if only Politicians can get in and out of Congress in four to six years before they are corrupted by the political industry in Washington DC.

The reality of course is that politicians use their experience for their own benefit, not for the benefit of the people. After learning "the ropes," representatives in Congress forget all about the people they are supposed to serve and they become powerful enough so that they can create corrupt deals. Sometimes this results in Pennsylvania grabbing taxpayer's money from Alaska or California or Missouri.

And when PA does get a small share of tax revenue back, it does not come back to the people because the politicians have to pay back relatives and cronies as we have seen in our own back yard over the years.

I do not think that being a representative is about getting the biggest grab bag of goodies possible and bringing the bag home and having a party. What happens when PA taxes go to fund Alaska, California, or Missouri? Such a philosophy hurts all states and the country as a whole, and eventually even if a Congressman makes a big grab one day, it will all come back to hurt Pennsylvania. It is a bad idea that has gotten even worse as politicians are brazenly corrupt today.

Ultimately, Pennsylvania is victimized and really not assisted by such a system that rewards corruption and back room deals. Where are the people, US, in all this "action." The people are soon left behind and the corruption is practiced openly as Congressmen and Congresswomen openly say, that's just the way it is! Sorry Dear Congress but when my constituents write me in for the US House of Representatives that is exactly the way it will no longer be.

It is a corrupt system, and over time, it corrupts our representatives. Today with Donald Trump running for the Presidency, we see entrenched establishment politicians no longer caring if the Democrats or Republicans win as long as it is a member of the establishment they know. If we can get rid of dirty politicians after a term or two, we won't have to worry about lifetime politicians becoming an establishment and working to ruin America, while serving themselves.

The more Congress-persons, who believe that their role is to bring more of the bacon home, are elected into office, the more the taxpayer's are cheated in all states. Their hide is whipped paying huge taxes for another politician to produce the bacon. At best, it is a lousy system. The representatives who learn the tricks are the ones who trick the people into thinking it is OK. It is not OK!

The federal government has no business messing with the states, especially favoring one over another. The people do not want one state to grab from another. So, if this is the system, it must be changed. We must not permit a system that lets a knowing representative steal from one who does not know the system well.

We must not permit special interests to rule over the interests of the people at large. I can assure you I will fight for these changes to help make our government serve the people. Of course if there are 434 other new Representatives in the 115th Congress, the thieves will have been expunged, including our own.

I know that this is a tough argument for any potential rookie to make. I think I can do well for Pennsylvania but while doing so I will work to make the playing field more fair for all representatives. One of my favorite movies is Mr. Smith Goes to Washington. In my personal ranking, it is just a bit behind Meet John Doe, and It's A Wonderful Life!

I am not suggesting that I can come anywhere close to the good work that Mr. Smith (Jimmy Stewart) or John Doe (Gary Cooper) did in those movies, but if I could just get close, and I will try, then maybe it would be a more wonderful life for us all. What would be wrong with no corruption in Washington?

Oh, it may be goody-goody to think like I do, but I can't believe that we must settle for what we now have in Washington. Go see Mr. Smith goes to Washington and see if it can bring some hope back in your heart that maybe it is OK to be goody-goody about important things. What is the alternative -- corruption, greed, graft, and back-room deals?

There is nothing written anywhere that says that Americans must give up on our country and our government by reelecting professional con artists every two years. Remember the naive Mr. Smith trying to convince the pros that their style of corruption was not good for the people and how he showed that even the most honorable representatives are often not honorable at all when they must make a choice for people or special interests.

If you choose to favor me with your write-in vote, I promise that I will use my conscience and my sense of honesty to put forth legislation, with no backroom deals, that will make us all proud. And when I do, you will hear my voice from Washington, and when you make your voice known to me, I will hear you and work for you and all the people of District 17.

Thank you for being part of the quiet populist revolution to save America.

Essay 25

Americans Are in Revolt.

Countervailing power is the only solution!

Those with power sometimes do not know how powerful they are while those without power know very well how weak they are. The have's always have and the have-nots, have not ever--but they do their best to survive. So it has been from the beginning of time as the major law of the universe dictates: "survival of the fittest."

Are humans above it all? Is there just a little bit in a human that is animal? Is it possible that part really is not as good in its spirit as man's best friend, the wonderful creature called dog. Are humans or dogs more inclined to do the right thing if called upon accordingly? Tough question! I look into my wonderful dog's eyes and I know which way he is going to go. When I look a human in the eye, it is my history with the person more than the look in his eye that matters. But, the look in his eye does matter. I admit that it is good to have a fine canine friend help out in the evaluation. Who is good; and who is bad? Dogs seem to know!

As we go back to the turn of the 20th century we find certain humans who had lots and lots of material goods as well as lots of power. These folks were truly captains of industry and they were referred to as "Robber Barons." That term was not very flattering to these people who went to church each week in fine clothes, hoping to charm even the priests into believing in their goodness. But, there was little goodness there!

Robber Barons was not a very flattering term for anybody at the time and it is not a well-appreciated term today. It implies that certain Barons are robbers. They rob the people. We all know who they are and who they were in real times from our unedited American History classes. John D. Rockefeller, Milton S. Hershey,

J.P. Morgan, Andrew Carnegie, and Cornelius Vanderbilt were the headliner robber barons of the period. They were all shrewd, cunning, and some might add heartless businessmen of the period. Even they may not have known they were so bad. .

These Robber Barons were indeed captains of industry and they were indeed, robber barons.

They had immense power and ran huge companies and hired many people to work in their facilities. For the workers, it was good because they had a job and they were able to provide for their families, though just barely. For the families, it was not so good because the head of the household had to work most of his waking hours every day of the week. The Robber Barons believed, perhaps even sincerely, that they were providing a modicum of wealth for the plebeians of the new America.

There is a very offensive term that has been used for some time to describe one of the worst acts of the Robber Barons. This term is "labor arbitrage." It came from this period of American History as the Robber Barons tried their best to assure that the wage they paid was the absolute minimal wage. And, they did pay only as much as legally required.

Only the Robber Barons held the power in the period before and immediately after the turn of the twentieth century. The irony is that the workers did not really understand their value in the wealth creation process. The workers were the means to the Barons' wealth. Yet, they had no power, and in most cases were living in destitute circumstances.

The worker had power but could not realize it individually. This enabled the barons to exact upon the workers whatever terms were favorable to the barons alone. The workers were mere resources. Though they were clearly the means to the barons' wealth, nobody on the Robber Baron team was about to reveal this to them.

In the power game, the barons had all the power and the workers had none. -- zero, nada, zilch as they like to say today. Thus, there was a power void. Whenever there is a power void, it will eventually be filled as the seemingly powerless realize that in numbers, they have power. In the days of the Robber Barons, the barons were able to essentially enslave the workers because there was no notion of a countervailing power, and no means of achieving it even if the notion were well known.

What is countervailing power and why is it important?

Wikipedia authors often get it right, "Modern economies give massive powers to large business corporations to bias this process, and there arise 'countervailing' powers in the form of trade unions, citizens' organizations and so on, to offset business's excessive advantage."

Corporations at the turn of the century were just becoming legal and powerful and this was coincident with the Robber Baron period. Corporations were like little dictatorships that created worker cities ruled mostly by tyrants all within the democracy of the United States. This was not a proud moment in American History.

The greed exhibited by one corporation during this period forced another corporation to be as greedy as the first or go out of business. So, corporations and the men (at the time) who ran them, chose to be as greedy as they could be. They viewed it as much a matter of survival as a means to success.

The conditions were perfect. There was a large supply of labor and many needy families willing to send any member into the factory. This set the stage for the ultimate labor arbitrage. So, let's examine this notion of labor arbitrage in light of countervailing power. Quite simply, Labor arbitrage is the movement of the wage which industry must pay for workers to the lowest possible level.

Labor arbitrage creates big hurts in lots of regular people. In many ways in 2016, the "new immigrants," undocumented workers," "illegal foreign nationals," or quite simply, "illegal aliens, are driving American wages down again to the point of labor arbitrage, and it is not by accident.

The Robber Barons are documented as having exploited Americans, using sweatshops with abysmally low wages. They were fully in control of the labor arbitrage. If workers had to work just 10 hours a day, it was an easy shop but sometimes the periods included 18-hour work shifts, without overtime pay. The abuses of the period included child labor; inadequate safety, minimal health and environmental safeguards; and of course, no pension or health benefits--for most Americans.

There seemed to be no escape. If a worker of that era tried to change his plight, he might be summarily discharged for union organizing. There were a lot of reasons for families to just accept their condition as it was dealt. The Robber Barons assured that those who accepted their dire circumstances were able to survive, though in the most meager ways.

Humans are animals and when animals are pinched and hurt and their young are hurting, life is different than when you and I are screaming at the TV set because of things as trite as that our favorite team did not score. If the team is Notre Dame, and if I (Brian Kelly) were the coach, then perhaps the screaming would be appropriate and responsible. But, that again is not the theme of this essay.

Eventually, when you are really hurting, finding a solution because of the gravity of a problem such as labor arbitrage with no countervailing power is far more important than the fear of repercussions. A solution must come one way or another. From every void a solution will come.

At the turn of the last century, however, there was a huge void. People were hurting and it seemed they were helpless. However, every now and then, brave men would come by to help. These were union organizers and they tried their best to fill the void. The union organizers intrinsically knew that giving power to the worker was the only solution to labor arbitrage.

Yet, employees knew that the best they could do would be to be able to barely make it if they made no waves at all. If they made some waves, such as fraternizing with a labor organizer, they might be left with nothing. The choice to organize was difficult as the risks were high.

The union workers were very brave souls with a real mission. They suffered and all suffered when trying to take the smallest action to avoid the tyranny of the Robber Barons. Can you imagine working for the Baron and trying to overcome the Baron at the same time?

There is an idea that if a decent wage were paid to the workers-- not substantially larger but seemingly generous, the Robber Barons would have been able to keep their gold and the worker would have achieved the opportunity to live more hours per week with family, rather than at the factory. But, with no countervailing power, the Robber Barons were more concerned about competing against other Robber Barons. They had no regard at all for the power of the worker who was merely part of the means of production. The worker simply had no power.

Wherever and whenever there is a power void, it will be filled.

Over time, unions developed strategies to face and to compete against the all-powerful captains of industry, the Robber Barons. They demanded better wages and better benefits for workers. The unions became the countervailing power against the Robber Barons / corporations that had been missing from the foray for far too long.

Soon after unions were integrated into the fabric of America, life got better for everybody -- workers and even the former barons. Though the sins of the Robber Barons were hard to forgive, the unions helped them to stop sinning against their fellow human-kind.

Enter the Politician

Political corruption is not new to our times. When the Robber Barons had the wealth, there were plenty of politicians who favored their way of life and benefited from it immensely. The people did not count. The political process has not changed much, unfortunately.

When the unions gained power, and perhaps as a means of that power, there were politicians who recognized the winds of change and prepared to accept their largesse from Unions as there had become a choice.

Once the countervailing power had been duly established, neither corporations nor unions controlled the scenario. Both were very powerful, and the unions did their best for the worker while the corporation did its best for the former baron class citizens.

Eventually both the corporations and the unions noticed that there was a very large and available third party that had entered the ring. Actually it had always been there but in the early days it represented only we the people. The third party was actually to have been the "people" as represented by the Congress, the Senate, the President, and the Supreme Court. Instead, the third party in its public face was just the government with all of its inelegant bureaucracy. Of course, when it chose to do so, and only when it was inclined, this third party known as the government, did claim to represent ordinary people. However, most of the time, as we have all come to realize in 2016, the temptation of the politician to feed himself from the public treasury is so overwhelming that he has little time to include we the people in his greed-driven thought process. Self-serving politicians are more visible today because they promise the people everything to get elected.

John Quinton called it right when he described the greed of a politician in this way: "Politicians are people who, when they see light at the end of the tunnel, go out and buy some more tunnel."

The corporations and the unions fought for the control of this powerful entity known as the government. Whoever won over the politician had the tie breaker on their side. For the most part, only at election time did the people matter. And, we know politicians love their perquisites. Depending on which politician was on-the-take or as they would like to have it said, "depending on which group got the politician's ear," things moved in that direction with a little help from government friends.

Meanwhile, though the forte of the unions was to organize workers, not all regular workers were in the union camp. These were the unorganized workers. There was no mistake then as there is no mistake today, when groups of people organize for any purpose, it is the unorganized people who are left behind with no power. There is only so much bounty and plunder to gain that those without organized power are always destined to become society's losers, giving up their meager holdings for those organized to take them from them with impunity. There really is no big pot, from which to distribute to all. When a union wage is exorbitant for example, the unorganized in society feel the pain in their purchasing power far more than do the union members.

For years, as unions grew more powerful, they represented the interests of the organized working people and the corporations represented the interests of the descendants of the wealthy Robber Barons. There were and still are classes of people in America but in America, since there are no classes permitted as all men are equal under God and the law; nobody talked about classes. So, we say there were / are no classes. But, there certainly were the rich and poor. There still are. There is no doubt about that.

One can conclude that from all of the good parts of the first major countervailing power, unions, came about a middle class. Without the good work of brave union organizers, the gap between poor and rich would be ever widening and thus the countervailing power brought by the unions helped all of America and all Americans. There was no longer just the rich and the very poor.

The middle class did not have enough to be rich and they did not have so little as to be poor. In some ways, they could see in both directions. Some middle class descendants became poor and some became rich and some stayed in the middle. Thus there were the nouveaux riche, coming from no-place to gain seats that had once been reserved for the rich alone. Unions were a major reason for enabling the emergence of the middle class.

How did this happen? Over time, from their emergence during the Robber Baron years, labor unions became stronger and stronger. Owners and management had to pay attention or they risked economic loss from strikes and other union actions. Unions thus became a strong countervailing power. They got big enough to shift some corporate profits from very wealthy owners to the middle class. The middle class gained better wages and unprecedented benefits. An economic side benefit was that money stayed in the hands of those most likely to spend it. Thus, with the middle class holding some of the country's wealth, this stimulated the national economy and provided more and more essential public services.

What about the poor?

The poor, however were still poor. Who represented the poor? Though supposedly representing all the people, in many ways government became a Robin-Hood type ally of the poor. The notion of one-voice, one vote meant, other than direct campaign contributions from the wealthy, that the poor counted just as much as the rich at election time, and this notion was not lost on the politicians.

And so there came massive initiatives directed at the poor. With programs such as Lyndon Johnson's "Great Society," the poor in the second half of the twentieth century seemed a lot less poor than those whose labor had been arbitraged at the "turn of the 20th century." There were programs that good Americans put together to help the poor and from this came plenty--from housing projects and food distribution centers, and even cash payments, often with no work requirement.

This assured that the poor could share in the health and wealth of the country. Some watching all this have humorously called the creation of so many agencies to serve the poor as Poor Inc. The rich again in one way or another were able to make money--this time, ironically, by serving the poor.

But, there was a problem. The poor still were isolated to the tenements and complexes that had been designed to make life more comfortable for them. Yet, everywhere in these complexes were poor people and their "poorness" became even more obvious. The people living in these facilities after a while began to refer to their neighborhoods derogatorily as "the projects."

Yet, despite the partial economic / neighborhood segregation, the poor for the most part shopped in the same stores and malls and paid the same prices as everybody else for their wares. So, they knew for sure that they were poor. Many of the children of the poor eventually, through major educational programs--college loans and scholarships, escaped to be successful but this story is not about that. And, yes, the middle class awaited all those who were able to make the great escape. Nobody forced anybody to be poor and the more opportunity that business produced, the more likely it would be for more and more poor to escape their condition.

As a point in time summary, during this period in the mid 1900's the three major forces were corporations, unions, and government. Together, the work of all three of these major forces has gotten the poor to understand the good life but in many cases the stubbornly poor know that the next step in the "good life" is difficult if not impossible to achieve for them. They have to work to achieve the next level.

Some knew they could change their lives but others felt that they had few choices. Television of course made it even worse to be poor as the poor were never exalted in TV shows such as "Leave it to Beaver." The heroes of the shows of the 1950's and 1960's were never somebody who had nothing before they became a hero. The "Beave" had that nice home with the white picket fence. It was nothing like the projects.

And, so, just like the void that caused the unions to form, and for government to take more of a role with the poor, there was another power vacuum. The poor were better off for sure but they had no power. They still did not feel good about themselves, but was that the objective of the assistance? The poor had people vouching and lobbying for them but on their own, they were powerless. The poor, other than having the inalienable opportunity of all Americans to choose to become successful, which somehow had left many of them behind, had little control of their destiny. Living in the "projects" was a continual reminder of that.

Wherever and whenever there is a power void, it will be filled.

And, so, seemingly out of nowhere for many in this situation, another power group emerged. These were called community organizers. This movement began, shall we say, with well-intentioned people in the US. They believed intrinsically that the people who had to live in complexes or the "projects" were left out of realizing the American Dream. As in all things, this conclusion was not hard and fast as many had climbed out of their poor life through education grants and job opportunities, and they had moved on. But, it certainly was not common thought. Community groups, once formed, never were successful if they actually helped the poor.

Community groups, such as Acorn served the poor?

To serve the poor, in this, their time of realized need, bands of people appeared, who called themselves community organizers. They believed that everyone, regardless of their status in life should have the opportunity to own a piece of the American Dream. The "dream" was symbolized by a nice house with a garage--preferably a two-car garage and a nice car.

Over time, the controversial group Acorn became one of the most powerful of these community organizing groups. Before too long, the community groups began to operate as much for the good of the community groups as for the poor. The poor gained single family housing though in most cases, they could not sustain the mortgage payments. The community groups became more cash-rich and more powerful as the poor had become their means for them to gain a lucrative financial end.

During Barack Obama's run for the presidency, many Americans were first introduced to the notion that there was an occupation called "community organizer," as the candidate president posited that was his profession. The major reason people would meet a community organizer from Acorn or from another group is if they needed help in getting a home mortgage. Thus, many people in the middle class had never even heard of the term.

To help poorer Americans have a shot at the American Dream, community organizers brought those with nothing, who were looking for the American Dream to the banks where the organizers helped them obtain a mortgage. So, the poor in this scenario were being lifted from the projects to a real home. The community organizers helped give the poor the status and the power to negotiate a home mortgage with neighborhood banks. In most cases, the poor had no real income, no assets, and they had no possible means of paying back the loan. None of this mattered to the government. So, they got the loan. Eventually John Q. Public, in the form of the American taxpayer paid the loan when the mortgagee defaulted.

The Acorn and banking Industry relationship really was not very symbiotic. Left on its own, the banking industry, in my humble opinion, would not have gotten in bed with Acorn for any reason whatsoever than that they were compelled to do so. Banks actually had no choice or else the government would take away their licenses. What was the result? Acorn made a ton of money. The poor got a piece of the American Dream. The banks were left holding the bag but nobody ever liked banks anyway. What's wrong with this scenario? Well, as we all know, in 2008, the bag of bad debt completely burst.

The overworked term, "perfect storm," applies here as the power structure was perfect for the American Dream to unfold for the poor. The government through the Clinton-backed Community Reinvestment Act (CRA) changes that became law in 1993, gained for the Democrats who have never been known to protect the taxpayer's money, the power to punish banks for not loaning to minorities. Minorities were known as the "plain old poor," as reported by hard neighborhood numbers.

Bankers who wanted to become truck drivers could have resisted. Those who wanted to remain bankers knew that if they chose to not loan to the poor; they were finished. Community groups figured out that if they became the tattle-tellers, and squealed at the slightest negative action of the banks, they were in a position to better their personal "business" financially.

And so, the groups extorted money from the banks and for the funds they received, they agreed to give the banks a good report card to the government auditors. The major forces in our government were complicit! Nobody was innocent but nobody went to jail.

Tracing through history we find that Mr. and Mrs. Clinton and many very liberal Democrats believed and many still believe that everybody is entitled to a home, and whether they can afford one or not should not be a consideration. I believe that everybody should have a home as long as the same everybody can afford it. The

Clintons did not add the qualifier. It really did not matter to these folks whether the mortgagee ever worked a day in their lives or, if the truth be known, whether they were in the U.S. legally or illegally.

Originally, there was nothing in it for the Republican Congress to give Bill Clinton this bill in 1993. So, there was Republican resistance but then Clinton figured a way to buy Republican support. Like politicians today, Clinton had to give the Republicans something to get them to go along. It may not have been the Louisiana Purchase but then-President Clinton promised the banks the repeal of the Glass-Steagall act.

This was a big concession to business but not necessarily a wise one. Without this post-depression law that had kept the financial industry stable for 60 years, banks were permitted to engage in much more risky ventures with depositors' money. The combination of mortgagees not being able to pay mortgages (toxic assets), and the ability of banks to play roulette with depositor's funds had a lot to do with the financial crisis in 2008. Moreover, the government knew it was destiny. The crash had to happen.

Acorn hustled the banks and banks willingly paid Acorn a "fee." This was pure extortion so that Acorn would not complain to have government probes launched against the bank's lending practices. The question has been asked many times, "Why would banks pay so much without even a small fight? Sol Stern, a famous consultant in the financial industry is quoted often with the best answer:

"The banks know they are being held up, but they are not going to fight over this. They look at it as a cost of doing business."

While ACORN et al was hustling the banks, unfortunately they were also hustling the poor in their communities. They charged a nominal fee in the neighborhood of $100 for their services in getting poor families mortgages, whether the families could afford the $100 or the mortgage, it did not matter as long as ACORN got paid.

Additionally, the new homeowner often got a mortgage with lousy terms. That as much as anything else created the conditions for eventual foreclosure. On top of it all, community groups like Acorn found other ways to get money from the taxpayers. In the last several years before its bust-up, for example, they received about 40% of their money from US. Various governmental agencies doled out big bucks to Acorn and others for one reason or another.

In 2010, Acorn's corruption and scandals finally caught up with the group and it went under. It filed for bankruptcy and seemingly was taken out. After four years of anonymity, Acorn seeds have been popping up all over the country and liberal veterans are pleased to tell conservatives that just like the big shark, they're back.

Conservatives thought they had ended Acorn once and for all. They had tapes of Acorn giving their low-income clients advice on how to engage in tax evasion, human smuggling, and child prostitution Now, as noted, dozens of mini-entities have sprung up with the same leadership and they are back doing their dirt all over again. Watch out, corruption breeds corruption.

The sub-prime bubble that burst in 2008, was inflated first by Clinton, and then George Bush did nothing to stop it. Bush knew that illegal aliens somehow were able to get mortgages for homes they otherwise were not able to afford. It got so bad that the banks were trying to prove the loans were worthy that they began to accept statements from Acorn that showed the "undocumented income" of "undocumented people" on the plus side of the books to help assure them getting a mortgage. Acorn referred to this as "under the table money.' They clearly were aiding in people avoiding paying taxes but no charges were filed.

Apparently George Bush liked the fact that illegal aliens were taken care of in the US as it seemed good for the businesses who would employ them. Unfortunately George Bush and now Barack Obama and the whole Congress are pleased to look the other way when non-citizens are fleecing the public treasury.

As hard as it is to believe, the government, in concert with the new countervailing power, the community groups, were responsible for delivering the American Dream to the poor. The CRA law actually encouraged community groups to market loans to targeted groups and they would collect various fees from the individuals and from the banks. It was more profit as a motive than altruism.

In essence, the "regulators" imposed an "Affirmative Action" approach to CRA. In most cases, to book the loan, bank officers had to relax the credit standards of the bank to get the loan approved. So, banks were trained to cheat by the federal government itself or pay the consequences. Banks also learned how to minimize their own risk. Yet, by 2007, as the price of housing began to drop, the financial party was just about over.

The community organizers had become the fourth great US countervailing power. Were they needed? They surely thought so. They orchestrated so many wonderful things for poor people that, after the down payment to them, many families actually believed that what happened to them was a miracle. It actually was but it was unsustainable. The Community Reinvestment Act gave the poor the advantage over the banks and said basically that sanity was no longer important in lending.

Eventually, as Banks were bundling and selling their mortgages to the unknowing investment community and the price of homes began to decline, or not increase, there was no escape for somebody who really could not afford the mortgage in the first place. They could not sell the property and win the game. They could not keep the property because they could not afford the monthly payments when they finally came due. So, what would they do?

They would ultimately default and hightail it out of town. This created what was almost a second great depression. It happened because Jimmy Carter in 1977 and Bill Clinton in 1993 created bad legislation, and because George Bush for eight long years, permitted it to be the law of the land.

So in 2009, the next President, Barack Hussein Obama, at a time of great financial trouble decided to solve the problem by throwing gobs of taxpayer money at it as had George Bush several months earlier. Words emerged that had seldom been used in the US lexicon, such as TARP, stimulus, bailout, and porkulus. These became bywords on the American landscape. The people were saying no tarp, no stimulus, no bail outs, and no porkulus, but our unresponsive representatives in Congress felt they knew better.

The fourth countervailing power, community organizers, were in it for the money and they directed the flow of profits their way. The unorganized, mostly from the middle class, were the ones hurt as they funded this largesse. The poor were clearly hurt as they had to give up their new homes that they never could have lived in if there had been reasonability tests applied to the loans. But, they were hurt anyway. For a while, it seemed like the unions, the corporations, the government, and the community organizers had already decided how to split the loot and they were going to get away with it. They were impervious to the people left out. Then, all of a sudden the market collapsed, and somebody said:

Look, up in the sky, it's a bird, no it's a plane, no it's Superman. Someone else said: "Mister Trouble always hangs around, 'til he hears this mighty sound, -- "Here I come to save the day -- that means that Mighty Mouse, is on his way. Then people began to gain the scent of TEA in the air. For a time, this was as pleasant a scent as the scent of freedom.

Remember wherever and whenever there is a power void, it will be filled.

But, just before the scent of TEA came in 2009, the United States had room for just one Superhero. His name of course is Barack Hussein Obama. Though some say that Obama is not a bad guy, watching him for seven years now, in 2016 Americans have learned that everything he touches turns out bad, and since Obama always wants to touch lots more than he has, things have gotten progressively worse, even in this, his last year, 2016.

With his thoughtful gifts in 2009 to US Citizens, such as a try at Cap and Trade, and Obamacare, and his 40 brand new Marxist czars, amidst the longest recession since the deep depression, regular Americans began wondering what was happening to America. Now we wonder what has happened to America. Another power void surely had been created.

Many people lost half or more of their retirement savings in just a few months. There was another need for countervailing power. This time, it was driven by the middle class in response to all of the shenanigans and the complicity of the Congress and the president. The middle class had emerged as the newest unprotected class.

Corporations were still for corporations and owners. Unions were still for unions and their members and leaders, and Community organizers, even though they began to be attack by conservative forces in Congress about 2010, continued to be for community organizers. The poor and the middle class, who were supporting this huge burden had been forgotten. And so, there was yet another power void.

Wherever and whenever there is a power void, it will be filled

Whenever there is a power void, it will eventually be filled as the seemingly powerless realize that in numbers, they have power. The poor still had nobody but the community organizers who were creating problems for themselves and were also fleecing the poor. The middle class and the small business people across the US as well as some from the ranks of the poor and the rich had become "mad as hell" about the pure buffoonery and reckless spending of our government.

The leaders of this government became caricatures of themselves. Hearing after hearing with one buffoon after another speaking in their patented buffoonish language, the government clearly showed that it had begun to believe that it had limitless resources. Worse than that, the government solution was always to spend every dime in sight to satisfy its perceived needs. Our government has not changed much though today's Republicans have simply decided to hand in the towel and let it happen. Government has gotten even worse since 2008. It is still hell bent on continuing to bail out every special interest so they cannot fail while adding so much national debt that the country itself is now in danger of failing and defaulting on its debt.

And, so people by the millions for years have been writing Congress and making their concerns known. Congress, for the first time that I can remember clearly told the people that the Congress knew better and it has simply ignored the cards and letters and the spirited debates that once occurred in Town Hall Meetings. Congress became completely unresponsive and it is still unresponsive though now it is controlled by Republicans. The cries of the people do not matter. The people continue to have every reason to feel completely helpless, at the mercy of a corrupt government, and without power.

Many hard working people are still being hurt today and will continue to be hurt by policies that elevate the needs of certain people over people who provide the work engine for the country. All citizens have a right to expect that by working hard for themselves, they should be able to keep the fruits of their labor.

Redistribution of wealth and the redistribution of healthcare has become the new mantra of Congress and the President. This has not been cutting it with the people at large. A look at the success of Bernie Sanders and Donald Trump shows the frustration with the Congress and the president. Redistribution is one of the basic tenets of socialism, and that is not the American way. Americans have decided that enough is enough, and neither elected representatives nor the establishment elite of both Political Parties can no longer control the people.

The people at large have been neglected by corporations, by unions, by government, or by community organizers and thus, there has been a large void to fill.

Before the hard left and the socialist corrupt press misrepresented, defamed, disparaged, villainized and dishonored the TEA Party, it was able to make a huge mark on the political scene as a countervailing power for middle class regular Americans.

What happened to the TEA Party? In 2009, it became the new countervailing power. Quiet for many years after a dishonest press smothered it with negatives, and the government's IRS harassed its leaders, it is quietly at work reflecting the discontent of the majority of today's American people.

The TEA has not only boiled; it has boiled over. The people are upset at elite politicians, the government and the media. The simple reason for its existence has always been that government had gone astray. Government has been taken too much from the people. People who liked TEA Party philosophies have not gone away; they still want their government and their country back. NOW!

The work of the TEA Party is happening today and it will go on in the future as this grassroots non-partisan network works to achieve many objectives. The TEA Party, without pushing its name, has gained power across the land. It is filling the void as a countervailing power. The slogans, precepts, objectives, desires, and love affairs of the people who would be classified as being TEA Partiers are many.

There are several hundred slogans, precepts, objectives, desires, and love affairs, within the philosophy espoused by the original TEA Party. Keep your eyes open.

Eric Olsen, organizer for the Billings TEA Party Group in Montana, as quoted in the Billings Montana Gazette in 2010 summed up his perception of the destiny of the TEA Party as a movement in an unconventional way. He knows the folks "of TEA" will not give up...ever:

"If someone gave me $1 million to leave [the TEA Party] , that would be tempting," Olsen said. "But then Jennifer would take over and they'd have to give her $1 million. And then someone else would take over".

TEA, the fifth and soon to be the controlling countervailing power never had a scent so sweet!

Summary of the Conservative Populist Movement. Can it be called The John Doe Party?

Some think that the Taxed Enough Already (TEA) Party, which was never a unified singular purpose group, has gone away. It could not be further from the truth. Since it was regular people and not elites that sponsored gatherings and created a conservative agenda, it was pretty easy for the TEA Party to slip under-ground for the last several years; but it has been active nonetheless.

The media and all the Lois Lerner's out there have had a tough time attacking conservative individuals since the TEA Party was more or less underground. The steam of the TEA of patriotism, however, is still hot. The believers in America-First are incensed at what has been happening to our country. Even more-so for many, the wimpy Republican response has been nauseating for those looking for somebody to stop our tyrannical president. . Donald Trump and

Ted Cruz's successful candidacies are a reflection of the sentiments of the people without having to use any particular name.

The new conservative populist movement is a result of a combination of budget compromises that funded Obama's wish-list 100%, while not rolling back any of his dramatic expansion in government spending. That's not all. The push for amnesty led by one-time TEA Party favorite Florida Senator Marco Rubio in the Senate, and the disintegration of trust in GOP House leadership, which brought down Boehner's speakership, changed the movement and made it more alive, and more tuned in; yet more subdued.

Instead of having fun with tri-cornered hats symbolizing patriotism and expecting that most Americans are patriotic, the people who once were Tea Party stalwarts transformed from idealistic babes waiting to get thumped by a corrupt media and government. They began to distrust more than trust even those politicians who promised that they mirrored their beliefs.

They are now a far more savvy and far more successful and a much more effective countervailing force. They have no label now other than a description as a much more cynical electorate. TEA Party groups were major victims of Obama's IRS abuses, and they were ignored by those they helped elect. Therefore, local TEA Party leaders and those citizens simply paying attention to what is going on in America are now challenging the very politicians who they pushed into office in 2010. Fool me once!

A young lady who was once a self-described TEA Party activist, when testifying before Congress on IRS abuses, captured the new essence of the new populist residual of the old TEA Party sentiment in these words: "I'm not interested in scoring political points. I want to preserve and protect the America that I grew up in. The America that people crossed oceans and risked their lives to become a part of, and I'm terrified it's slipping away. Thank you very much."

And, so it is the people against the establishment today. The new countervailing power is alive and well, and it is driving the 2016 Presidential Election Campaigns but nobody is drinking any more TEA. To join the movement, all one has to do is believe in

America. Nobody needs to tell anybody. I would call it the John Doe Party if it needed a name.

The people in the TEA Party returned to their roots. It is no longer an organized political machine as it once was. Instead, it is simply a movement of people who believe that America can and needs to do better. Those politicians, once trusted in 2010 and 2014 have used up their chances. And so, the people, not a group easily picked off by a corrupt media, have found alternatives to elite Republican double-dealers.

They have found a brazen-faced New York real estate mogul who plays by the people's rules. Additionally, they have Ted Cruz, another outsider with grand eloquence and no shortage of guts. Cruz sticks to his guns, and does not play the elite Republican game. That's why his fellow Senators, the same Senators whose greed drives their very being, fear Senator Cruz. They do not want their gravy train to end.

By the way, I am a Democrat and my populist conservative view is right in line with this thinking. More and More Americans from all Parties, are deciding that the power of the politicians needs to be minimized and the power of the people expanded. That's why Bush, Rubio, and John Kasich never had a prayer. The people are sick of politicians. Insider, elitist politicians create an extra revulsion in the caring citizenry.

So, is there a TEA Party left to fight as a countervailing power? There does not need to be a formal group as the people are together on this one. Look around and you can see that the spirit of the TEA Party is the new heart and soul of the Republican Party. This is much to the shock and chagrin of too-comfortable GOP Congressional majority. It is not nice to fool the people.

Thank you for being part of the quiet populist revolution to save America.

Essay 26

US Education Gets Failing Grades

U.S. Education is odiferous!

Eliminating federal involvement in K–12 education is one of my top domestic priorities for education. The Constitution offers no provision for federal meddling in education. Ron Paul says that, "It is hard to think of a function less suited to a centralized, bureaucratic approach than education. The very idea that a group of legislators and bureaucrats in D.C. can design a curriculum capable of meeting the needs of every American schoolchild is ludicrous."

As the federal government has exerted more control over education, what has happened? I don't need to tell you because you know. "The deteriorating performance of our schools as federal control over the classroom has grown shows the folly of giving Washington more power over American education." Do you really want an American bureaucrat determining the education your child receives?

When were the children of your favorite last politician, from state offices to the White House so pleased with the system they created that they insisted that their children realized the benefits? Actually, that's Washington-speak for saying, "hey, they won't send their kids to those schools." Doesn't that tell it all?

Ron Paul is my second favorite political hero after Alan Keyes. Paul has been thinking about solutions all his life. He is not right on all issues but he is right on most. He suggests that a constitutionalist president looking for ways to improve the lives of children should demand that Congress cut the federal education bureaucracy. And, that's just a down payment on eventually returning 100 percent of the education dollars back to parents.

In other words, Paul says and I say eliminate the US Department of Education and send them all back for remedial training. Put parents back in charge of their children's education. Parents can do a much better job than Washington?

Education is critical in a democracy. It is also critical in a dictatorship as the despot wishes to control the thoughts of the population begin with the young. So, watch indoctrination direct from Washington. I assure you I do not like 'mmm mmm mmmm' Barack Hussein Obama' being sung in grade schools as much as I do not like the idea that "Adolf Hitler is our savior, our hero" as was sung by the Hitler Youth.

Tell me why Obama is now in charge of college loans. Is it so he can influence the curriculum? There are many bad signs.

There's the story of the old guy walking by and he sees something on the ground that intrigues him. He says, "Looks like it.!" He picks it up and says "Feels like it!" He takes a whiff and he says, "Smells like it!' Then he takes just a little taste, makes a bad face, puts it back on the ground and says, ""Tastes like it! --- Boy am I glad I did not step in it.! If it looks like it, it probably is it and Obama has been giving us a lot of that for a seven years plus now, and none of it smells good.

Education, without indoctrination is the ONLY thing that breaks the cycle of poverty that traps kids into a life of low wages, followed by single parenthood. Lack of education likewise robs them of their future. We spend more than any nation yet we lag far behind in terms of results. Students at every level from K to 12 are outperformed by students in other industrialized nations.

What happened to our education system? Why does Obama want more control when federal control has failed the schools and our education system miserably? Why are Obama's own children not going to public school?

Along with the dumbing down of our kids, look at the colleges and universities (yes, I was part of the problem there as a college professor) where semi-socialist grading has been on the front-burner for some time -- far too long. Professors who do not go along with the high grade giveaways, get poor student evaluations and therefore never get tenure or they get fired. That, ladies and gentlemen means they are fired after six years so that the school can keep its accreditation.

Why is accreditation not based on results? By the way, my department chairman's student evaluations were almost perfect. Mine were not so bad but I had some that were not good at all as my student grades were not all A's. The University was crawling with liberals that cared nothing about students and learning. After seven years, when I ran for Congress in 2010, Marywood University eliminated my position.

When we cut to the chase it says that professors who do not give lots and lots and lots of A's get fired. Students have no real incentive to apply themselves when the fix is in. Now, with Obama in charge of the funding for all of higher education (passed in the Obamacare Reconciliation by all Democrats) and the Department of Education is undermining our youth with a weak core curriculum and Obama songs, the future looks like a world in which Americans will not be able to compete. Don't you want to ask yourself -- is this by plan?

In the school districts that support K to 12, have our tax dollars been channeled to the cronies, relatives, and supporters of corrupt politicians, rather than to education itself? Why do we have substandard schools with high paid teachers?

Why is it that the high school dropout rate nationwide is at 33% and worse in big cities? Why are employers reporting that the fresh high school graduates they hire, regardless of their grades are typically just fair to poor in basic writing, reading, and math skills?

Why are good university professors like those of us that were once at Marywood University wondering why many students who came to us, who were otherwise intelligent, did not know how to think critically or write in complete sentences?

We pay huge taxes and yet we taxpayers and our children are not served by the best of the best. Our school boards have accepted that equalizing politically correct notion that children should not compete because somebody then has to lose. Teachers are pressured to give little Johnny an A, even though little Johnny still cannot read the room number on the classroom on the last day of class. The objective has become that everybody gets an A in every course. In this scenario good students are not challenged to try to get a real A. Worse than that, they do not learn as they should, and not even more than a generation later America suffers from not producing the best of the best as in days past.

The school boards do not want students to feel bad while they are supposed to be learning. For twelve years, they don't give them the basics needed to get a job. This does not help Americans trying to better themselves. It has really been a disservice to our youth for some time now.

By the time these kids get to College, they continue to expect A's, and that is another problem. Even small countries around the world now show greater achievement than Americans, and we think we can solve the problem with money! To whom should we give the cash?

We spend enough money so that our education system ought to be perfect. So what is wrong? Perhaps teachers are selected based on who they know rather than what they know? Can we even find out if the bottom of the barrel teachers can pass achievement tests their students are asked to pass? If not, why not? Can we even get rid of the bottom part of the barrel? Surely if you are going to teach something, you first should understand the subject matter yourself. If it could be solved with money it would already be solved.

Having said that, I am surely for good education provided by competent teachers who believe in excellence. "If you think education is expensive, try ignorance." -- Quote attributed to both Andy McIntyre and Derek Bok.

We are all responsible but there was little we could do in the past. This phenomenon seemed to sneak up on us. Yet, we--all of us, have permitted the dumbing down of our children compared to the rest of the world. This will bring our great country to her knees. I believe there is still time to stop it. Education should not be free of accountability.

While we profess that no child should be left behind, we must figure out how to put that notion into practice with some reality. We need accountability for where these taxes are being spent because our children will be left behind as they are not being taught to compete in the global economy. We must hold our schools and our teachers accountable.

Parents, are the key voice needed to assure the best education in our communities. Unfortunately, once parents vote in the local school board, the educators, and / or the local leaders, they often abdicate their responsibilities and let the PTA take a back seat to local politics. It's time to get involved in a big way. Accountability needs to rule the day.

Most of us just entering our senior citizen years and beyond probably did not pay attention back in the 1980's, when our public schools were run and paid for by each state. Back then, local school districts controlled the curriculum, teachers' wages, retention, and school schedules. Then, as if to create a perfect Obama state as we experience today, the big hand of the Federal Government reached into the states to extend its power over our lives in education.

Was this part of the plan overall and is Barack Obama and the open progressives in our government the culmination of the plan. I think they showed their cards a little early on Obamacare but after six years of delays we can even get this back on course. But, it won't necessarily be easy.

It is ironic that the takeover of student education funding was in the health bill. Quite frankly, it does make me sick. How about you?

The Bureaucrats and the equalizers created the Department of Education and all of a sudden came standardized testing and lots of other things that appeared innocuous. Parents, teachers, and administrators complain that the current system sends our education tax dollars to Washington where just a portion of that money is returned to us conditionally. Nobody could have done such a poor job with our children's education if they intended to do so.

Georgia's roughly 46% drop-out rate is but one indicator that their system statewide is not functioning. Other states are worse. Pennsylvania is at 18%. Federal control is definitely not the answer. Please say you understand that in spades. It is the problem. Whatever the Feds touch turns sour. Control needs to be returned to the people at the state and local level.

I promise to vote to eliminate the Department of Education when you send me to Congress. Our kids are smart and they can be as productive as the system that we create for them. Let's start building that system. Let's also let the best be the best, and let's call them the best. What's wrong with a little truth? Maybe it would be really good for America. I surely think so!

Essay 27

Saving America from Recession

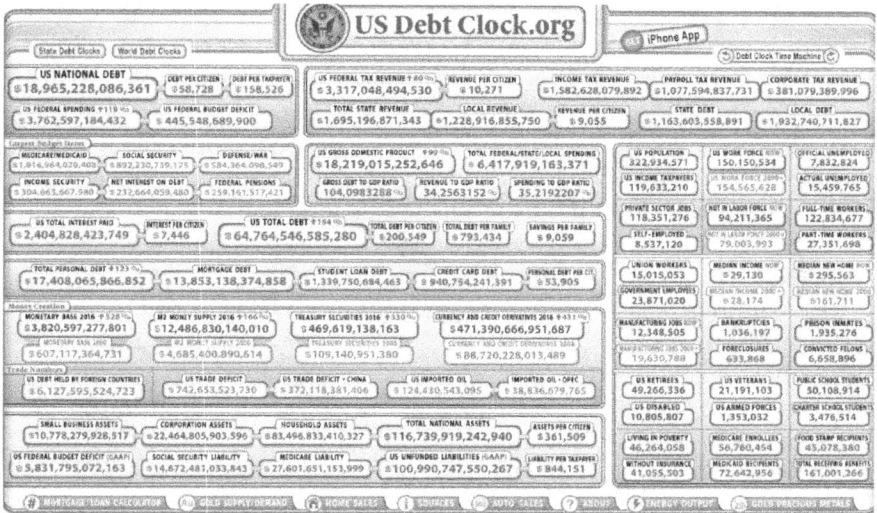

In other essays on the web site, www.briankellyforcongress.com, an
in this book, I have discussed the problems of a recession, which, by
the way, still has not ended. We have also discussed innovative
solutions from cutting red tape to solutions for offshoring and illegal
immigration and others. This essay is the bottom line on how to get
the inertia rolling the other way. This is the road to recovery from
this unprecedented never ending Obama / Cartwright / Casey
recession.

We are clearly suffering under a mountain of debt and there are
deficits scheduled from here to eternity.   A Congress controlled by
my party has permitted the deficit to skyrocket to over a trillion
dollars. The National debt is up six-fold to over $20 trillion. With
these big numbers it is easy to get zero fatigue. Take a look at the
debt clock in the figure above from usdebtclock.org/ to get a picture

at how the me generation has robbed the future. The number of zeroes are staggering.

There are only two groups in America it seems who do not know the basic way to get the United States out of a recession. The two groups are the Legislative Branch (Congress) and the Executive Branch (the President and the Czars and the Bureaucrats).

We have been in recessions before and they were almost all solved by doing two simple things. The government must stop spending and it must cut taxes. It is the only way. Then, and only then will the people be able to have money to spend on real stuff. Though the budget is a trillion out of whack, it must be balanced or be on its way to being balanced to escape a further deepening recession, and the ultimate demise of our nation.

Instead budget deals between corrupt Democrats and Republicans that will increase spending forever, radio talk show-host Sean Hannity has solved the problem. Number one, eliminate this madness called baseline budgeting, which projects increases in government spending in every program, six, seven, eight, nine, ten percent a year. That is insane.

Instead, Hannity's "penny plan" proposes that Congress insists that government cut just one penny out of every dollar that government spends every year for five years. At the end of five years, things will be in balance. Our Congress however, both Republicans and Democrats like to spend money we do not have.

One of the dumbest things the two know-nothings (Legislative and Executive branches) bring up when the people are sleeping is something called a value-added-tax or VAT. We must fight this with all our muscle as the fiscal end is near if a VAT is passed. Why? It is an unseen tax and dishonest Congresses love bringing pork home unnoticed.

The VAT will not reduce the deficit anyway. In fact, it would cause the debt to continue to rise because the President and the Congress have insatiable spending appetites. They will take any money we give them to make the economy better and they will throw it away on expanding the welfare state. They will make government bigger and less responsive to the people.

This will be another tool with which the government can redistribute wealth and spend much more on stupid and frivolous projects. Maybe if they spent some money on NASA, along the way it would not be so bad but NASA is not part of this government's spending plans. Team Obama with Matt Cartwright and Bob Casey Jr. right alongside him, has given up on the US being a leader in Space technology. NASA's prime function today is counting up the contributions of Muslims.

Rasmussen, the polling people, has found the public to be well aware of how to solve the problem. Voters agree that tax cuts would help the economy lots more than increased government spending. We have seen the spending side and it does not work. The economy remains un-stimulated despite the stimulus bills and seven years, almost eight years of Obama policies. Job losses continue at a record pace.

Why do they not say enough already. Instead the Congress voted in Obamacare, which at a minimum raised expenditures by $1 trillion and many are suggesting that it will eventually be more like $3 trillion. Meanwhile, Americans are paying more and more because of Obamacare, for basic healthcare.

Though interest rates are being kept artificially low, inflation is already taking hold. Please do not use the consumer price index as a guide to knowing the inflation rate as it is a formal instrument for government lying. Bureaucrats use it to dupe the public to suit their purposes. One place it is used all the time is to set the social security take home amounts.

Despite major inflation and food costs spiraling, seniors again got no raises. Politicians in Congress and the President lie like rugs. Go buy a rug and see if it is less expensive when the CPI is low. Better yet, go try to buy a grocery cart full of food. How is everything more expensive and yet the government tells seniors there is no inflation. Again, get its straight, they lie to suit their purposes.

Another hidden tax that seems destined to be here sooner than later is the raising of the minimum wage to $15.00. In PA right now, it is $7.25. So, the wage of unskilled workers will more than double.

How is this a tax? Well, if low wage earner gets a double increase, prices will go up almost immediately. Let's say for this plus 100% wage increase that prices go up 50% just as an example.

Will Social Security wages increase so that seniors can afford paying 50% more for the same stuff? Will Medicare costs go up to pay for the increased labor expense of services? Who gets stiffed? Does anybody really gain? Will those who have worked their way up to $14.00 per hour not want a differential of at least $7.00 over those at the bottom pay scale? When would it end?

Taxation through currency devaluation is how this all happens and it is very easy to do. Moreover it is the politically expedient course; but it is also more damaging as your dollars become the size of the one dollar bill in Gordon Liddy's famous Rosland Capital commercial as shown below:

ROSLANDCAPITAL.COM

Government cannot continue secretly taxing through borrowing (a.k.a. deficit spending) yet they persist. Is the Fed secretly printing money? Inflation is socially and economically destructive in that it wipes out fortunes for those who are not invested in hard assets. if you want to know the pace at which the dollar is devaluing, look at the price of gold. Since 2008, the stock market has risen strangely enough but that too is because there is nothing worse to own right now than cash.

Inflation is taxation but silent. Though taxation is not the answer, if citizens were forced to pay through direct taxation up front, the voters would be shocked. They would immediately see that there really is no free lunch as promised. Though more and more people understand that nothing is free, still others think government creates money from thin air.

They secretly believe that in Fort Knox and its surrounds, the US plants the whole world's supply of money trees. The dollar is the world's currency right now because these trees grow various denominations of dollars. The trees cannot grow Euros, for example. Congress would not be able to go out in public if some of the public really knew that the trees do not exist. Politicians spend the people's money. Those who think the government creates money just cannot see the problem.

Before we continue let's review the notion of a tax. A tax simply is money collected by government directly or indirectly from the people to cover the expenditures of government.

How does the government get the people's money? Though tax systems are supposed to be voluntary, the Government gets its money by force. We know that intrinsically. The IRS may very well be toting heat in the future when the citizens stop coughing up the cash willingly. There was a time when FBI Agents did not carry weapons so don't be surprised if your friendly IRS begins to get a bit more forceful if you hold out on them. What force is typically applied today?

Government decrees that you and I and businesses will pay a percentage of our income to the Tax man (the IRS). If you or I or any business refuses, we are faced with fines, imprisonment or both. Since a business per se cannot go to jail, its officers may be held liable and they would be sent to the Big House by the IRS as necessary for it to collect what it believes is due.

If somebody else took your money by threat or force, it would be stealing. Government confiscates funds and does with them as it wishes. Your dollars often wind up in the pockets of your neighbors. And, yes, it is stealing.

Let's explore this question briefly: "If government can borrow instead of tax, isn't that good for the people? It's not like the people are borrowing, right?" Let's review how the government gets its money one more time. They take as much as is politically possible by force through the tax system. However, if Congress raises taxes too high, they don't get to come back to serve their next term in Washington.

So, since politicians believe that they serve because they deliver the pork to the home folks, they have figured a way to bring pork home without raising taxes. As we noted above, they know they can borrow and who cares if it is Russia or the Chinese from whom we are borrowing. One would expect Iran not to be on the list of lenders.

This idea called government borrowing is a misnomer. Why the Chinese think they are going to get paid back is a mystery unto itself. There is no chance at all that the government will ever repay any of its debt. Who are they kidding? You may know that there was hardly any debt at the turn of the 20th century. It went from $2 billion to over $20 trillion in this past century, and there are at least $60 trillion in SS pension and Medicare promises via worthless IOUs that will never be paid back. The US Congress as custodians of the treasury have served no better than a pack of charlatans. They assure their reelections by robbing the treasury to provide pork to their people. When the people take the pork, the people get the government they deserve.

Do the people get hurt when government borrows? The word again is price inflation. When government borrows, and when the Fed is operating normally instead of under Obama constraints, interest rates rise and the Fed lowers those rates by monetizing the Federal IOUs. When there is more money in circulation, your money loses its purchasing power. So, yes, the people do get hurt even when the government borrows instead of raising taxes. It is the most unfair form of taxation. It is called inflation.

If the dollar were forced to be reduced in size to match its value, Gordon Liddy would in fact have the first printed bill at the correct size for 2016. Whenever the Liddy Ad would come on TV, I stopped and would call my wife's attention to it. It is the face of the future. If the government had to continually reduce the size of the dollar to match inflation, eventually people would need tweezers to hold on to the dollar bills used to purchase their wares. The smaller the bill, the less it would buy.

As people traded in their huge dollars for smaller and smaller sized currency, Congress's game would be up. If they taxed us, we would know it and if they had to re-size the currency such as the Liddy Dollar Sizing System, to match its new spending power, we would also know it. And in all cases, G. Gordon Liddy would forever have the first reduced sized dollar. Just as the one we show above. Inflation without dollar re-sizing makes it very difficult and probably more like impossible for both consumers and businesses to plan ahead.

When businesses cannot plan ahead they like to have as few employees around to pay if they are not sure that they will need their labor. So, Jobs! Jobs! Jobs! does not occur in times of economic uncertainty. Since this is a time of uncertainty, one would rightfully ask, "Why is the government intentionally devaluing our currency?" Only the President and Congress can answer that one. It makes no sense.

When businesses cannot plan, their growth is impeded and when business growth is impeded you can forget about having progress in every aspect of society. Society is dependent on many things. For example, at its simplest, society is dependent on things being good.

If the people were taxed outright and honestly, we would revolt. Well, at least we would fire our politicians. Right? However, the slow sting of inflation is just what the doctor ordered for a Congress more interested in snookering constituents than representing them. What is unseen is never blamed. There are no champions in the 114th Congress, therefore none of us should lament when all of them are fired by the people.

You Won't Believe This!

You know that technology is such today that it would be easy for the government to set up an electronic wallet for everybody so nobody would be forced to carry dirty, slimy, cash. Though I do not know the man, something tells me that Bill Ayers would not want the government knowing how much walking around money he was carrying. And, let's face it, the government is the least secure entity on the planet. So if somebody wanted to know your wallet contents at a given moment, they too could hack the government system. Why bother taking on the cash-rich before you know they have gotten to their ATMs?

How innovative and how beneficent that would be of the government to take on the responsibility for managing all of the wallets in the country. It is such a powerfully fulfilling thought that it almost wants you to stand up and declare that banks are no longer needed. The imperial government can handle the cash and one would suspect it can also give a better interest rate. But, would it?

Unless, of course, like Bill Ayers, on some matters, we too are realists.

The government would own you even if they did not charge a dime for the service. When the "Big Government" chose to levy a new fee or a "simple" adjustment of a prior adjustment of an adjustment, once the paper trail looked more like oblivion than the Olive Garden, they could just take the funds immediately from your electronic wallet. Under this system, Government would not need

to process those long and nasty lies (tax returns) sent in every year by taxpayers.
Rooting for the Government to Win the End Game?

Real radicals would ask, "Why should the government have to wait until April 15th to get their money." Hey, for historical purposes, if the tax code ever changed for the good, that could be the day of reckoning or the day of accountability or the close day or whatever you would like to call it. I predict April 15 will always have historical significance.

It would be more difficult for the government to fleece you if paper cash were used. But some might say it would be a grand day if the government were able to remotely lift your wallet from your pants-- even as you were watching. Then, it could riffle through the bills and the change, perhaps even read the credit card stripes and even check all your accounts. You would never have to fear being audited again. Auditing would become a daily idea.

The hard left might propose an even slicker idea. Why should you have to go to the Post Office on April 15, to fulfill a duty? The government could electronically spare you the trouble. In a perfect world, the physical dollars could be activated to flow from your wallet to the closest mailbox and they could be electronically identified as coming from you -- perhaps via a dollar / retina-like scan.

Then the postman, in addition to doing regular mail, could pick up the cash from your mail box and turn over to the US treasury. It may not really be able to be done now (2016) with real dollar bills but if Obama has his way, this can all be done electronically. You would then have to spend only what the government has not taken. Can you imagine how easy it would be to contribute your "fair share?" Nobody would be left out of the reach of the automatic electronic hand of the IRS.

Why did nobody think of this before Obama? Why should government be the last served? In the new system, when government needs anything, the electronic dollars, though in worth they may be the size of the Liddy Dollar Bill, would be electronically lifted from your electronic wallet. You "vill" be happy. These dollars will then head down an electronic speedway to the electronic national treasury where you can visit them once a month but -- no touching.

The bottom line is that if every dollar spent by government came immediately out of taxpayers' wallets (your wallet), Congress might just find it impossible to fund their vast pork-barrel spending programs. You would not stand for it.

Life would become better as we would definitely throw the bums (Congress) out when the first pilferage occurred. Then, we'd all be able to plan for our future, knowing that our savings would be there and the bills would be able to be paid.

Congress gets away with this only because we the people accept it. Only conservatives line up against this and liberals, though not stupid by any means, hear our arguments but do not buy them. The far left cannot accept that these exploding deficits mean that they are laying the burden of this huge debt pile on their children and grandchildren.

Maybe they are right! Do you think that the real hard left liberals think the next generation (grandchildren) will solve this financial dilemma? Let me ask a different way. If they felt that their grandchildren were going to be asked to pay up for grandpa's excesses, would they not stop the excesses? Unless they think their offspring will be so smart they can figure a way out of it, or they think that money grows on trees, they can't want to dump this on the grand-kids.

Since they really do not want to dump all this debt (our debt) on the next generation my logic tells me they should be complaining about how Congress and the President no longer respect their contributions. Even liberals are conservative when it comes to keeping their own money. The government is all consuming and all-eradicating. Don't look for anything to be left when the administration finally gives up on socialism.

All of us have been duped into thinking it will take a long time --- why else would there be references to children and grand-kids.? All US citizens will be paying what can only be called a fraud tax in the months ahead as price inflation soars. It is not waiting for the grand-kids to be born It is right around the corner. When it breaks loose, who are you going to blame?

Most will not blame the government. Yet, the big culprit is the government. If the people rose up and blamed the government, we could actually solve the problem. The government is the problem. Yes, we have met the enemy and it is the government of the US.

The government is the culprit, and the good news is that we have the ability and the authority to change the government. The tool we use has a simple name. It is called a "vote."

Of all the big economic issues the most serious problem is the amount the US government owes to US citizens, corporations, foreign instruments, and of course the Government Sponsored Enterprise's -- GSE (Social Security, Medicare, etc.).

This cannot be fixed with monetary policy as it will lead to hyperinflation. The losers will be those with cash or treasury bonds. The holders of such bonds would never receive fair value market value for their investment. The dollars they would receive would be Liddy-sized and if China were shipped a pile of Liddy dollars in a small bag for their trillions in holdings, they might create a different kind of economic crisis.

I am a man looking for a solution that might even be quicker than the offshoring solutions explored in other essays. This solution would be very painful for a lot of people so even if they get a vote, the good from it will never happen. Some of this stuff has already been explored in other essays but let's look at it all together one more time:

Among the suggestions is to replace the income tax with the FAIR Tax. I like that an awful lot. Get rid of the Income Tax completely as we have been suggested in prior essays. Replace it with the FAIR tax.

Instead of businesses protecting their earnings by eliminating jobs, they could pay as they go and be able to plan. A consumption tax such as the FAIR tax removes the disincentive for business to invest and it creates Jobs! Jobs! Jobs! Additionally, it has the effect of making products and services seemingly more expensive, and this encourages saving.

Some might call this a "virtuous cycle" as it adds to the pool of invest-able business credit; it lowers real interest rates; and it creates further business investment and jobs.

The financial experts have analyzed government spending patterns, especially as they relate to defense. Many, many good Americans worry that the President is too naive about the dangers in the world. Many think that he believes that the US should unilaterally disarm.

They view him, the President, in his usual and customary role of the Pied Piper enabling all other nations who are apt to follow the Piper, to disarm. Some even believe he hates America and Americans.

If we can get past that without totally ignoring Obama's propensity to do good even if it is bad for America, the analysts have calculated that major savings could be garnered by getting it all done quickly in Iraq and Afghanistan, and wherever we may be wasting defense dollars, countless billions and billions could be saved.

There are also solutions for Medicare and Social Security that will not bankrupt anybody and not stiff any current beneficiaries. The more important future scenario is that America still exists and America is still a capitalist country!

So, then what is the simple secret?

Herbert Hoover's Treasury Secretary Andrew Mellon cut taxes in the mid 1920's and the economy healed. For Roosevelt, all of the wonderfully progressive notions he enacted helped a lot of people but did nothing to bring the economy back to the good days after the Mellon tax cuts. After World War II, the economy finally began to revive but Truman was President by then.

In the 1960's John Kennedy cut taxes and the economy healed. Ronald Reagan in the 1980's cut taxes and the economy healed and boomed. George Bush, after 9/11 (September 11, 2001) was faced with a stagnant economy and he cut taxes three times over the years, and the economy came back but died down near the end of his last term when Democrats took over both houses of Congress. The Bush solution should have been even more tax cuts and less spending but he did not do it, and President Obama continued relive the big Bush mistake. Additionally Obama did away with all cuts he could and added more taxes, which had a negative impact on jobs and the economy.

The 2008 collapse should have been predicted by banking regulators.

A number of poorly conceived economic policies were forced upon the financial sector and they had been softening the strengths in the financial industry for a twenty year period before the 2008 collapse. Force, remember that word from earlier in this essay was the perpetrator. The strong arm of the government caused the problem.

The government forced the banks to do things that could not work in the long haul. The banks never would have gone this far if left to their profit motives. The bureaucratic regulators, charged by a dysfunctional and too altruistic Congress forced the banks to break sanity rules. The message from Congress to the banks was, "Loan to anybody who wants a home, or else!" When the banks began to fail, Congress blamed the banks even though it was the same Congress who forced them to endure the losses they experienced from making so many bad loans.

A few administration soldiers, strac, and brave did appear from the Congress. These "brave" men, a full trio of "Mighty Mice," included Barney Frank, Christopher Dodd, and NEPA's own Paul Kanjorski back then. Thank God these three are long gone. They decided to help the banks while the proletariat (We the People) were screaming, "No Bailouts!" These three believed they knew better than the people and they acted accordingly.

Their work helped cause the crisis and has led to a lengthened recession. Their CRA (Community Reinvestment Act) and poor banking regulations along with poor oversight caused the problem. Spending money on a failed GM, failed banks, Freddie Mac and Fannie Mae, exacerbated the problem. It helped keep the economy at a standstill long after it hit bottom. The people wanted no part of it.

If all these deals were so good, you and I know that the three politicians in charge would have figured out some way to put some of their own money into the investment pot to assure their getting some of the returns.

The verdict on a lot of this has been in for some time. We know the bailouts and the stimulus packages all were ill conceived and doomed to failure. Only a fool would have invested in a deal that would cost more than it was worth. Barney, Chris, and Paul stuck the American people with the bill for their ill-advised largesse.

No matter what we do, GM will have cost the taxpayers $billions that will never be returned. GM would be out of business if the government were not continually buying GM products. They will go out of business without more government help.

No sane person would have gone for the Frank / Dodd/ Kanjorski deal. These three stooges stuck John Q. Public with the tab for their unsupportable and unprecedented schemes. For everybody in government and politics, the bailout decisions were good. The people have been remembering the members of Congress in the past three elections, but somehow forgot Obama's role.

Ironically as if nobody would remember the truth, all three Congressmen lined up to take credit in their campaigns for their sheer brilliance in avoiding a catastrophe. When I looked around I saw something far different. We are still living through a catastrophe.

Freddie and Fannie are still bottomless pits fully subsidized by the people. Who are they kidding? The problem is not gone. None of the three charlatan congressmen were reelected thankfully.

Fannie Mae and Freddie Mac still have a big role in what some would call the welfare state mentality in Congress but it goes even further. What do these financial cousins, Fannie and Freddie actually do? Their mission is to buy mortgages from savings and loans, banks and other lenders. The bank makes its profit on writing the mortgage up front and Freddie and Fannie assume the mortgage. This gives more cash for banks and other lenders so they can make many more home loans.

Unfortunately for Americans, Fannie and Freddie together, right now either hold or guarantee $5.5 trillion of mortgages. This is about half of the US's outstanding home loans. Think of how big this trough can become. Thank you again Barney, Chris, and Paul. By the way, Hillary has ties to Freddie so expect little reform is she makes it to the White House.

Many know that President Obama has an easy time of taking issues which he either created or has permitted to fester and to comment on them as if he is an innocent bystander. Recently, he commented on Freddie and Fannie.

Yes, President Obama actually said that these two government sponsored companies had to be abolished, because it was, heads they win, tails, taxpayers lose. What the President meant by that was that, in good times, executives and shareholders of these companies would make money, but, in bad times, taxpayers would be left holding the bag.

And that is sort of how it panned out. And, so Obama, who can get rid of them with a stroke of his pen pretends that he has no role in their survival. Perhaps, if we checked their executive's donations we might find a good reason for the President's lack of potency regarding these two shill organizations.

So what gets these institutions in trouble with taxpayers? Well, as home prices fell, foreclosures go up, and lenders run into trouble. So also with Fannie and Freddie. The loans they back go bad; capital becomes harder to come by and it is thus more difficult for Fannie Mae and Freddie Mac to find buyers for their loan packages. So, what did they do? The politically correct answer is that they compromise and compromise and this leads to lower and lower standards.

Eventually, they are "forced" to back even riskier mortgages. As we learned in 2008, and as continues today, all this comes back to bite them. Barney, Chris, and Paul were there from the beginning, but none took credit for helping to cause the collapse of the market.

The politically incorrect answer for the 2008 debacle is that Congress repealed depression era legislation designed to prevent catastrophes such as this. Additionally, Congress passed multiple versions of the Community Reinvestment Act (CRA) -- the last update was in the Clinton years.

This was so that even people without a dime could qualify to get a mortgage for a home. The main criteria was reduced to whether the potential mortgagee was breathing or not.
The CRA more or less forced banks to loan at 105% or 110% of home value to people who could not even afford a rented apartment.

The joke in states like Florida was that not only did they get a house that they could not afford but there was a Lexus in the garage when they moved in -- all financed by their no down-payment mortgage.

While property values were rising, this was not a bad deal as everybody was a winner. As home prices fell, it all blew up in everybody's faces. Barney, Chris, and Paul Kanjorski, all Democrats, were supposed to have been watching. They are gone now but their legacy is not forgotten.

Barney, Chris, and Paul had the banks as well as Freddie and Fannie over a barrel so they squeezed them to take on bad loans. The system had to break. These Congressional caretakers actually broke it.

These are the kind of loans in which the mortgagee brings nothing to the closing and if need be his lawyer, at the closing, types up a fake W-2 and other needed documentation to assure the loan.

Everybody at the closing and the approving bank officers all knew this was a sham. But, by getting the documentation correct, at least the bank would have a record of why they approved the loan to the applicant. It was forced institutional fraud. Everybody knew it was a joke, but they had to commit fraud in order to be in compliance with the banking laws. In the last twenty years or so, being a liar was essential to being trustworthy in the financial industry.

There is no secret anymore. The government knows what happened. Yet, Barney, Chris and Paul in their last terms were still trying to pass legislation that makes permanent the notion of too big to fail, subtitled, the government will bail you out if you fail.

In the last third of April 2010 as I was finishing up my first version of a new book at the time, Jobs! Jobs! Jobs!, the Republicans were trying to figure out how to tell the American people that the big three—Barney, Chris, and Paul, but mostly Chris, were really not trying to regulate the industry. They were actually trying to set up the country to have to pay for the next bailout.

With President Obama out on another campaign tour to sell "banking regulations" to the people, the Republican dilemma is that the people want good banking regulations. Nothing that helps Americans will ever come from this administration.

Unfortunately, many people still trust Obama, Pelosi, and Reid. They still can't or won't believe that Congress can intentionally perpetrate a fraud on the American people. The fact is that Republicans and Democrats had a deal going to make sure the legislation stopped Wall Street in its tracks when the Democrats, my political party, with Chris Dodd, a big part of the original financial crisis in charge of negotiations, pulled out and softened the legislation.

Among other things, they created a $50 billion slush fund to bail-out any banks that failed. When that $50 billion was gone, the legislation authorized Congress to grab another $50 billion for the next of the "too big to fails," would not fail. The people want them to fail when they squander the people's assets. Bad banks need to be purged from the US banking system rather than rewarding their crony investors.

The legislation did not do that. Yet, it must for the stability of the future. Despite the facts, with Obama on another whirlwind campaign tour, Republicans had a tough problem convincing the loyalists in the Democratic Party that Congress has set the people up again for a round of perpetual bailouts. Some things never change.

To make matters worse, one of the sticking points that caused Dodd to get up from the negotiating table with Republicans and strike out on his own was the treatment of Fannie and Freddie. Dodd completely let them out of his bill. Fannie and Freddie and government control of the mortgage industry had a lot to do with all of the financial failings. The Republicans were right. Leaving them out of the legislation to wreak more havoc was dumb-headed, but it helped a lot of cronies. .

The not so secret solution to ending recession

Do you think banks who do not make it should fail? What if their failure is because they trusted that the government would protect them when they acted irresponsibly? I say yes they should fail. Should Fannie and Freddie Fail? I say yes again. Maybe housing will get so affordable that regular people can afford to buy homes again without the Fed devaluing the dollar every week. We need to get all this bad debt off the books and let the people who gained pay the price -- not the taxpayers.

Besides dealing with "too big to fail" in a responsible way, the secret to solving the recession is to simply cut spending and lower taxes. I would recommend corporate reforms for offshoring and we also need to correct the problem of illegal immigrants taking and keeping American jobs. Both of these are well covered and explained in other essays in my book, Saving America!. If we do all that, we can get this ship floating again without using Gordon Liddy dollars.

How do we know this will work? it has worked every time it has been tried from Andrew Mellon to JFK to Ronald Reagan to George Bush. Obama could have made history if he did what he should have done. Veronique de Rugy of the Cato Institute, a Conservative Think Tank sees it this way:

"Changes in marginal income tax rates cause individuals and businesses to change their behavior. As tax rates rise, taxpayers reduce taxable income by working less, retiring earlier, scaling back plans to start or expand businesses, moving activities to the underground economy, restructuring companies, and spending more time and money on accountants to minimize

taxes. Tax rate cuts reduce such distortions and cause the tax base to expand as tax avoidance falls and the economy grows. A review of tax data for high-income earners in the 1920's shows that as top tax rates were cut, tax revenues and the share of taxes paid by high-income taxpayers soared. "

Don't expect fundamental change until this fundamental law is followed (enforced) by the current administration or we are able to change the Congress and the President again. Additionally, we cannot permit Hillary or Bernie to ever take the office of the Presidency... ever... ever... ever...

To repeat, the bottom line on ending the recession is to cut spending and reduce taxes. Neither of these will occur, I am afraid, if it is left to this administration or one modeled after it. Keep the penny plan in the back of your mind. It can be done.

Essay 28

Speak Softly and Carry a Really Big Stick

National Defense

In this essay, Brian Kelly answers a big Question, **the answer of which many in Northeastern PA and across the entire US have been considering. Why is it that we no longer seem to be willing to win the wars in which we choose to engage? As you would expect, Kelly has a thoughtful answer. His essay title is:**

"Speak Softly and Carry a Really Big Stick!"

Please enjoy this essay by Mr. Brian Kelly, written in the "first person."

I support a Constitutional approach to foreign policy that ensures a strong national defense. Who can argue that at this moment in time, we have the most powerful, most advanced military in the history of the world, despite the work our current president has done to reduce its apparent strength.

One can conclude that if we were to fight a war and if we chose to fight to win, boldly, quickly and conclusively, there would be minimal US casualties, and the notch of victory could be hailed. If we ever received the OK to do so in these times, the most surprised at our victory would be our president, Barack Hussein Obama.

However, it seems that we are no longer in armed conflicts to win them but instead after decades with no declarations of war by Congress (required by the Constitution) we have been snookered into permitting wars to continue unabated. Why not just win them and then they are done and we can go home for good?

These conflicts are often begun in the name of defending our national interests, but then all of a sudden we are running guerrilla policing campaigns that cost us our precious soldier's lives, and we seem to give terrorists exactly what they want. Why can we not figure out how to avoid all American deaths as a condition to assist the countries that call upon us for help? And Donald Trump is right. We should not bear all the expenses for helping save the world from terrorist forces.

You may know that we have troops in over 120 countries. Can you imagine that? Isn't that a little much? If we are helping so many countries, why do so many hate us? Why is the president's tactic to apologize for America instead of gaining respect by winning wars and helping all who we can? Does he care? Why do we care? If we do so well overseas in 120 countries, then why are our own borders unprotected? Does it make sense to fight terrorists abroad on their home turf when our own front door is wide open and unlocked?

How is it that we permit over a million illegal aliens (perhaps as many as three million) to cross our borders each year without our knowledge? Is this not a clear threat to our nation's security? And when we have no jobs for Americans, is it not stupid for us to give foreign nationals American jobs -- our jobs?

American Independence v Entangling Alliances

The Founding Fathers warned us that concern for other countries above America sacrifices our independence and integrity as a nation. Jefferson was the most vocal. In his first inaugural address, he proclaimed that America should have "peace, commerce and honest friendship with all nations - entangling alliances with none."

Today, America's interests are undermined by subtle deference to foreign entities such as the International Monetary Fund (IMF), World Bank, World Trade Organization (WTO), and the United Nations (UN). It's time to end the things that do not make sense for America. Who sold us out?

Foreign Policy -- War and Peace -- Ronald Reagan

Here is what Ronald Reagan had to say about that:

"Now let's set the record straight. There's no argument over the choice between peace and war, but there's only one guaranteed way you can have peace -- and you can have it in the next second -- surrender."

"You and I know and do not believe that life is so dear and peace so sweet as to be purchased at the price of chains and slavery. If nothing in life is worth dying for, when did this begin -- just in the face of this enemy? Or should Moses have told the children of Israel to live in slavery under the pharaohs? Should Christ have refused the cross?

"Should the patriots at Concord Bridge have thrown down their guns and refused to fire the shot heard 'round the world? The martyrs of history were not fools, and our honored dead who gave their lives to stop the advance of the Nazis didn't die in vain. Where, then, is the road to peace? Well it's a simple answer after all.

"You and I have the courage to say to our enemies, 'There is a price we will not pay....'There is a point beyond which they must not advance.' And this -- this is the meaning in the phrase of Barry Goldwater's 'peace through strength.'

"Winston Churchill said, 'The destiny of man is not measured by material computations. When great forces are on the move in the world, we learn we're spirits -- not animals.' And he said, "There's something going on in time and space, and beyond time and space, which, whether we like it or not, spells duty."

In this speech in the 1960's Reagan also said, "You and I have a rendezvous with destiny."

What will be our destiny?

Will the US die because our leadership no longer cares about the people about whom, their oaths were sworn?

Teddy Roosevelt was a Rough Rider and he believed we must speak softly and we must carry a big stick. Today there is a lot of tough rhetoric against Iran and North Korea, and a theoretical non-country named ISIS. For some strange reason, however, there is also tough rhetoric against Israel from an American president. Who does that help?

When was the last Israeli terrorist bombing in the US? What is wrong with this President? What does he see that we do not see and why will he not tell us why he sees what he sees? Does he see a future for America with policies that permit us to be easy targets? Does he see America having a right to freedom? If I knew the answer my friends, I would not be asking such questions? Who knows the important answers to those questions?

We live in a strange world. Right now we have wound down a war in Iraq in a wrong-headed way, and because of our President's promises, we fired up another war a lot more than a few notches in Afghanistan. But before our definite and total victory in Afghanistan could be achieved, the same president called for a withdrawal again, just as in Iraq. Why is America prohibited from winning wars and calling it quits?

Because we have a poor leader as a president, history will find that we have lost both wars because that was his plan. In my experience as a computer scientist, I have learned that logic is the key to making systems work. If logic does not apply with Obama's intentions, that does make sense. Real logic when given the facts would definitely conclude that our President is simply not happy having to protect Americans when so many other citizens of the world have a tough time every day.

Should we have foot soldiers in any of these lands for any extended period? I say no unless we protect them at all costs by our men being permitted to kill all the enemies who fire upon them. Once I believed these wars were necessary but the rules of engagement by white collar executives (of all skin colors) that prevented us from using our might and winning--are what killed so many of our soldiers. Why send our boys and men into battle with their hands tied? If we go, our mission is a simple one --- we win!

The courage of the US Fighting Man from the days of the Revolution is what protects us. But, good leadership would never send anybody into harm's way if the soldiers are not permitted to inflict the greatest harm upon our enemy. If we have no enemy we should not be at war.

And, Congress should be declaring the wars in which we engage. Congress, not a milk-toast president should be working on the terms of engagement rather than permitting the commander in chief to kill our soldiers in meaningless acts. When at war, from my perspective, one American is worth a million enemies.

Ask Harry Truman-- a Democrat! He is the only guy I think ever knew who blew up a world first that would have blown up the US if they had had their chance. What would today's Democrats do? Why do we show weakness instead of strength when strength wins and weakness emboldens the enemy. No American soldier wants to put a smile on an enemy's face! Americans are winners and we want to be able to win!

I am not against the efforts that are underway and I do appreciate the work of our brave armed services. I am against wars in which we offer our young as potential casualties because we choose rules of engagement that cause Americans to die. I say we either fight to win and we fight the war like it is a war and not a police action, or we get the hell out. Each American who perishes in battle needs to have a tribunal about how his death will be eliminated in the next round. No American deaths are acceptable....PERIOD! No mistakes about American lives are permitted!

Win and leave would be my strategy in ending the Afghanistan conflict, which continues regardless of Obama's declarations, and of course the worldwide ISIS war. Let the peace-keepers then come in when the battle is over and the dead and maimed need caring. Let them all be from other nations. If we engage, our mission should be get in, win, and then get our warriors out, and bring the peace-keepers in. I don't have access to the information that the President has available so I don't see all that he sees. BUt, we have not won much of anything recently and our country is now threatened from within.

Something is wrong when we can't win or choose not to win against puny little countries. Even sillier is giving them billions of dollars to stockpile nuclear bombs to use against us. What's wrong is that we either have chosen bad wars or we have chosen not to win. And when I am your Congressman, and we finally have a President who loves America that stuff will quickly end.

Until George Bush decided to win the Iraq war, with the surge, we were sending our boys to be slaughtered by roadside explosives or picked off by snipers in a country that wasn't sure if they even wanted us there or not. We should back countries who are our friends like Israel and we should not trust countries with whom we do not have a long standing history of trust. We should not bear the price tag for all these wars either. If the Saudis and others are benefiting from our involvement in the Middle East, they should be presented a bill for our services as we exit stage right.

Essay 29

Jobs! Jobs! Jobs!

Hopefully you will elect me your next Congressman and we will not have to fear the lack of jobs anymore. I know how to bring Jobs back to Northeastern PA and the USA at large. I am a regular citizen and not one of the elite. Why not give me the opportunity to help all the people -- US!

When I ran for Congress in 2010, I wrote a book for all Americans. The title is **Jobs! Jobs! Jobs!** The subtitle is *Where Did They Go? How Can We Get Them Back?* In 2016, I revised and updated this book and it is available for free on the briankellyforcongress.com web site.

The original soft cover paperback of the book is available for sale at www.bookhawkers.com. Check out the BookHawkers site to find other great patriotic books. Scroll on the site menus right on the Congress site to find all the chapters in the Jobs! book available as free downloads. The book is a compendium of many essays about the Jobs! Jobs! Jobs! problem in the US and NEPA.

Enjoy it for free or buy a hard copy from bookhawkers.

You can read these essays, which are much of the substance of the book, free on the web site. You never have to buy this book unless you want hard copy. Kelly has packaged a deal for you that you won't believe. Your friends and family can read the updated book right on www.briankellyforcongress.com for free.

Since the time he ran for Congress, Brian has written two more books on the subject. One is called the RRR Plan, a very comprehensive plan for reestablishing America as a business leader and Saving America, a detailed plan for saving America from financial ruination. These books are available in hard copy on the BookHawker site (www.bookhawkers.com).

As noted, the revised text of Jobs! Jobs! Jobs! is also on this site packed in up-to-date essays. Each essay that is in the book is available on the right side of the home page under the Jobs! Jobs! Jobs! Heading.

Yes, it's free. No kidding. Even the book's Preface, a worthwhile read as an essay unto itself is on this site. The Preface is also included in the hard copy of this Brian Kelly for Congress book that you are now reading.

It is where you should begin as it is another important essay on the Jobs! Jobs! Jobs! Landscape. If you would like to get the book in paper form, feel free to take the link to bookhawkers.com or www.trumpbookshop.com. Otherwise, it is on the web site for you to read and to enjoy.

Thank you for choosing to visit the Brian Kelly for Congress web site.

By reading the full content of Jobs! Jobs! Jobs! just like author Brian Kelly, you too will get an appreciation about jobs that you may never have had before. Kelly wants to create jobs in the US and in NEPA in particular and he outlines how it can be done when Congress finally wants it to be done. So far, it seems Congress is disinterested in anything that is good for America. They get their cues from President Obama.

So far, as you well know, Congress has avoided its responsibility of helping Americans in need of jobs. For years, they have either taken no action or given more rights to foreigners and International Corporations.

Instead of being a force to help the American people, Congress, especially this 114th Congress, now in session has chosen special interests over the needs of the American people. Along with Matt Cartwright from Northeastern PA and Barack Obama, they have permitted unbridled crony capitalism with huge corporate profits to the friends of Congress and cronies of the President.

Meanwhile, the same corporations are shipping jobs overseas or bringing in foreign workers to replace Americans in their enterprises. This is not fair.

That is why Brian Kelly is running for Congress -- to change the jobs scenario and many other scenarios that work against the people. Kelly thinks jobs are more important than special interests.

Don't you agree?

Why not pick a person for Congress like you, who thinks like you do?

Essay 30

The FAIR Tax

The Fair Tax -- An Essential Element for Jobs!

"The Congress shall have power to lay and collect taxes on incomes, from whatever source derived, without apportionment among the several States, and without regard to any census or enumeration."

Way back in February, 1913, the 16th Amendment was ratified by the states and thus it became a part of the Constitution. As such, mostly everybody who is affected by the income tax law would like it to go away. Yet, if we listen to them and believe their lies (Matt Cartwright's lies et al), even Congress cannot get rid of it. It will take another amendment to the Constitution to make that happen and that is not easy. But, it will be worth it! We can do it!

When I am elected your representative, you will be throwing out Matt Cartwright as a bonus in the deal. You can then be assured that I will push to get the ball rolling on the FAIR Tax. And, as another bonus, the corporate and personal income tax are eliminated along with the entire IRS. There are other notions about the corporate income tax discussed in other essays.

The problem of the day in 2016 (It was in 2010 when I ran for Congress the first time), is clearly Jobs! Jobs! Jobs! It's been bad since 2008 and getting worse as time goes by. How does the 16th amendment help business? How does the 16th amendment help Jobs? How does the Sixteenth Amendment help you and me and the next guy assure that tomorrow will be a better day than today?

Obviously it does not, or this essay would never have been written.

The 16th Amendment to the Constitution authorizes the "progressive" income tax. We all know that more than a mechanism to feed the government's need to defend us, and to enable highways to be built and other things that individuals cannot do, the income tax has more recently been used as a mechanism for wealth redistribution and thus a means of an unconstitutional presidency to gain more dictatorial power. This is what killed the goose that laid golden eggs in the US for an awful long time.

The income tax was not new in 1913 when enacted. It had been used to fund the armies of the north in the Civil War. No country can conduct war without cash. So, to bring in a lot of revenue as necessary in 1861, Congress introduced the Revenue Act of 1861 with a flat tax of 3% on annual income above $800.

The original income tax self-destructed in 1866 but was almost brought back a number of times by the Socialist Labor Part in 1887, the Populist Party in 1892, and the Democratic Party in 1904 and again in 1908. Notice the Republicans were never openly for the personal income tax. Moreover, for Pennsylvanians, it is nice to know that along with Virginia and Florida, Pennsylvania never took up the proposed amendment that ultimately permits government to do things never intended by the Founding Patriots. It's time for this monster to go, along with 435 members of the House and 33% of the Senate.

On the treasury site, it says, "By 1913, 36 States had ratified the 16th Amendment to the Constitution. In October, Congress passed a new income tax law with rates beginning at 1 percent and rising to 7 percent for taxpayers with income in excess of $500,000. Less than 1 percent of the population paid income tax at the time. Form 1040 was introduced as the standard tax reporting form and, though changed in many ways over the years, it remains in use today."

Lawyers like to use the term *slippery slope* to mean "give them an inch and they will take a mile." The tax slope was so slippery that when John Kennedy cut back income taxes to save the economy in the early 1960's. The highest tax rate had risen to over 90%. No matter who you are, that is ridiculous. Whether my gross income ever goes to $100,000.00 or not, I do not deny those people clever enough to beat the business system and become utterly successful. None of us want to pay taxes. Only a fool would so submit.

Without those who make a lot of money from their inventions, we would not have the radio, the TV, the computer or the iPad, and an awful lot of other wonderful things. Surely, the buffoons in the government would never have brought us such innovations, and so I question any person thinking we should turn to government for hardly any of our needs other than National Defense. Putting the government in charge of healthcare is like finding the worst player on the team when the championship game is tied in the bottom of the ninth, and substituting the worst player for the best player on the team. You're going to lose. It's a certitude. That describes Obama's America to a tee.

The 16th amendment like most things that may once have been perverted over the years, especially by this administration, now apparently openly declares that an individual's wealth is not his. Instead, it should be redistributed merely because government is all powerful. So, they steal from the rich and the disappearing middle class to seemingly give some alms to the poor. This then makes the poor dependent on the state and lovers of Obama.

In the newest trick with Obamacare, the government in trying to equalize everything between the workers and non-workers decided to redistribute healthcare. The "person" in charge of anything so important should be competent. Yet, competent Americans are expected to give up control so the government can assume all of their responsibilities except for paying taxes. Have the seeds of another American revolution now been planted?

In the redistribution schemes, those who work for a living do not like the deal but the non-workers like it fine. It is definitely good to help the poor as individuals. That's why charity is a virtue. It is not good for government to help make poor people out of those who otherwise would be fruitful contributors to their own lives. That destroys hope. You can have faith in that.

The notion of giving to those who should not need anything returns nothing to the people. The government really does decide too much. The income tax is used for social engineering. Government uses it as a tool to manage people's purchases via tax exemptions, credits, and deductions. Watch how much beer you drink; sugar you eat; and toilet paper you use because one of those video cameras that Uncle Sam is installing everywhere is going to tell on you one day soon.

People may ask, "How does a bureaucrat from the government know what is good or bad for you or for me?" We all know they do not because most of them are unfortunately asleep or too inept to make a positive difference. The last person anybody would call if in need would be a person from the government.

Some Elements of Government Are Good

Since we need taxes to support the good parts of government that we the people control, the best tax is clearly a consumption tax. You have seen waitresses and waiters that treat your family well. I sure have. You and I know that they prefer to get cash, rather than have the tip on the bill. Why is that? It's because it is non-reportable income to the government. A consumption tax would get them to pay and you and I would pay only when we spend a dime. If they spend their tip, they would then pay a tax regardless of whether you gave them some cash or it was on your charge card.

So, a Fair Tax can save the money the government uses for the IRS to find the tips that these folks might hide. Though the drugs that a dealer sells may not get taxed, the drug dealer's purchases are all subject to the FAIR TAX. The IRS can be eliminated because nobody will have to find the dollars that are earned under the table. Instead the tax will occur when the hidden loot is spent.

So, a consumption / sales tax would force those operating outside the current income tax system to pay their fair share -- whether they are legal or illegal. In this way, nobody gets public services for free. Nobody! Why is that not something that we all like? Anybody with a job and those who receive money from those with a job all pay taxes. This lifts the burden from only those who work.

Opponents of the Fair Tax love the idea of socialism and social engineering. The income tax is their tool that is why they love it so much. So, they will lie about the FAIR Tax such as telling you that it will hurt Senior Citizens on Social Security. That is another lie that government likes to tell.

Has government ever lied to seniors? How about no COLA because the CPI (a.k.a. the inflation rate) is zero. Is that a joke? Seniors know that is a big and unforgiving lie perpetrated by Obama and this Congress and they are angry as hell about it. What Bureaucrats say about the Fair Tax is another pack of lies.

We're hearing more and more about big cuts in Social Security and Medicare. Hopefully, the cuts will not affect those over 62 or anybody who is collecting already. But, if you are 54 or below, expect that the government will be telling you that you are no longer in the real Social Security fund. Your net contributions will be reset to zero and you will be starting over. Watch and see. Raises in Social Security may also be a thing of the past regardless of the inflation rate. The fact is the government is broke.

A consumption tax like the Fair Tax is visible and thus government will be accountable. Don't compare it to the Value Added Tax which the liars in the government may be implementing in addition to the punitive personal income tax. When you hear the bureaucrats tell you the Fair Tax is bad for you, please remember that it is one of the ways to save Social Security and Medicare as everybody will be contributing. So you don't get snookered by the myths, here are a few facts from fairtax.org to chew on so you can win the argument:

1. The FairTax ensures Social Security's soundness by funding it with a progressive, broad-based national retail sales tax, rather than the current regressive, narrow payroll tax.
2. The FairTax rebate zeros the retail taxation of necessities, up to poverty-level spending, for seniors.
3. The FairTax repeals the taxation of Social Security benefits and adjusts Social Security indexing to protect seniors.
4. The FairTax ends all record keeping and income tax filings of any kind for seniors, totally insulating them from the high costs and abusive tactics of tax preparers.
5. The FairTax does not tax used goods, giving low-income seniors choices.
6. The FairTax reduces manufacturers', services', and retailers' costs, allowing them to lower costs to seniors.
7. The FairTax delivers a tax holiday on IRAs and other tax-deferred plans.

8. The FairTax ends gift and estate taxes, along with all of the unfairness to heirs and complex planning for those who earned the money.
9. The FairTax allows seniors to sell their homes and pay no capital gains taxes.
10. The FairTax generates an economic boom, which eases future budget pressure on seniors' entitlements.
11. The FairTax lowers average remaining lifetime tax rates.
12. The FairTax ensures your grandchildren have the same opportunity you did.

There is another notion that a sales tax such as the FAIR tax can be a very practical measure by which we will gradually wean ourselves off of our dependence on federal and state services. By slowly lowering the percentage of the tax over time, the size of the government overall can shrink and government services can eventually be returned back to state control where they belong or perhaps, other than those deemed extremely essential, they can be ended entirely and people can keep their own money. How can that be bad?

So that you understand the salient components of the Fair Tax Plan, I have captured from the http://www.fairtax.org/ site, some of its essence below.

What is the Fair Tax Plan?

The Fair Tax Plan is a comprehensive proposal that replaces all federal income and payroll based taxes with an integrated approach including a progressive national retail sales tax, a prebate to ensure no American pays federal taxes on spending up to the poverty level, dollar-for-dollar federal revenue neutrality, and, through companion legislation, the repeal of the 16th Amendment.

That last notion, ladies and gentlemen means that Congress sets in motion the repeal of the 16th Amendment and with it goes the IRS.

There actually has been an act proposed called the Fair Tax Act (HR 25, S 296). It is nonpartisan legislation. It abolishes all federal personal and corporate income taxes, gift, estate, capital gains, alternative minimum, Social Security, Medicare, and self-employment taxes and replaces them with one simple, visible, federal retail sales tax administered primarily by existing state sales tax authorities.

Because the best approach would be a small corporate income tax in the 10% range and an offshoring penalty of another 10%, I am almost in full agreement with the FAIR TAX as proposed and would be happy to vote for it as is. The 10% tax would still make the US the lowest taxed nation in the world at the corporate level and this would create major investment in the US. If the FAIR Tax as proposed is enacted, I would introduce legislation to permit a 10% tax penalty for American corporations that offshore jobs.

The Fair Tax taxes us only on what we choose to spend on new goods or services, not on what we earn. The Fair Tax is a fair, efficient, transparent, and intelligent solution to the frustration and inequity of our current tax system.

According to the bill, the Fair Tax:

- Enables workers to keep their entire paychecks
- Enables retirees to keep their entire pensions
- Refunds in advance the tax on purchases of basic necessities
- Allows American products to compete fairly
- Brings transparency and accountability to tax policy
- Ensures Social Security and Medicare funding
- Closes all loopholes and brings fairness to taxation
- Abolishes the IRS

To save you the effort of going out to the Fair tax site, http://www.fairtax.org/PDF/PlainEnglishSummary_The FairTaxAct2007.pdf, I have copied the summary into this essay. If there is one thing one can say about the Fair Tax that cannot be said about the Income Tax, it is that it is *Fair* and politicians cannot mess with it to make it unfair. . .

The Fair Tax Act of 2007 – HR 25/S 1025 plain English summary

"The Act is called the "Fair Tax Act of 2007." As of Dec. 31, 2008, it repeals all income taxes and payroll taxes, specifically:

1. The individual income tax (including capital gains taxes and the alternative minimum tax)
2. All individual and employer payroll taxes including Social Security, Medicare, and federal unemployment taxes
3. The corporate income tax
4. The self-employment tax (a self-employed person pays both the individual and the employer portions of Social Security and Medicare taxes)
5. The estate and gift tax

"Effective January 1, 2009 [or whenever it went into effect] it would replace the above taxes with a national retail sales tax on all goods and services sold at retail. The tax rate is set to be revenue neutral – at the level necessary to replace the revenues generated by the repealed taxes.

"A 23-percent (of the tax-inclusive sales price) sales tax is imposed on all retail sales for personal consumption of new goods and services. Exports and the purchase of inputs by businesses (i.e., intermediate sales) are not taxed, nor are used goods or any savings, investment, or education tuition expenses. The sales tax must be separately stated and charged on the sales receipt. This makes it clear to the consumer exactly how much they are paying in federal taxes.

"There are no exemptions under the Fair Tax, meaning that no lobbyist, corporation, con man, or other individual can obtain tax advantages that are not available to the general public. Also, everyone pays the same rate, but those who spend more pay more total taxes than those who spend less.

"The Fair Tax provides every American family with a rebate of the sales tax on spending up to the federal poverty level (plus an extra amount to prevent any marriage penalty). The rebate is paid monthly in advance. It allows a family of four to spend $27,380 tax free each year. The rebate for a married couple with two children is $525 per month ($6,297 annually). Therefore, no family pays federal sales tax on essential goods and services and middle-class families are effectively exempted on a large part of their annual spending. It really is fair!

"Funding for Social Security and Medicare benefits remains the same. The Social Security and Medicare trust funds receive the same amount of money as they do under current law. The source of the trust fund revenue is a dedicated portion of sales tax revenue instead of payroll tax revenue.

"States can elect to collect the federal sales tax on behalf of the federal government in exchange for a fee of one-quarter of one percent of gross collections. Retail businesses collecting the tax also get the same administrative fee.

"Strong taxpayer rights provisions are incorporated into the Act. The burden of persuasion in disputes is on the government. A strong, independent problem resolution office is created. Taxpayers are entitled to professional fees in disputes unless the government establishes that its position was substantially justified."

As the song ends, "Who could ask for anything more?"

Essay 31

Worker Visas Take Many American Jobs!

Worker Visas Take Way Too Many American Jobs. They should take about zero.

This essay is part of the Jobs! Jobs! Jobs book as it surely applies to the jobs situation. The US Visa programs have been used by corporations and a complicit Congress & President to sell out American intellectuals and skilled service workers in recent years.

The scam continues even while Americans are unemployed in record numbers. The "worker Visa" program had noble beginnings and there is no obvious problem with the type of people who come in on visas. However under certain visa types, employers get a big bonus as they can access foreign technical talent for slave wages, and there are no penalties for firing Americans to gain lower wage foreign nationals. It may even be worse when unscrupulous employers are inclined to scam everybody for a buck.

When I was an active IT Consultant, one of my clients were able to obtain an H-1B visa for a top-level, bright executive. I watched him and I can confirm he was a very bright guy. He was thrilled to be in America so he let himself be scammed by his employer. I was a contractor and a citizen so they had no control over my earnings.

They were not the nicest of employers. His salary was about 1/3 of the other executives. Why was that? Because he was in many ways an indentured servant to the company. If he messed up or made any demands, they held his right to his visa, and he would be back in South Africa at the drop of a hat.

As a demonstration of how endearing this company was to the foreign worker, when he finally became a citizen, he immediately gave his notice and moved to Florida from Pennsylvania. They could not do without him. Payback is a bi----. He commanded a full executive salary while in Florida and he had a full time job there at the same time. His skills were non-replaceable for some time even for the proper wage. Some stories work out well.

The point is that legal foreigners will gladly work for substantially less wages than their American counterparts in high tech jobs. Engineers, computer techs, and many people in many other occupations want to live in America. They make lots more than where they came from and most are placed on a track to a green card and ultimately citizenship.

As with my friend, those on such Visas do not have a real picnic before they get citizenship. Their job is to please their masters who know their plight and they know they are ripe for abuse in the workplace. They will do almost anything not to be deported and so they do what they must to satisfy the whim of their often nasty corporate sponsors.

One of the first spigots to get shut off when the US entered this recession ten years ago was the influx of legal foreign workers. Who needs them? But, your Congress took no action even as the unemployment rate shot up to 10%. Their donors demanded they keep the flow of cheap labor coming. Senators and House members care lots more about their next campaign than they do about their jobs representing the people.

So, yes, your Congress has been complicit in the Visa programs that kill American jobs and which also take advantage of the job receivers. It is only fair that this pitiful Congress should be left jobless after this next election and perhaps somebody will pick them up for the minimum wage, or hopefully a lot less!.

In my book, Taxation Without Representation (available at www.bookhawkers.com), I wrote a chapter on how American corporations exploit foreign workers as well as Americans with their special government sanctioned visa worker programs. As difficult as it may be to believe for those that think government is needed for survival, there are over 80 different Visa programs, and none are fair to Americans. The H-1B is just one program that brings in 65,000 otherwise illegals at a clip each year and they all get jobs.

For a few years they were enticing over 100,000 a year. Meanwhile IT people and engineers were and still are getting laid off. Thank you Congress. Thank you Matt Cartwright and thank you Bob Casey, Jr.

Recently some of our trade agreements, such as the WTO, have insisted on language that forced the US to continue to use the H-1B program to help foreign nationals come to America with the intention of robbing Johnnie or Susie, your kids, as they graduate from a $40,000 per year university, from getting the jobs they should be offered. Consequently those who about donors more than Americans suggest that we cannot summarily stop the H-1B spigot. I say we are a sovereign nation and we are in a recession and we can damn well do what we please to help our country and our people who are in fact, Americans.

As with most trade agreements, we were out-snookered by our "adversaries: unless we went in with a give-up strategy, which is more likely. I joked with my Marywood classes that in trade talks, the US negotiators are the worst able at the table. It is as if they were programmed at the top to lose.

I suggested to my classes that it would be far better for the US to ship in a huge block of granite and place it in the area in which the US team of negotiators would have been placed. The block of granite would serve America's needs far better than the losers who actually sit at the table, supposedly representing Americans.

The H-1B is a terrible loss for America's best workforce, its college graduates -- our best and brightest. It is a program that at any point in time is sapping almost 400,000 American jobs from the economy. It is a travesty for American college graduates but especially bright students graduating from America's finest Universities, who actually want to be paid more than the burger and salad tossers at McDonalds.

The cream of the crop are unemployed while they find their potential jobs taken by foreigners on Visa programs so that corporations can save money on wages. And, yes, there are times when the new H-1B worker comes in and replaces an American making two to three times as much income. The American has the pleasure of training the foreign national prior to his or her getting fired. It's not the way it is supposed to be.

H1B Visas for FY 2017

For the Fiscal Year 2017 (FY 2016), the US is currently accepting applications for H1B visas. I find that hard to believe. The H1B is a nonimmigrant classification used by an alien who will be employed temporarily in a specialty occupation or as a fashion model. Too bad nobody in the US can fill the bill. This really is unfair to Americans and is perpetrated by the lobbyists and future lobbyists (Congress).
Our Congress is still bringing in 65,000 foreigners a year under this one of 80 Visa deals to take American jobs. Ask your representative or Matt Cartwright about that!

The filing deadline for H1B visas for Fiscal Year 2017 (FY 2017) was April 1, 2016. Under current law, an alien can be in H-1B status for a maximum period of six years at a time. After that time an alien must remain outside the United States for one year before another H1B petition can be approved. Certain aliens working on Defense Department projects [Does this make any defense sense having a foreign national be essential?] may remain in H1B status for 10 years.

In addition, certain aliens may obtain an extension of H1B status far beyond the 6-year maximum period. The premise is that Americans cannot do those jobs. Meanwhile 85% of college graduates go home to live with mom and dad each year. Can it be that they do not want to find good jobs or that foreign nationals are preferred?

The current law limits the cap of H1Bs to 65,000 as the number of aliens who may be issued an H1B visa or otherwise be provided H1B status in a given year. There are 80 plus other Visa programs. Why is this permitted when Americans cannot get jobs?

BTW, because Visa holders are documented, is that why border jumpers are called undocumented? What about the Visa holders who just never go back, and then just blend into the US landscape? Does documentation really matter to the unemployed American worker?

The following quote is from my book, <u>Taxation Without Representation</u>.

Onshore vs. Offshore

"The big difference between losing your job to a person with an H-1B Visa and having your job offshored is whether the person who gets your job will be playing a home game or an away game. If they get to work in their own country, say India for example, then for them it is a home game. Your job has been offshored.

If instead, they get an H-1B Visa, then they get to come to the U.S. to take your job. In the latter scenario, however, your company or the company that would have hired you first lies about your availability to work or they would not get the H-1B Visa slot. The next lie is that they will pay the H-1B Visa worker or any other work Visa employee the same wage for the same work that you would have done. Do you believe any of that?

Have you heard the Brooklyn Bridge is again for sale at a bargain rate? Government lies and accepts liars as if their own rules do not matter.

The book continues:

Visa Alphabet Soup

"We can always thank the Greeks for the alphabet, because overall, the U.S. Visa problem is not stuck on the letters H1B. There are several visa types for just about as many letters fashioned for us by the Greeks and Phoenicians many, many years ago. As you would expect, in addition to H1B, there is an H1A, and there are visa types that start with A and go to T with many variants within those letters.

"Right now, there are 81 different visa types, each promising somebody in the world the opportunity to come to the U.S. for one reason or another to take a job—which of course is an American worker's job!

"I have reworked a table from a government site and it is shown below n Table 7-1. To see the whole table, rather than type the four line URL, just type *Immigration Classifications and Visa Categories* into your browser and you can see the full chart and all of its meaning.

"Actually there are so many Visa types that foreigners interested in coming to the U.S. often use the one type of Visa that they can get rather than the type of Visa that they actually should get for the type of work or study that they are hoping to do. It is a bureaucratic nightmare that only a desperate non-citizen or a lawyer could be paid enough to want to fully understand. That's why the latter make a lot of money on the former trying to squeeze them in."

It is clear that corporations have figured out that they do not have to export production to less developed countries to achieve low labor costs and to find a nice place in which health, safety and environmental enforcement is merely a wink and a nod away.

Finally, they don't have to look to developing nations to find a vulnerable, exploited worker class since they have been able to create one right here in the good ole U.S. of A. The huge pool of illegal workers combined with those on visas accept low wages and the depress the entire wage scale so that Americans formerly engaged in these industries can no longer earn a decent wage.

What is the solution?

Would it not be nice if all the billionaires gave some thought to whet they are doing? The solution for the non-billionaires, like you and I, who theoretically own the congressional representation in the country really is simple. The only reason that these programs exist at the numeric levels they do is that corporations own our Congress.

The solution is not to shut off the opportunities for Americans to mix with foreigners but to limit their numbers so that they do not become inexpensive replacement players for standout academics.

When has Matt Cartwright or Robert Casey Jr. suggested that this might be an issue for Americans?

Who has ever told you this is an issue? Let me be the first. I wrote about it four of my books, and I say it again for all to hear. The way this program is used is a travesty. We are not talking about students.

Sometimes, however, we are talking about Professors who will work for peanuts. Academia gets a lot of cheap labor on special visas and they help foreign students get jobs that American graduates otherwise would get.

We are talking about employees who are foreign nationals who get positions in advanced areas and for the promise of a green card or the right to eventually live in America, they forego six years of great wages. Instead they work for pauper's wages while stealing American jobs while American graduates either more so or at least equally qualified remain unemployed, because Americans think the American game is fair. It is not!

Americans expect to make a decent wage and none of us are depending on the good will of a corporate manager to decide whether we get put on a fast track to citizenship. Thankfully we are already citizens but our Congress denigrates us and denies us our natural opportunities. What a shame! What a sham! Cartwright has denied many graduates of NEPA universities their day in the sun. Are you planning to reelect him?

Can we not all agree to send all 435 members of Congress and the 100 Senators home packing--most in November and the rest when their time comes--for the harm they cause American workers and visitors who should go home loving America.

As with all the problems we identify as we discuss the poor jobs situation in America, there are many solutions. Your current Congress would not consider making it better because they are owned by donors who want foreigners taking away any chance that your children might have great careers. They have sold those careers to foreign nationals. The donors make more money when your children suffer the consequences of believing in Democrats who promise the moon even though they know God owns the moon! Ask Matt Cartwright or Bob Casey if any of these donors have sent either of them big checks to go along to get along?

So, let's make sure Cartwright and in two years, Casey do not have the opportunity to hurt your children ever again. For Northeastern PA, our time of reckoning is April 26, 2016 and then again November 8, 2016. Make sure you take the time to vote. Write in Brian Kelly both times if you do not see him on the ballot. Thank you.

Essay 32

Americans Need Not Apply!

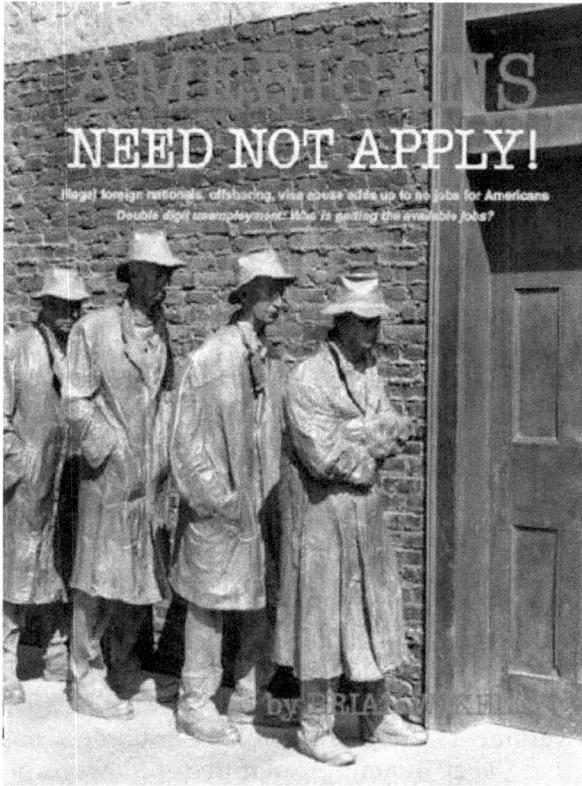

Irish Need not Apply! Syrians need not apply! Italians need not apply! Spanish need not apply! Polish need not apply! How many of our parents went through tough times in the USA finding bigotry instead of work when they sought employment?

You've heard the stories at the dinner table. Eventually our parents all got jobs and America toned down its ethnic prejudices. Today, however, all American citizens are feeling a new kind of prejudice in the workplace. It's an economic prejudice carried out by greedy businesses. It cries out that Americans Need Not Apply! You're wasting your time.

Please note, just like it was not the Irish, the Syrians, the Italians, the Spanish or the Polish who were the problem in our country's infancy, the Mexicans, the Costa Ricans, or the Guatemalans are not the problem today. It is greedy businesses and a greedy political class and in this book, we will show you how and why.

Brian W. Kelly is one of America's most outspoken and eloquent conservative protagonists. He is the leading published non-fiction author of today in the US.

His books include Taxation without Representation, Obama's Seven Deadly Sins, Jobs! Jobs! Jobs! The Constitution 4 Dummmies, Saving America, and many other books. Brian has written several hundred articles to help America.

Like many Americans, Brian Kelly is fed up with a progressive liberal agenda in Washington that places the needs of illegal foreign workers in front of the needs of Americans. Endorsed by the Independence Hall Tea Party in 2010, Kelly ran for Congress against a 13-term Democrat and, in a three way race he spent just $4500 of his own money and, as a virtual unknown, he captured 17% of the vote.

Kelly then supported Republican challenger Lou Barletta, a conservative leader on immigration policy, and helped him win a resounding victory in the general election.

Kelly wrote this book to help Americans know what we can do to force our government to regain control of our borders, ensure our national security, keep our culture, enforce our laws, protect American jobs, and keep all Americans from being overwhelmed by illegal foreign nationals with no allegiance to the USA.

Like you, Brian is frustrated with the devastation that illegal immigration inflicts on law-abiding Americans and likewise he finds the destitution brought upon the illegal class by corporate America to be the greatest sin of all.

He's read the intelligence reports, has researched and written about the topic for years, and he knows how intolerable illegal immigration can be within our neighborhoods.

Today's economic story can be spelled out in three words, Jobs Jobs Jobs. American workers are losing their jobs and the big reason for that in the USA is that greedy corporations and corrupt politicians have teamed up in an unholy alliance to use illegal and legal foreign nationals as a means to feather their own nests.

US corporations are the major perpetrators as they try to compete with slave shops in Asia and hellholes across the world. In all of these industries that reluctantly hire Americans, the workers are paid slave wages. Yet, the corporate titans of today have no problem taking the seats in the first pews as they worship their Lord each Sunday. Is their Lord, the god of greed?

Americans Need Not Apply is a book that needed to be written, but which no one had the guts to write until Brian Kelly took up the task. For all Americans, who care about the USA, Kelly offers a compelling plan to keep us safe, and to get Americans back to work. Few books are a must-read but Americans Need Not Apply is at the top of the list.

Isn't it nice that Brian Kelly has agreed to be a write-in candidate in Pennsylvania's 17th District to fight the corruption brought about by the incumbent? Matt Cartwright never utters a bad word about the donors that pad his campaign war chest and exploit the illegal class in America.

Too many other Congressional Representatives across the country care nothing of their constituency. I hope to change in District 17, but chances are nobody will find my message anywhere. Ask the Times Leader or WVIA Public TV or WBRE, or WILK in NEPA why nobody has ever told you that you have a choice.

Matt Cartwright was not sent by God to make the fourth estate shudder if they mention a challenger's name. I. Brian Kelly challenge Matt Cartwright's supposed right to do what he wants for the donor class rather than representing the people of NEPA. Thank God for the Citizens Voice, who have also not endorsed Brian Kelly's write-in campaign. However, the Voice at least acknowledged that Brian Kelly is running and that those of us in NEPA do have a choice in D17!   God bless you all!

Essay 33

No Amnesty! No Way!

Why the Rubio Plan is Amnesty

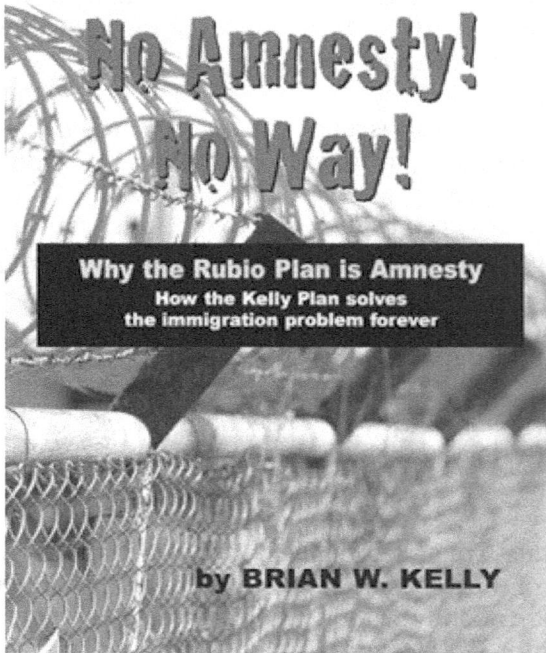

No Amnesty! No Way!

Why the Rubio Plan is Amnesty
How the Kelly Plan solves the immigration problem forever

by BRIAN W. KELLY

Shall we just let them come with no repercussions so that we can forgive them?

The gang of eight tyrant's amnesty plan, of which Marco Rubio was a chief spokesman, was designed to kill America. There would be no jobs left; but worse than that, there might be no more America if we permit the tyranny to persist without protest.

Our country will be owned and overrun by illegal foreign nationals from Mexico and China, and elsewhere. Americans will be paying them to live here for free. If you think things are bad for your kids now, wait until this legislation from the most corrupt politicians in America is rammed down your throats. Wait until Obama acts on his own and it sticks!

If you want foreigners to be voting in American elections, and you want newly minted citizens to be taking American jobs, and you want the average wage in America to keep going down, down, down, and you want Congress to consider changing our national language from English to Mandarin, and you want to pay the cost of welfare cash and food and housing and medical for the new owners of America, that's where we are heading.

If you also want China and Russia to be the only superpowers left in the world, please encourage your legislators to bring back and quickly pass the Senate's gang of eight tyrants plan so we can quickly move forth with the destruction of America the beautiful and the once grand. I think these last two paragraphs ask our existential question quite well. I'd rather it not be so simple to see.

Yes, this situation is that severe!

Brian W. Kelly is one of America's most outspoken and eloquent conservative spokesmen. Your author, Brian Kelly is no stranger to controversial yet patriotic topics.

BK is the author of Taxation Without Representation, Obama's Seven Deadly Sins, Saving America, Americans Need Not Apply, and many other patriotic books.

Like many Americans, Brian is fed up with a progressive liberal agenda in Washington that places the needs of illegal foreign workers in front of the needs of Americans.

Kelly wrote this book to help Americans know what we can do to force our government to regain control of our borders, ensure our national security, keep our culture, enforce our laws, protect American jobs, and keep all Americans from being overwhelmed by illegal foreign nationals with no allegiance to the USA.

Essay 34

The Lifetime Guest Plan

A Long Term Immigration Fix that Puts Americans First!

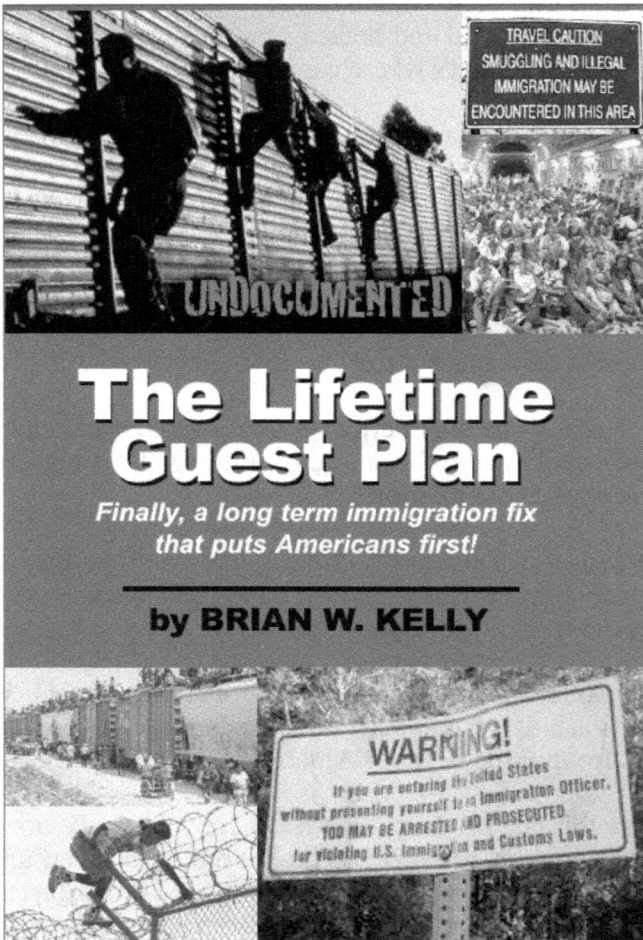

The Lifetime Guest Plan (LGP) was developed by Brian Kelly in 2013 and released originally as a notion called The Kelly Plan.

Brian examined the gang of eight plan, existing law, and other notions about how to solve the nation's problem with illegal residents. He found none that addressed all of the issues that having 20 million to 60 million illegal foreign nationals in residence brought to America.

Brian did his research. He read the gang of eight plan in 2013, and easily noticed that it smelled a lot like it was purposely designed to kill America. No jobs would be left for Americans; newly unemployed Americans would have to pay for newly minted citizens; voting in national elections was not ruled out; 33 million more foreign nationals would be invited in; it would cost over $6 trillion.

It was a terrible deal for the country. Yet, the corrupt press gave none of these facts to regular Americans because they were on the take for the deal.

Kelly looked at all of the things that Americans did not like about the idea and he looked at what the interlopers liked. He figured out a way to permit well-behaved interlopers to stay in America while giving Americans priority in all ways. This plan actually will work and it will solve the problem and take a huge financial burden off the backs of Americans. That's why you have never heard of it.

Brian W. Kelly is the leading conservative author in America. He has written 64 books so far and there is no living published non-fiction author that has equaled his output. He is an outspoken and eloquent expert on immigration solutions. Though a Democrat, he is a JFK Democrat. One of his pet peeves is the chicanery and deceit of RINOS on conservative Americans and DINOS on liberal Americans. Kelly asks why we cannot simply tell the truth.

Kelly is the author of Saving America; Taxation without Representation; Americans Need Not Apply; No Amnesty! No Way!; Jobs! Jobs! Jobs!; The Constitution 4 Dummmies!; and many other conservative books. Like many Americans, Brian is fed up with a stifling agenda in Washington that places the needs of foreign nationals in front of the needs of Americans.

He wrote this book to help Americans know what we can do to force our government to regain control of our borders, ensure our national security, keep our culture, enforce our laws, protect American jobs, and keep all Americans from being overwhelmed by illegal foreign nationals with no allegiance to the USA. In addition to showing why amnesty is not the right medicine, Brian Kelly explains the best plan (LGP) for America again to become a sovereign state.

This is Brian Kelly's 60th book. He has written four more since this book became popular. You are going to love this book and the LGP plan, since it is designed by an American for Americans. Few books are a must-read, but The Lifetime Guest Plan will quickly appear at the top of America's most read list.

Tell me more about the notion of a plan that makes existing illegal foreign nationals happy but makes Americans even happier. Here goes:

Brian Kelly's Lifetime Guest Plan brings 60,000,000 illegals out of the shadows

Every Congressional solution to the occupation of the US by 60 million illegal foreign nationals is trumped by the idea that border security must come first. Yet, as perhaps this is merely a ruse by Congressmen in the pockets of lobbyists and donors, border security never comes. Have you seen it? I have not either!

Since 1986 in the Reagan amnesty at a clip of about 3 million per year, interlopers have chosen to cross the southern border or simply overstay their visas in order to gain residence in the US. I challenge anybody to show proof that there are less than 60 million interlopers living and working in the US today. The corrupt press lies about it and your congressman lies about it because telling the American people the truth does not get the Congress reelected in these days of chicanery.

Over time, because Democrats like the idea that the new dependent foreign class will vote Democrat one day, and Republican political operatives and elites want so much to please their donor class, who employ these "residents" at sub-minimum wage rates; that our government again intentionally has chosen to ignore the wishes of the American people to serve their own greed.

President Obama thinks that the game he plays is "How many executive orders authorizing illegals in the USA can I get through before the people notice?" But, the game he is really playing is

"How can I, the Emperor destroy America quickly while the people are looking someplace else for solutions?"

The Donald Trump and Ted Cruz plans will definitely stop the new potential illegal foreign nationals at the border. Both are good and that is why the corrupt media tried to make both Trump and Cruz appear to be (A-holes) so the low information folks think Hillary or Bernie would make better presidents.

However, though Trump has proven that we all care about the infestation we face, the supposed fourth estate does not seem to care about those illegal residents who are beginning to think they own significant parts of America.

My solution addresses the latter and it is the product of a lot of research and thinking. It is called the Lifetime Guest Plan and it should be passed and implemented ASAP. I will work with your Congressman to assure it happens.

Over the last six years, I wrote two books, *Americans Need Not Apply*, and *No Amnesty! No Way!* These books captured the essence of the problem of 60,000,000 foreign interlopers living in America. Initially I had no solution so I kept researching and thinking and researching and thinking and finally it came to me. What if we made a deal with the interlopers and the American people within which both parts of the puzzle could live and be OK! Here is the essence of the Lifetime Guest Plan but there is lots more. I admit the current law says all interlopers should be deported but do many of us have the stomach for all that if we can solve it differently?

Suppose a registered designee with credentials as a lifetime guest is well behaved, and we get to define what that means, would it not be OK if they get a right to live in America and hold a job for which an American citizen is not competing. Lifetime guests will be 100% out of the shadows and will live like you and I within our neighborhoods, paying for housing as we do. Their kids will go to our schools as they now do but now, they will pay school taxes like you and I.

In order to gain their status they must promise not to be a burden (defined as costing taxpayers) or they must voluntarily deport. The government will help in their deportation and in fact may offer a substantial stipend of $5,000 to $10,000 for those who agree to go and not come back without paying back their to-date burden.

Americans will no longer pay a dime for lifetime guests for education, healthcare or general living. Iron clad identification databases and ID cards with biometrics will be issued and those without such identification will be deported immediately when they show disrespect for a program built to benefit them.

Once the program is in full implementation, EMTALA will still be provided but the lifetime guest receiver must immediately self deport if they cost taxpayers a dime or work out a payment plan with their new Healthcare Accountability Record. No freebies!

Lifetime Guests (LGPG) must begin their freedom in the US by registering at no charge at one of many US facilities. No tricks! When the process is completed, US officials will know all illegal foreign nationals at that point and their status will be legal. Having not paid a dime for anything after registration, they must immediately apply for a lifetime guest visa and be approved to stay a lifetime under our code.

Of course, they may also agree to be deported if they do not wish to be a lifetime guest. Any who choose exodus from the US will receive a stipend to help them live in their old country with a grub-stake. It will be well-worth the trouble and the cost for the US tax payer. But, the former interloper, who becomes a voluntary deportee is not welcome back ever!

Americans believe the influx of illegal foreign nationals hurts them and from my own observations, we Americans are 100% correct. The table is turned in this program with the citizen now holding all the TRUMP cards. LGPG's will have no welfare or health benefits other than those provided by their employers.

If they seek US benefits, they will agree to be summarily deported. They will not be able to vote in any election in the US for any office local, municipality, state, or federal. Unless they return to their home country, and begin a process like all others from that country, they can never become a citizen of the US.

Registration will be free for a period until it is obvious all should be registered (perhaps 3 months) at which time registration will have a charge of say $50.00. All registrants must pay $100.00 to apply for lifetime guest status and go through a vetting process. Those granted lifetime guest status merely have to be well behaved.

In year two, each lifetime guest must appear in front of US officials to be vetted again and pay their annual guest fee of $100. The fee is $100 per year every year unless it costs more to process them. Each year until the plan is proven. LGPG's must make personal appearances and pay their $100.00 to get their card renewed.

The key point is that these folks are guests of American citizens. They are not American Citizens or ¼ citizens, or ½ citizens. They are guests. Once registered and approved, they have a special right granted by the citizens of the US to remain in the US as long as they are well-behaved, and no longer.

They have no special privileges. American Citizens have all the privileges of citizens in their own country / state.

There are other advanced notions in the plan that may help US officials deal better with the ongoing issue of people wanting to crash into America uninvited for various purposes.

For example, The Lifetime Guest Plan should never cost the US more than if the plan were not in force. Illegal foreign nationals who choose to be lifetime guests and are granted permission are not permitted to ever become a burden, financial or otherwise on the citizenry of the USA.

You have read a very light introduction to a very detailed plan intended for the benefit of Americans, but nonetheless accommodates over 60,000,000 foreign interlopers simply because America is a kind nation, and Americans have big hearts.

There is no reason for Americans to pay for guests in any category, though the burden for such interlopers has been very large for taxpayers over the years.

And so, a look at the costs of not having a lifetime guest plan v having such a plan; it is obvious that there will be some special things that can be done to help keep families together.

For example, suppose an anchor baby through his or her parents could choose to take a $50,000 stipend to give up anchor baby citizen status and go home with his or her parents. What if the US also provided a large stipend for the mother and father to be resettled in a safe area of their home country?

They could start anew with a bankroll and become big-shot entrepreneurs in their home country. There may be families who could gain a grub stake of as little as $70,000 to several hundred thousand dollars, depending on the # of children, to start fresh in their home country with their families intact. Why would they want to stay in America with no grand prize?

The idea of the Lifetime Guest Plan is to help those stuck in America doing meaningless labor for peanuts. It is also a plan to help Americans subjugated to the effects of a new but clandestine wage scale that comes before all minimum wages, for which they cannot compete.

Essay 35

Healthcare Accountability

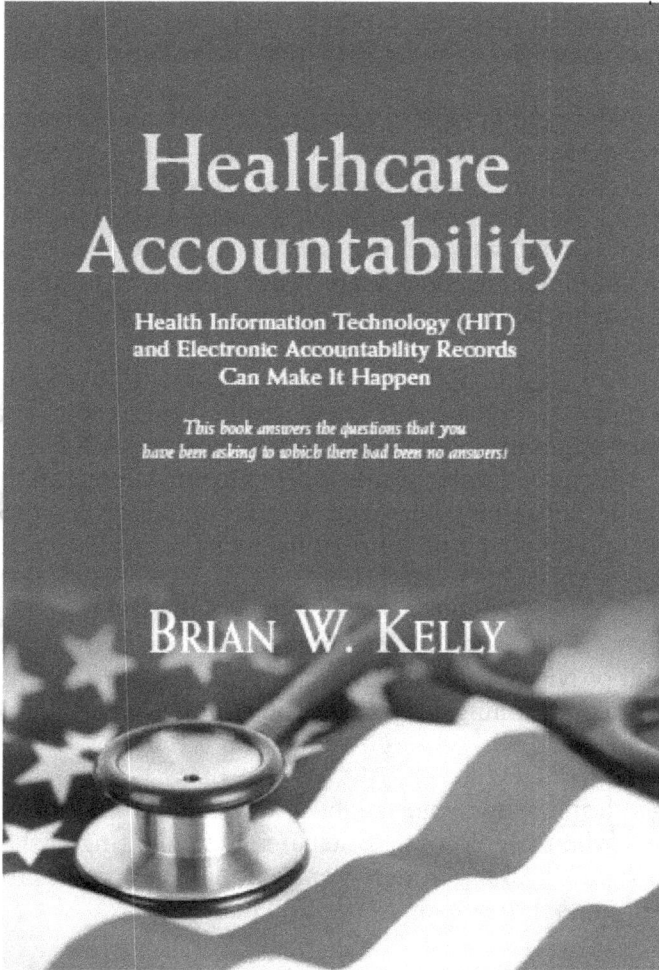

Healthcare Accountability

Healthcare is a right! How can it not be? Why should some have healthcare and others not have healthcare? Are these issues not at the center of the debate about who gets the bounty produced by the workers in America? In days gone by there would have been no dispute, the workers would get their bounty. Almost sounds piggish to mention that in these days--when rights trump work.

The Barack Obama Healthcare plan which is aptly shortened to Obamacare could never have passed muster with the greatest Americans of our time, the founding fathers. These guys and the 5 million population that were around in the post 1750 era had a tough time asking the Crown for a Crown, if you get my drift.

So, what is the right of man to healthcare? What are its origins? Did the right come from Adam and Eve? Did the Apple bite mean that we all became winners in the big fruit lottery? Which of the two were doctors, Adam, the observer, or Eve, the Apple biter? Or perhaps it was God, who deemed it so? If there were no Doctors than how could there be healthcare at that time in our human history? Maybe the hospitals would handle the traffic? Whoops! No hospitals yet!

Is heat a right? Is food a right? Do the animals come to man asking to be eaten so that man can survive? If so, why are there hunters? When the farmer plants is he concerned about all the others besides his family who need to be fed by his crop -- pro bono? Should he till a little more or throw more seed because others may want of his harvest?

Is air a right? I think you got me on that one. Yes, I think air is a right. God provides air. Is milk a right? Are chocolate cupcakes a right? Is air conditioning a right? Is protection from earthquakes and tsunamis a right?

Is sitting at home while your neighbor works a right? Is sharing in the harvest when you do not participate in the planting or the harvest a right? Is taking from a friend's home the things that should have been yours if they had not become his, a right?

How hard do you think the founding fathers had to reach to come up with the few rights that they believe all of us possess? Has two hundred and a quarter years separated us from the love of freedom that those who died so that we could live free gave to us: How about these rights:

"We hold these truths to be self-evident, that all men are created equal, that they are endowed by their Creator (who's that guy?) with certain unalienable Rights, that among these are Life, Liberty and the pursuit of Happiness." The only enunciated rights and please note healthcare was not one of them, nor was chocolatecare -- keep listening—that to secure these rights, Governments are instituted among Men, deriving their just powers from the consent of the governed, [US]

That whenever any Form of Government becomes destructive of these ends [THE GOVERNMENT WHICH NOW LISTENS NOT TO THE PEOPLE], it is the Right of the People to alter or to abolish it, and to institute new Government, laying its foundation on such principles and organizing its powers in such form, as to them shall seem most likely to affect their safety and happiness!

Who would have ever written a piece like that? Well, recent historians have tried to disguise this patriot as a slave owner who cared little about mankind. In fact, the name of the writer is Thomas Jefferson, a man who loathed all attempts to subvert freedom and who loathed the realities of government by "mortal men" even more.

All one has to do is keep reading and just like Harry Reid can gain accord with the President about nascent remarks in our time, how about a real patriot? The Patriot of whom I speak, stubborn as he was, was as good as it got even in disagreement, and he helped us all be what we are. And more importantly, he helped us know what we can be

Accursed as it is in less understanding circles, his name of course is Thomas Jefferson, and we would do well to have him among us today. No, he was not the sole author of the Declaration against England. Many other brave men stood the task and did what needed to be done. The Declaration of Independence of course is a formal explanation of why Congress had voted on July 2, 1776, to declare independence from Great Britain. Surely it would have been sooner if Tony Blair were King!

So, as we evaluate our rights versus our privileges for living in the United States, it is better for all of us to think of all of our wonderments as privileges, reserved by our founding fathers of course only for citizens of the United States of America. Let others ask and they may receive but if they demand there shall be no receipt. There are no rights in which one man may appear and demand the rights of another.

And, to be more specific, which founding father would you suspect suggested that the work of the many shall provide for the lack of will to work of the few?

I did not think you could find that one so I will give it to you below:
....

Healthcare is something that one should expect if you have paid into the system. If Doctors were slaves of the state, indentured to serve without complaint, then many things could be asked of them.

But, they are human beings just like you and I and so we shall not!

Thinking I had created a notion about individual accountability for healthcare as well as a new idea for funding as much care of those with no insurance as we can, I wrote a book called Healthcare Accountability. When I originally wrote this brief essay, the printed book titled Healthcare Accountability was in my hands. You'll love it

www.letsgopublish.com
This book is sold at www.bookhawkers.com
The best in life to all!

Do you realize that for all the help that we taxpayers give to so many -- Medicaid, EMTALA, CHIPS, etc, there is no mechanism to account for it all? In other words if upon being treated, the patient gaining help from Medicaid or EMTALA were to become a millionaire within the next second, there would be no way to know and thus no way to collect because we immediately forgive the bill / debt.

EMTALA hospitals do try to collect but when they cannot, they give up. No matter when the patient becomes a millionaire, because there is no accounting by the government that uses taxpayer dollars from the treasury, there is no accountability. Tough to believe isn't it!

The cover text on the book is as follows:

Most Americans are aware of the major battle regarding health insurance and healthcare "reform" that was at its peak in the fall of 2009. Congress was getting ready to spend more than a trillion dollars on a government take-over of healthcare.

The purpose of the take-over was, purportedly, to improve the lives of just 17% of the people -- those that the government determined to have no access to healthcare (a determination with which many constituents tend to disagree).

What about those 17%? What do you think? Should they be on the public tab forever regardless of their status in life? In order to attain accountability, we must keep track of things. President Bush and President Obama both agree that a database of citizen health records needs to be compiled and it is, indeed, a very good idea. In such as system, there would be records for each citizen in the United States. In this way, it would be much easier to get a full picture of a patient in any medical provider's setting. Clearly this helps in all aspects of healthcare.

With all the rhetoric about reform, there is little to no talk about accountability. This book not only broaches the subject, it shows that it can be done and how it can be done in a lightly technical but mostly amusing style. Americans need a logical and clear blueprint that defines the terms for organization of online records and discusses the objectionable entities that are positioned to "own" your health data. Let's keep them forever locked out.

I hope you enjoy reading this book and that you will remain vigilant and take the actions necessary to ensure that all the people as individuals, and not the government in groupthink, determine the fate of US healthcare.

Not one person whose life is saved would deny the people of the US their just payback once they are well. It just makes good sense. Learn how inside! [Book = Healthcare Accountability available at www.bookhawkers.com] I wish you the best!"

Sincerely.
Melissa L. Sabol, Editor in Chief

Essay 36

Obamacare 101 -- A Tough Pill to Swallow

Nobody wants to hurt anybody even when they are hurting them!

Do we all need health care? You bet we do! But even before the big March 21, 2010 Pelosi / Obama/ Stupak takeover, the citizens of the US already had health care. Few needed government to intercede. It would have cost a buck, three eighty to solve their mini-dilemma if the government was interested in solving anything! Do you remember those days? Obama was not even in the equation. When we were sick, we went to the doctors. How is it that with Obamacare, *not being able to go to your doctor* somehow is a better deal?

Hard to believe now but it is fact that our illegal alien friends also have health care. It is better care than we will get when we choose not to pay the Obamacare penalty. Illegal care has been the Federal law since 1986. Can you think of the expense that would be saved if the freeloaders and deadbeats from other countries were not chewing as much out of our system? Maybe we could actually afford more than just emergency room care for all citizens.

By the way, I am for care for the helpless but that is where it ends. I am not for Government being the only health broker in the country because that is where individual freedom ends, and real healthcare is right behind it.

In mid -arch 2010 before the March 21 bill passed the house, I had been reading about the supposed myths of Obamacare. In a New York Times article by Paul Krugman, he cited what he thought were the three myths of Obamacare. From reading Paul Krugman one could get the idea that he does not read newspapers because he is too busy writing his opinion. He happens to like anything the President and Pelosi and Reid have to say. That is no myth for sure. His writings are pure Obama propaganda.

Do you want to know a real myth? You won't get this from the New York Times. It is a myth. It is a myth that 30,000,000 people do not have healthcare. Do you know any of the 30,000,000? None of my family, and we are a heartland PA family without many white collar workers. Do any of us know any who cannot use EMTALA or choose not to use the free ER care? Seems like ERs are full so why do we need Obamacare. Will it make them fuller? Let's stop now and take a quick look at EMTALA so that we know that Obamacare was not needed unless the idea is to give Cadillac plans to the poor, the indigent, and/or the illegals.

The Emergency Medical Treatment and Labor Act (EMTALA) was part of the very large Consolidated Omnibus Budget Reconciliation Act (COBRA) of 1985 and was in response to a perceived crisis in patient "dumping" by hospitals denying emergency medical care to patients with inadequate or no insurance. Although only 4 pages in length and barely noticed at the time, EMTALA has created a storm of controversy over the ensuing 15 years, and it is now considered one of the most comprehensive laws guaranteeing nondiscriminatory access to emergency medical care and thus to the health care system. And, folks, this was here long before Obamacare. So, why the 2010 emergency? Why did Bart Stupak have to sell his soul to help Nancy Pelosi pass this in the cover of darkness?

I do have relatives who have no health insurance policies but they and everybody else has healthcare because of EMTALA. They know they have healthcare. They had it before Obamacare passed. It has been the law of the land since 1985. Everybody gets healthcare either through their own money, their own insurance, Medicare, Medicaid, or EMTALA. Obamacare was and is a lie, the intention of which is to give government control of your healthcare. It was not and is not an idea to help make care better or more affordable. In fact, it does just the opposite.

Again, I do not advocate EMTALA if you can afford healthcare or if it is provided for you, but it certainly proves that there was and still is healthcare for all without Obamacare bankrupting the US and denying care to the middle class. Obamacare. The court of last resort is EMTALA and it is the law of the land. Nobody is left out. Nobody! And, yes, the term active labor means that if you are in labor, you get to have your baby in the hospital. And, all of this has been in effect without an ounce of Obamacare.

Why was nobody telling this to the people? Because the objective of Obamacare was not healthcare but for government to control the 20% of the economy which makes up the e-healthcare industry. When government controls healthcare, it owns you.

I do not mean to suggest that the ER doctors all appreciate the freeloaders who come in for running noses or drug addiction. Often, their interests are as simple as getting a sandwich and a drink and they require no treatment. I don't know why. There are food kitchens that can help them better.

Hospital administrators, whose hospitals have figured out how to cope with the law of the land from 1986 have adapted or they would be out of business. I know it is hard to believe that something productive may have actually been accomplished in the pre-Obama days. But, it is true.

Obamacare has actually reduced the funding for EMTALA, the greatest benefit the US could give to its citizens and to any interlopers. Now that Obama has taken over healthcare, who feels comfortable getting sick in the US. Probably note our illegal interlopers who once got everything.

In larger hospitals, there are often two ERs. One is for triage etc. and the other is used as a clinic and a place to rest for the indigent who know the address of the ER by heart. This keeps costs down substantially. It is actually geared for the type of person that comes in for help. I mean they are really not emergencies.

They sometimes come in for healthcare, not just a drink, and they get it. If the hospital so much as discusses payment with them, before they receive treatment, they can report the hospital to HEW, and the Hospital can be sued. It is against the law to harass a patient for money in the ER before the person is treated.

When they receive the treatment, they may be admitted. If it is a pregnancy and the mother is in labor, they get a room and they have a delivery like anybody else in the OR. (Active Labor Act). In addition to treatment, they are given a drink and something to eat. If they have a baby, they get the same amenities though perhaps the room is not as private. Perhaps.

For the patient it is not such a bad deal. For the hospital, when the patient is finished, they typically just leave and the hospital does not get to collect anything for their service. So it is not such a good idea for the hospitals. Some patients are pure charity and some are funded one way or another by taxpayers.

Hospitals have figured out how to give those in need of healthcare the care they need without it costing a $trillion dollars. So, if everybody is already covered, why do we need to cover 30,000,000 more plus the 60,000,000 illegal aliens who get their free healthcare via EMTALA? For me, it does not compute! There is only one answer to that question. The goal of Obamacare is not about healthcare. It is about government control of your life.

At one time, hospitals were so concerned about Medicare audits that they would not ask if the person could pay before delivering service. Now, they do ask if one can pay. If the patient states that they cannot pay they must agree to a medical screening exam by a physician to determine if what they have is really an emergency.

Most hospitals are still concerned about government retribution and so they just see everyone due to liability. Pregnant women must be seen and stabilized. Many note that this is one of the big reasons why it is assured that illegals are born future Democrats.

Part of Obamacare is to make all people equal in terms of healthcare. In other words, it is not good enough for somebody to be able to be made well by the system -- via charity or by merely slipping out before the hospital gets the billing information. The goal of Obamacare is that everybody, regardless of their status in life or country of origin should have your insurance policy. That is how I see it.

If you have a good insurance policy. Obama wants that policy in his stash so he can give it away to somebody else. No, he does not care if you worked for it. Pelosi and Matt Cartwright and Bob Casey Jr. from PA have been convinced by Obama that he is right on this. Hey, don't you have a heart? If you do, you should be glad to give your healthcare to somebody else.

The EMTALA is a very charitable act. It is the catch-all. It is America at its best. A little improvement to EMTALA and no Obamacare is necessary. Let me ask again. If everybody at a minimum has some healthcare, what is the issue? Sometimes I really do think the issue for the hard left is that those who get care in ER clinics don't have your (the reader's) insurance policy.

They may not have your employer-provided policy because maybe they do not work; but they all do have healthcare, legal and illegal among them. It really bugs the health redistribution crowd of lefties that you have your own insurance policy and they cannot get you to give it willingly to one of the "disadvantaged" in need of a handout. If you give up your insurance policy to somebody else, nobody from the Obamacare institute will ever bug you again. But, what if YOU get sick? You won't be able to reach them!

When I think about EMTALA, I think it is pretty generous of the medical community to provide it.

Speaking of generosity, after Obamacare passed in March 2010 a proponent of the bill noted that there more than likely would not be an overfilling of doctor's offices with new patients because as he said, "Doctors typically see between eight and ten charity patients a week." My hat is off to the doctors in the US medical community who have been so kind to us all for so long. I think the government should treat them far better.

What a shame that doctors will have to depend on the Federal Government soon as their major employer, making rules that are not favorable to doctors or patients.

By the way, with EMTALA, charitable clinics, and charity care by doctors has become the practice of the land. So, where was the emergency requiring? There was none and there is none. Obamacare is a fraud perpetrated on the American people with health insurance policies to get them to give them up by force. If doctors see so many charitable patients a week, can it be that the goal is to have the people via the government pay -- rather than permit the doctor to provide charity?

It doesn't make sense! Well, maybe now it does because Obama did not like this argument so he has in fact requested less funding for EMTALA. Maybe he sees it a a competitor to Obamacare? What do you think?

The Affordable Healthcare Act (ACA) which is also known as Obamacare and the EMTALA are in practice, incompatible statutes. Enacted in 1986, EMTALA mandates that hospitals treat anyone in need of emergency health care, regardless of his citizenship status or ability to pay for treatment. Obamacare competes with EMTALA and therefore the government analysts figured they would shortchange the competitive program to avoid the competition. They cut funding by 75%.

Hospitals depend on these funds to offset the costs of of providing the care required by EMTALA law. Obama did not get rid of EMTALA. He got rid of most of the funding. Why? Because EMTALA was more affordable; was just four pages; and all the sweet deals for Obama cronies would be cut off if all that changed was another four pages added to EMTALA.

Obama does not see it that way. His minions' project this Obama theory: Because Obamacare requires everybody to have insurance, hospitals will treat fewer uninsured patients who require emergency care that they cannot afford, incur lower uncompensated care costs, and therefore, require less government funding. However, like most government theories this theory is dangerously flawed. It actually may wind up denying care to 3/4 of those who once received it.

Al Aviles, President and CEO of the largest municipal system in the US explains this phenomenon: "That calculus doesn't work in places lick New York," where undocumented immigrants make up a large percentage of uninsured patients and are excluded from the coverage expansion.

Under Obamacare, deferral funding to hospitals will decrease while the number of uninsured undocumented immigrants will remain roughly the same or increase at the rate of entry. Illegal foreign nationals contribute to a significant portion of hospitals non-reimbursed costs; thus, the reductions by Obama to EMTALA will impose serious financial burdens on states and hospitals. Think about this.

There was an affordable program that worked and now it is unaffordable and Obamacare itself is unaffordable. Why did government have to touch our healthcare? Once might conclude that our legislators were unaware of EMTALA and Obama did not like it because it did not give government the control of the people that it sought.

When we ask the rhetorical question: "So, if there was no real emergency, why the big push?" The truthful answer and the only logical answer is that it has nothing to do with healthcare. It is about government control.

In a redistributive type of state, what you as an individual possess, such as an adequate health insurance policy, it must be confiscated and be given to someone else. Why should you have something that another person who is not leading your life does not have? That ladies and gentlemen is the essence of Obamacare -- redistribution of healthcare. Soon, you will see it playing at a medical facility near you…if you have not lost all of your healthcare options by then.

What is universal healthcare?

The United States has no reason to play by Lewis and Clark rules regarding Obamacare. There is no need to send out scouts and settlers into unexplored lands to find out how Obamacare would work out. Obamacare is already practiced throughout the world. Until March 21, 2010, it was forbidden in the US because the US had higher standards.

That's why those who can afford real healthcare come to the US for the best care anywhere in the world. Don't let anybody tell you differently. If you don't believe me, try another country. But, then again, you only have one life so you better guess right. That is why

76% of the population is against Obamacare. Each of us have only one life and we like it the way it is, --- living.

Obamacare everywhere else is called Universal Healthcare. As good as it sounds, it never quite works out the way people hope. It is much less in reality than it is in theory. The Europeans and the Canadians and the Russians had great notions of equality before implementing their programs. Like many things that are kept equal, when everything is equal, there is no room for excellence. Based on the success in these other countries, nobody should want Obamacare.

The government loves it because they are in control but the people hate it because if they do not have a ton of money and they get sick, it is OK to die. Government lends an unsympathetic ear. In the US, when we are hurting health-wise, we expect to see doctors, not government bureaucrats whose mission is to save the state money.

Look at Europe before you as a potential healthcare patient vote for EURO-style healthcare for Americans. Don't worry, Congress has already voted your opinion out of the matter. You do not count in determining what is right for your body. No, this is not an abortion speech. Just as the government is willing to throw away these things called "fetuses" that are the youngest of human lives, they are just as happy to throw away "old-asses" (that's the over 62 crowd) before you start costing them big time.

The truthful reports on the issue indicate for sure that citizens in countries with nationalized healthcare never would have accepted this system had they known up-front about the rationing of care, the long lines, and often the lack of excellence. Oh, and did I say, the unnecessary deaths.

Why is it that our leaders do not see the obvious? Or perhaps they do. Socialism may be theoretically fair but it is not known for having heart with empathy for the masses. Go up to any government counter anywhere for any purpose and look at the face you see. Now, envision a big NO, comping from that same person when you ask about a medical procedure that you need in order to live. Get used to it. That's how government works. Our leaders know; they just do not care if it does not affect them.

You do know Obamacare does not affect Congress or their staff. Why has our government done its best to try to coax all of us into giving up the best insurance and care we will ever have? Can it be so they can have a legacy and because some deadbeat someplace, who will never complain about government, can have equal care to those, such as you and I who have worked all their lives? Damn their legacy! And, let the deadbeat get a job.

The government wants control and that control means they want to give your healthcare that you worked all your life to maintain and preserve -- they want the power to give that care, your care, to somebody else who you do not even know. They are not as concerned about what care you get in return for giving yours to the healthcare pool. Are you? By the way, it is OK to not feel guilty about not wanting to give up your healthcare so somebody else can take it. Please keep your house also.

As bureaucrats take over medicine, you know intrinsically that costs will go up and quality will go down because doctors spend more and more of their time on government paperwork and less time helping patients. When the post office succumbs to UPS and FEDEX, will Congress come up with a means to keep the lines at the hospitals shorter. Perhaps there can be an ER stamp with a notable person on the stamp. This would permit the bearer of the stamp to have ER care. Maybe there can be a doctor stamp and a nurse stamp and a drug stamp and when you are out of stamps, you are out of Obamacare.

As stamp costs skyrocket, the government could hire other inefficient bureaucrats to take the reins. If necessary, and only if necessary, government may choose to confiscate cash or print more money or maybe just print stamps to somehow pay the Obamacare bills. Can you even trust that government will pay the bills? Perhaps Congress will choose as in social security to shift any resources that they gain for Obamacare and use that money for some nice pork projects to help get themselves reelected? Hey they do run the country!

The weekend in which Obamacare passed, Obama himself proclaimed that this would reduce the deficit, solve long term issues, give everybody a car, and put a chicken in every pot, or so it seemed. If you had a problem, this bill passing was the solution. Some said it was like Christmas in March it was so good. Oh, Obama and his minions in the media were all lying and they still are.

On Monday morning, however, when the exhilaration had ended over the huge progressive "victory," and Obama was not on the airways thirty times a day for at least a few days, other people got to say something about how truthful the President and Ms. Pelosi were with the American people.

Caterpillar, once cited incorrectly by the Obama machine as having created or saved a gazillion jobs more than the US population, rained on the PP parade (President and Pelosi) Caterpillar Inc. in the last week of March 2010 announced that the Obamacare that had just been passed by the U.S. House of Representatives would increase the company's health-care costs by more than $100 million in the first year alone.

Yes, Virginia, there is a US government filled with liars. Later in the week, Caterpillar teamed up with John Deere to say that together it would cast them $250 million. Nobody from the Obama team showed up to take pictures. It was almost as if they were from Israel.

Tort Reform

The huge cost of healthcare is a major issue keeping all from having the best. If there were no cost and the care were unlimited, why would we not all opt for the best. The irony is that affordable and high quality health care for all with thousands of new features is possible only if government can be stopped from interfering with the marketplace. Even on a good day however, somebody's healthcare package is going to be better than yours or mine. And, I think that is OK. In a world of all beautiful blondes, a brunette would stand out.

But those on the far left want equality. They want all grey haired pimply faces. They are so tuned into equality that they almost lost union support when they decided to one-size-fits-all the unions on health insurance by whacking their policies with a huge luxury tax. Yes, they will bite the hand that feeds them. Unions in 2016 are not too angry because Obama has delayed the Cadillac Obamacare tax until after he is out of office. But, it is still on the books.

They are obsessively and compulsively trying to work some equality magic on insurance policies but they backed off the unions' or they would not have gotten the bill passed. Their goals of equal, lowest common denominator health care remain. When that comes, our healthcare will be just good enough to give patients free admission to a pay toilet.

Who wants one of those policies? That may sound cute but the fact is the policies are so bad that the people who wrote Obamacare determined their government employee classifications and those who helped them, are excluded. They do not have to worry nor do the rest of their cronies from participation in Obamacare. They are too important for Obamacare. No, I am not kidding.

The Republicans via amendments tried to get them back in but the Democratic controlled Senate at the time defended them as did the president and so, they now operate on the only different healthcare plan in the federal government. If Obamacare is so good, why doesn't Obama and his family as well as the people that wrote the bill want it to replace their policies?

If the government is so concerned about the cost of healthcare, don't you wonder why Congress is not energetically advocating tort reform (malpractice suit reform?). You and I know that the cost of health care is directly affected by all the frivolous lawsuits that lawyers just love to file. It is also affected by the monstrous awards received.

Granted some incidents are tragic but there are others in which the patient somehow thinks they have drawn the winning lottery ticket and nothing but a big payoff will suit their needs.

Additionally, you see lawyers advertising for clients looking to create issues, often when there are none. Why then in this healthcare battle, where health costs and quality of care are supposedly the prime motivators, why is there no tort reform in the bill? Tort reform can save unneeded tests and tremendous litigation costs adding up to billions and billions of dollars? Let me give you the answer without suspense. This bill is not about healthcare or its high costs. It is about government control.

Doctors are cutting out of their practices at an early age often because of the cost of malpractice insurance. This puts pressure on the whole system as good doctors choose not to practice. Obamacare will not make it any better. Independent doctors have no real reason to work for the government health insurance company. You know that many doctors do not take Medicaid today. Some won't even take Medicare.

Who are we kidding thinking that things will get better, not worse for doctors? They will either go out of business or go back to CASH only now that this insane health care plan has passed. Watch as the whole bill eventually sneaks out after Obama is gone.

Tort reform can help keep doctors in the business of healthcare as it lowers their cost to provide care. But, that is not the goal. Government control is the goal and the trial lawyers support the Progressive agenda so limiting their opportunity to realize their greed is off the table. Ask John Edwards.

Without even touching on the notion of malpractice insurance costs, "defensive medicine," admittedly is practiced by doctors regularly so they do not get sued. This has a huge cost, estimated to consume 4 percent to 9 percent of the nation's total health care spending.

The Big Numbers that Defeat Obamacare

If you are scoring at home folks, that translates to between roughly $92 billion and $207 billion annually that is wasted on unnecessary tests and procedures that doctors perform simply to avoid the threat of a lawsuit. Eliminating just half of this waste would be enough to cover all uninsured Americans with about an $8,000 per year insurance policy. I am not kidding!

So, do you ever ask yourself why is the healthcare bill priced at $1 trillion. Who's getting that money -- or is it just to pay for the bloated healthcare bureaucracy? Oh, maybe it is not about healthcare at all. Maybe it is about government control!.

Healthcare Expenses

Malpractice insurance costs for physicians run anywhere from $15,000 per year to $100,000 with the average being about $40,000. Physicians are only one part of the malpractice formula as all healthcare providers / practitioners need liability insurance. There are between 500,000 and 600,000 physicians of all types in the U.S. today and so the amount taken from the healthcare industry for malpractice insurance in the US is huge. In other words, the cost of just the physician insurance is between $20 billion and $25 billion per year.

Considering that physician cost is only one component, let's assume all other costs are equal to the physician cost of malpractice insurance. The total becomes $40 billion to $50 billion. I am not proposing that such insurance be eliminated but it can sure be reduced with Tort Reform.

If half of the savings were secured, that would pay for about 40% of the uninsured. Together both components of healthcare add up to more than 140% of the cost to insure all of the uninsured citizens.

YOU can see how important tort reform is in the total healthcare cost equation. Yet, the Congress chose not to include it in its plans. Why is that? Can it be campaign contributions from trial lawyers? If Congress is not reelected, they cannot be in control. You know what you must do with Congress, including Matt Cartwright and Robert Casey Jr. They no longer serve us so let's send them home in a bum's rush.

Obamacare is designed to ruin the medical system.

Can one say that the more money and power that government has, the more power it will abuse? Will anybody out of the chute, just agree to that or does that have to be proven? There are very frightening aspects to all this. Is it possible that by cutting costs, which government will inevitably do when tied against the wall that this will create a situation in which the denying of vital health services becomes part of the government cost plan?

Sorry sir, your food costs and medical costs were too high this year, you will be terminated on April 8, 2018. The government thanks you for helping us meet our budget.

If it is OK to deny care, would that not save money? Will you be able to obtain private insurance? Will you just be asked to die, even if your wallet is full? Will the insurance companies be here ten years from now or will you have to get both stamps and doctor's appointments at the post office. Well, at least stamps. And, yes, those death panels are in the bill.

Here is the scoop. The government will be paying all the bills. This will force doctors and hospitals to dance more and more to the government's tune. Can you imagine the number of government ringmasters and impresarios who will be needed to fully claim our freedoms? They will be everywhere.

Insurance companies will go out of business. Obamacare says that you pay about $695 in 2016 as penalty for not doing the mandated care "thing." Now that we hit 2016, the Individual Shared Responsibility fee for not having insurance is $695 per adult and $347.50 per child (up to $2,085 for a family), or it's 2.5% of your household income above the tax return filing threshold for your filing status – whichever is greater.

You pay 1/12 of the total fee for each full month in which a family member went without coverage or an exemption. The fee increases each year until it ends up being about the price of getting the cheapest health plan. Everywhere you go, since it is now 2016, you hear people grumbling about this. Everything... I mean everything ... about Obamacare will get worse. It is timed to all kick in when he is out of office and the elections of 2016 are over.

So, you do not need a policy if you pay the fine / tax. God forbid, but for example, let's say you get real sick. The bill says you can go get a policy even with your poor prognosis / pre-existing conditions. Can you tell me why anybody should carry insurance at all? Just get an Obamacare policy when you get sick. Then, when you are better drop coverage and pay the fine again. Think of the losses insurance companies will go through.

Well, surprise—surprise, this is not totally true. If you get sick in 2016 after the open enrollment period ends, you must not be so sick that you die before the fall when the next open enrollment period for 2017 begins. You will have to wait eleven months for insurance if you chose to pay the penalty for 2016. That is how the government is minimizing its losses on pre-existing conditions. They hope you are gone in 11 months so you will never get insurance.

This is a great plan devised by Moe Larry, and Curly, Shemp, and Curly Joe. Within a few years after people catch on, insurance companies will no longer be an option. They will be gone. They make their money when nobody gets sick.

If all their customers are terminally sick when they go to them, there will be only one provider left that can fill the bill. Gummy Gumment will step to the plate like the mustachioed messiah saving the damsel on the tracks: "I'll pay the costs." Only the government will be left.

I wonder if that has been the plan all along. Government control and healthcare redistribution will then be able to run unimpeded. Of course once your healthcare plan is redistributed, more than likely you won't see it again.

The great irony is that in turning the good of healthcare into a right, your life and liberty are put in jeopardy. That which you worked for is gone but somebody who never worked is now in a position to outlive you.

End of essay

End of full compendium of Essays

Best wishes in all you do!

LETS GO PUBLISH! Books by Brian W. Kelly
www.letsgopublish.com; Sold at www.bookhawkers.com
Email info@ letsgopublish.com for specific ordering info. Our titles include the following:

Great Moments in Notre Dame Football The story of the most storied football program ever. Great coaches, great players, great seasons, great history. You won't want to put this fine sports book down.

Thank You IBM The story of how IBM helped today's technology millionaires and billionaires gain their vast fortunes

WineDiets.Com PresentsThe Wine Diet Learn how to lose weight while having fun. Four specific diets and some great anecdotes fill this book with fun.

Wilkes-Barre, PA; Return to Glory Wilkes-Barre City's return to glory begins with dreams and ideas. Along with plans and actions, this equals leadership.

The Lifetime Guest Plan. This is a plan which if deployed today would immediately solve the problem of 60 million illegal aliens in the United States.

Geoffrey Parsons' Epoch... The Land of Fair Play Better than the original. The greatest re-mastering of the greatest book ever written on American Civics. It was built for all Americans as the best govt. design in the history of the world.

The Bill of Rights 4 Dummmies This is the best book to learn about your rights. Be the first, to have a "Rights Fest" on your block. You will win for sure!

Sol Bloom's Epoch ...Story of the Constitution This work by Sol Bloom was written to commemorate the Sesquicentennial celebration of the Constitution. It has been remastered by Lets Go Publish! – an excellent read!

The Constitution 4 Dummmies This is the best book to learn about the Constitution. Learn all about the fundamental laws of America.

America for Dummmies!
All Americans should read to learn about this great country.

Just Say No to Chris Christie for President!
Discusses the reasons why Chris Christie is a poor choice for US President

The Federalist Papers by Hamilton, Jay, Madison w/ intro by Brian Kelly
Complete unabridged, easier to read version of the original Federalist Papers

Bring On the American Party!
Demonstrates how Americans can be free from Parties of wimps by starting our own national party called the American Party.

Saving America
This how-to book is about saving our country using strong mercantilist principles. These are the same principles that helped the country from its founding.

RRR:
A unique plan for economic recovery and job creation

Kill the EPA
The EPA seems to hate mankind and love nature. They are also making it tough for asthmatics to breathe and for those with malaria to live. It's time they go.

Taxation Without Representation Second Edition
At the time of the Boston Tea Party, there was no representation. Now, there is no representation again but there are "representatives."

Healthcare Accountability
Who should pay for your healthcare? Whose healthcare should you pay for? Is it a lifetime free ride on others or should those once in need of help have to pay it back when their lives improve?

Jobs! Jobs! Jobs!
Where have all the American Jobs gone and how can we get them back?

IBM I Technical Books

The All Everything Operating System:
The story about IBM's finest operating system, its facilities, and how it came to be.

The All-Everything Machine
The story about IBM's finest computer server.

Chip Wars
The story of the ongoing war between Intel and AMD and the upcoming was between Intel and IBM. This book may cause you to buy or sell somebody's stock.

Can the AS/400 Survive IBM?
Exciting book about the AS/400 in an System i5 World.

The IBM i Pocket SQL Guide.
Complete Pocket Guide to SQL as implemented on System i5. A must have for SQL developers new to System i5. It is very compact yet very comprehensive and it is example driven. Written in a part tutorial and part reference style, this book has tons of SQL coding samples, from the simple to the sublime.

The IBM i Pocket Query Guide.
If you have been spending money for years educating your Query users, and you find you are still spending, or you've given up, this book is right for you. This one QuikCourse covers all Query options.

The IBM I Pocket RPG & RPG IV Guide.
Comprehensive RPG & RPGIV Textbook -- Over 900 pages. From afar, it looks like a brick. This is the one RPG book to have if you are not having more than one. All areas of the language covered smartly in a convenient sized book Annotated PowerPoint's available for self-study (extra fee for self-study package). Depending on your size, you may be able to fit this 900+ page baby in your front pocket! It is big because it tells the whole story!

* 9 7 8 0 9 9 6 2 4 5 4 6 3 *